Entertainment Directo

ATLANTA TRAVEL GUIDE 2015

SHOPS, RESTAURANTS, ARTS, ENTERTAINMENT & NIGHTLIFE

The Most Positively Reviewed And Recommended Places In The City

EGP Editorial

ATLANTA
TRAVEL GUIDE
2015

SHOPS, RESTAURANTS, ARTS, ENTERTAINMENT & NIGHTLIFE

ATLANTA TRAVEL GUIDE 2015
Shops, Restaurants, Arts, Entertainment & Nightlife

Printed in USA.

ISBN-13: 978-1505232226
ISBN-10: 1505232228

EGP
Editorial

INDEX

ATLANTA TRAVEL GUIDE 2015

Shops, Restaurants, Arts, Entertainment & Nightlife

This directory is dedicated to Atlanta Business Owners and Managers
who provide the experience that the locals and tourists enjoy.
Thanks you very much for all that you do and thank for being the "People Choice".

Thanks to everyone that posts their reviews online and
the amazing reviews sites that make our life easier.

The places listed in this book are the most positively reviewed
and recommended by locals and travelers from around the world.

Thank you for your time and enjoy the directory that is
designed with locals and tourist in mind!

TOP 500 SHOPS

The Most Recommended by Locals & Trevelers
(From #1 to #500)

#1
Young Blood Boutique
Category: Jewelry, Gift Shop
Average price: Modest
Area: Poncey-Highland
Address: 632 N Highland Ave NE
Atlanta, GA 30306
Phone: (404) 254-4127

#2
Bound To Be Read Books
Category: Bookstore
Average price: Inexpensive
Area: East Atlanta Village
Address: 481 Flat Shoals Ave
Atlanta, GA 30316
Phone: (404) 522-0877

#3
Perimeter Mall
Category: Shopping Center
Average price: Modest
Address: 4400 Ashford Dunwoody Rd
Atlanta, GA 30346
Phone: (770) 394-4270

#4
Lenox Square Mall
Category: Shopping Center
Average price: Expensive
Area: Buckhead
Address: 3393 Peachtree Rd NE
Atlanta, GA 30326
Phone: (404) 233-6767

#5
Doubletake Recycled Luxury Boutique
Category: Used, Vintage, Women's Clothing
Average price: Modest
Area: Old Fourth Ward
Address: 659 Auburn Ave
Atlanta, GA 30312
Phone: (404) 935-8253

#6
The Beehive
Category: Accessories, Women's Clothing, Jewelry
Average price: Modest
Area: Edgewood
Address: 1250 Caroline St
Atlanta, GA 30307
Phone: (404) 581-9261

#7
Phipps Plaza
Category: Shopping Center
Average price: Exclusive
Area: Buckhead
Address: 3500 Peachtree Rd NE
Atlanta, GA 30326
Phone: (404) 261-7910

#8
The Gear Revival
Category: Luggage
Average price: Modest
Address: 955 Marietta St NW
Atlanta, GA 30318
Phone: (404) 892-4326

#9
Ten Thousand Villages
Category: Stationery, Home Decor
Average price: Expensive
Area: Virginia Highland
Address: 1056 Saint Charles Ave NE
Atlanta, GA 30306
Phone: (404) 892-5307

#10
Donna Van Gogh's Artist Market
Category: Art Gallery
Average price: Modest
Area: Candler Park
Address: 1651 McLendon Ave NE
Atlanta, GA 30307
Phone: (404) 370-1003

#11
Ambrose Vintage
Category: Used, Vintage
Average price: Modest
Area: Little Five Points
Address: 1160 Euclid Ave NE
Atlanta, GA 30307
Phone: (404) 688-4929

#12
Costco
Category: Wholesale Store
Average price: Modest
Address: 500 Brookhaven Ave
Atlanta, GA 30319
Phone: (404) 460-1915

#13
Junkman's Daughter
Category: Costumes, Women's Clothing
Average price: Expensive
Area: Little Five Points
Address: 464 Moreland Ave NE
Atlanta, GA 30307
Phone: (404) 577-3188

#14
Pin Up Girl Cosmetics
Category: Cosmetics, Beauty Supply, Session Photography
Average price: Modest
Area: Grant Park
Address: 566 Blvd SE
Atlanta, GA 30312
Phone: (404) 688-7468

#15
Phidippides
Category: Shoe Store
Average price: Modest
Address: 1544 Piedmont Ave NE
Atlanta, GA 30324
Phone: (404) 875-4268

#16
Cherry Bomb
Category: Shoe Store, Women's Clothing
Average price: Expensive
Area: Little Five Points
Address: 1129 Euclid Ave NE
Atlanta, GA 30307
Phone: (404) 522-2662

#17
City Issue
Category: Furniture Store, Antiques
Average price: Expensive
Area: Old Fourth Ward, Poncey-Highland
Address: 325 Elizabeth St NE
Atlanta, GA 30307
Phone: (678) 999-9075

#18
Target
Category: Department Store
Average price: Modest
Area: Atlantic Station
Address: 375 18th St
Atlanta, GA 30363
Phone: (678) 954-4265

#19
REI
Category: Bikes, Outdoor Gear, Sports Wear
Average price: Modest
Address: 1165 Perimeter Center W
Atlanta, GA 30338
Phone: (770) 901-9200

#20
Atlantic Station
Category: Shopping Center
Average price: Modest
Area: Atlantic Station
Address: 1380 Atlantic Dr
Atlanta, GA 30363
Phone: (404) 733-1221

#21
HomeGoods
Category: Home Decor, Department Store
Average price: Modest
Area: Lindbergh
Address: 2625 Piedmont Rd NE
Atlanta, GA 30305
Phone: (404) 949-9186

#22
REI
Category: Sports Wear, Outdoor Gear, Bike Repair/Maintenance
Average price: Expensive
Address: 1800 NE Expy NE
Atlanta, GA 30329
Phone: (404) 633-6508

#23
Lululemon Athletica
Category: Women's Clothing, Accessories, Men's Clothing
Average price: Expensive
Area: Westside / Home Park
Address: 1168 Howell Mill Rd
Atlanta, GA 30318
Phone: (404) 898-0774

#24
Rag-O-Rama
Category: Used, Vintage, Men's Clothing, Women's Clothing
Average price: Modest
Area: Little Five Points
Address: 1111 Euclid Ave NE
Atlanta, GA 30307
Phone: (404) 658-1988

#25
The Cook's Warehouse
Category: Appliances
Average price: Expensive
Address: 1544 Piedmont Ave NE
Atlanta, GA 30324
Phone: (404) 815-4993

#26
Wish
Category: Men's Clothing, Women's Clothing, Shoe Store
Average price: Expensive
Area: Little Five Points
Address: 447 Moreland Ave
Atlanta, GA 30307
Phone: (404) 880-0402

#27
Bang-On
Category: Fashion
Average price: Modest
Area: Little Five Points
Address: 1152 Euclid Ave
Atlanta, GA 30307
Phone: (404) 222-6466

#28
Sole Shoes & Accessories
Category: Shoe Store, Accessories
Average price: Modest
Area: Edgewood
Address: 1245 Caroline St
Atlanta, GA 30307
Phone: (404) 523-1777

#29
Tease
Category: Sports Wear, Men's Clothing, Women's Clothing
Average price: Inexpensive
Area: Little Five Points
Address: 1166 Euclid Ave NE
Atlanta, GA 30307
Phone: (404) 584-0220

#30
Metro Computer
Category: Computer Repair, Mobile Phones
Average price: Modest
Area: Midtown
Address: 950 W Peachtree St NW
Atlanta, GA 30309
Phone: (404) 865-3435

#31
Publix Super Market
Category: Grocery, Drugstore
Average price: Modest
Address: 2451 Cumberland Pkwy SE
Atlanta, GA 30339
Phone: (770) 437-7000

#33
Living Walls
Category: Art Gallery
Average price: Inexpensive
Area: Reynoldstown
Address: 170 Chester Ave SE
Atlanta, GA 30316
Phone: (404) 000-0000

#32
IKEA
Category: Furniture Store
Average price: Modest
Area: Westside / Home Park
Address: 441 16th St NW
Atlanta, GA 30363
Phone: (404) 745-4532

#34
Abbadabba's Little Five Points
Category: Shoe Store
Average price: Expensive
Area: Little Five Points
Address: 421-B Moreland Ave NE
Atlanta, GA 30307
Phone: (470) 226-5205

#35
EnvyATL
Category: Women's Clothing, Makeup Artists, Hair Salon
Average price: Expensive
Area: Little Five Points
Address: 1143 Euclid Ave NE
Atlanta, GA 30307
Phone: (404) 525-3689

#36
Aperturent
Category: Photography Store
Average price: Modest
Address: 6065 Roswell Rd NE
Atlanta, GA 30328
Phone: (404) 963-2750

#37
Criminal Records
Category: Comic Books, Music, DVDs, Vinyl Records
Average price: Modest
Area: Little Five Points
Address: 1154-A Euclid Ave NE
Atlanta, GA 30307
Phone: (404) 215-9511

#38
Bloomingdale's
Category: Department Store
Average price: Expensive
Address: 3393 Peachtree Rd NE
Atlanta, GA 30326
Phone: (404) 495-2800

#39
Brushstrokes
Category: Books, Mags, Video, Adult
Average price: Modest
Address: 1510 Piedmont Ave NE
Atlanta, GA 30324
Phone: (404) 876-6567

#40
Half Moon Outfitters
Category: Sports Wear, Outdoor Gear
Average price: Modest
Area: Virginia Highland
Address: 1034 N Highland Ave NE
Atlanta, GA 30306
Phone: (404) 249-7921

#41
Crystal Blue
Category: Arts, Crafts, Flowers, Gifts
Average price: Modest
Area: Little Five Points
Address: 1168 Euclid Ave NE
Atlanta, GA 30307
Phone: (404) 522-4605

#42
Psycho Sisters
Category: Used, Vintage, Costumes
Average price: Modest
Area: Little Five Points
Address: 428 Moreland Ave NE
Atlanta, GA 30307
Phone: (404) 523-0100

#43
Nordstrom Rack
Category: Accessories, Men's Clothing
Average price: Modest
Area: Buckhead
Address: 3495 Buckhead Loop NE
Atlanta, GA 30326
Phone: (404) 736-2230

#44
Paris on Ponce
Category: Antiques, Venues
Average price: Expensive
Area: Virginia Highland, Old Fourth Ward
Address: 716 Ponce De Leon Pl NE
Atlanta, GA 30306
Phone: (404) 249-9965

#45
Plaza Fiesta
Category: Shopping Center
Average price: Inexpensive
Address: 4166 Buford Hwy NE
Atlanta, GA 30345
Phone: (404) 982-9138

#46
Cost Plus World Market
Category: Furniture Store, Beer, Wine, Spirits, Home Decor
Average price: Modest
Area: Buckhead
Address: 3330 Piedmont Road NE
Atlanta, GA 30305
Phone: (404) 814-0801

#47
Highland Row Antiques
Category: Antiques
Average price: Modest
Area: Poncey-Highland
Address: 628 N Highland Ave NE
Atlanta, GA 30306
Phone: (404) 815-8830

#48
Leather & Luggage Depot
Category: Luggage
Average price: Modest
Address: 1151 Chattahoochee Ave NW
Atlanta, GA 30318
Phone: (404) 351-7410

#49
Petals A Florist
Category: Florist
Average price: Modest
Address: 1422 Woodmont Ln NW
Atlanta, GA 30318
Phone: (404) 350-8108

#50
CB2
Category: Home Decor, Furniture Store
Average price: Modest
Area: Midtown
Address: 1080 Peachtree St NE
Atlanta, GA 30309
Phone: (404) 894-3763

#51
Mitzi & Romano
Category: Women's Clothing
Average price: Expensive
Area: Virginia Highland
Address: 1038 N Highland Ave NE
Atlanta, GA 30306
Phone: (404) 876-7228

#52
The Letterbox
Category: Coffee, Tea, Jewelry
Average price: Modest
Area: Downtown
Address: 134 Peachtree St NW
Atlanta, GA 30303
Phone: (404) 521-9063

#53
West Elm
Category: Furniture Store
Average price: Expensive
Area: Atlantic Station
Address: 260 18th St
Atlanta, GA 30363
Phone: (404) 541-9310

#54
INTIMACY - Bra Fit Stylists
Category: Lingerie, Women's Clothing
Average price: Expensive
Area: Buckhead
Address: 3500 Peachtree Road, NE
Atlanta, GA 30326
Phone: (404) 261-9333

#55
Cumberland Mall
Category: Shopping Center
Average price: Modest
Address: 1000 Cumberland Mall
Atlanta, GA 30339
Phone: (770) 435-2206

#56
All Fired Up
Category: Arts, Crafts, Art School
Average price: Modest
Area: Emory Village
Address: 1563 N Decatur Rd NE
Atlanta, GA 30307
Phone: (404) 270-9048

#57
Costco
Category: Department Store
Average price: Modest
Address: 2900 Cumberland Mall
Atlanta, GA 30339
Phone: (770) 431-1702

#58
T.J. Maxx
Category: Department Store
Average price: Modest
Area: Buckhead
Address: 1 Buckhead Loop
Atlanta, GA 30326
Phone: (404) 467-9772

#59
Kai Lin Art
Category: Art Gallery, Arts, Crafts, Jewelry
Average price: Modest
Area: Buckhead
Address: 999 Brady Ave
Atlanta, GA 30318
Phone: (404) 408-4248

#60
Buckhead Thriftique
Category: Thrift Store
Average price: Modest
Area: Lindbergh
Address: 800 Miami Cir
Atlanta, GA 30324
Phone: (404) 365-8811

#61
Pink Sky Boutique
Category: Women's Clothing
Average price: Modest
Area: Grant Park
Address: 880 Glenwood Ave
Atlanta, GA 30316
Phone: (404) 549-7047

#62
SoKai Salon
Category: Hair Salon, Makeup Artists, Cosmetics, Beauty Supply
Average price: Modest
Area: East Atlanta Village
Address: 559 Flat Shaols Ave
Atlanta, GA 30316
Phone: (404) 586-0737

#63
Wonderroot
Category: Music Venues, Art Gallery, Cultural Center
Average price: Inexpensive
Area: Reynoldstown
Address: 982 Memorial Dr
Atlanta, GA 30316
Phone: (404) 254-5955

#64
Macy's
Category: Department Store, Men's Clothing, Women's Clothing
Average price: Modest
Area: Buckhead
Address: 3393 Peachtree Road
Atlanta, GA 30326
Phone: (404) 231-2800

#65
Hur's Wholesale Mart
Category: Jewelry, Accessories
Average price: Inexpensive
Address: 5316 Buford Hwy NE
Atlanta, GA 30340
Phone: (770) 936-0948

#66
The Fainting Couch
Category: Antiques
Average price: Modest
Area: Midtown, Old Fourth Ward
Address: 434 Ponce de Leon Ave NE
Atlanta, GA 30308
Phone: (404) 872-6698

#67
Target
Category: Department Store
Average price: Modest
Area: Lindbergh
Address: 2539 Piedmont Rd NE
Atlanta, GA 30324
Phone: (404) 720-1081

#68
Paper Source
Category: Cards, Stationery
Average price: Modest
Area: Virginia Highland
Address: 1052-54 N Highland Ave
Atlanta, GA 30306
Phone: (404) 575-4400

#69
Meringue
Category: Women's Clothing, Accessories
Average price: Expensive
Area: Morningside / Lenox Park
Address: 1393 N Highland Ave
Atlanta, GA 30306
Phone: (404) 724-0960

#70
Onyx Consulting
Category: Computer Repair, Computers
Average price: Modest
Address: 3296 Northcrest Rd
Atlanta, GA 30340
Phone: (770) 451-8223

#71
Artistic Designs
Category: Framing
Average price: Modest
Area: Morningside / Lenox Park
Address: 903 Courtenay Dr
Atlanta, GA 30306
Phone: (404) 872-4076

#72
Zara
Category: Women's Clothing, Accessories
Average price: Modest
Area: Buckhead
Address: 3393 Peachtree Rd NE
Atlanta, GA 30326
Phone: (404) 948-1516

#73
Atlanta Vintage Books
Category: Antiques, Bookstore, Wholesale Store
Average price: Modest
Address: 3660 Clairmont Rd
Atlanta, GA 30341
Phone: (770) 457-2919

#74
Anthropologie
Category: Women's Clothing
Average price: Expensive
Area: Westside / Home Park
Address: 1207 Howell Mill Rd
Atlanta, GA 30318
Phone: (404) 355-4889

#75
Anthropologie
Category: Women's Clothing, Accessories
Average price: Expensive
Address: 4400 Ashford Dunwoody Rd
Atlanta, GA 30346
Phone: (678) 320-9892

#76
Target
Category: Department Store
Average price: Modest
Area: Buckhead
Address: 3535 Peachtree Rd NE
Atlanta, GA 30326
Phone: (404) 237-9494

#77
42 Degrees South
Category: Tobacco Shop, Art Gallery, Accessories
Average price: Expensive
Area: Little Five Points
Address: 453 Moreland Ave NE
Atlanta, GA 30307
Phone: (404) 521-3420

#78
Target
Category: Department Store
Average price: Modest
Area: Edgewood
Address: 1275 Caroline St NE
Atlanta, GA 30307
Phone: (404) 260-0200

#79
Goodwill Industries of North Georgia
Category: Thrift Store
Average price: Inexpensive
Address: 3337 Buford Hwy
Atlanta, GA 30329
Phone: (678) 891-0100

#80
Atlanta Chinatown
Category: Shopping Center
Average price: Inexpensive
Address: 5383 New Peachtree Rd
Atlanta, GA 30341
Phone: (770) 986-9827

#81
Lila
Category: Women's Clothing, Accessories
Average price: Modest
Area: Lake Claire
Address: 240 N Highland Ave
Atlanta, GA 30307
Phone: (404) 584-5452

#82
The Lucky Exchange
Category: Used, Vintage, Accessories
Average price: Modest
Area: Midtown, Old Fourth Ward
Address: 212 Ponce De Leon Ave NE
Atlanta, GA 30308
Phone: (404) 817-7715

#83
Eye Elements
Category: Eyewear, Opticians
Average price: Modest
Address: 4505 Ashford Dunwoody Rd NE
#1, Atlanta, GA 30346
Phone: (770) 399-0488

#84
Raw Denim Boutique
Category: Women's Clothing, Men's Clothing, Accessories
Average price: Expensive
Address: 77 12th St NE
Atlanta, GA 30309
Phone: (404) 949-0068

#85
Target
Category: Department Store
Average price: Modest
Address: 5570 Roswell Rd NE
Atlanta, GA 30342
Phone: (678) 704-8120

#86
Tiffany and Co.
Category: Jewelry
Average price: Exclusive
Area: Buckhead
Address: 3500 Peachtree Rd NE
Atlanta, GA 30326
Phone: (404) 261-0074

#87
Fantasyland Records
Category: Videos, Video Game Rental, Music, DVDs, Antiques
Average price: Inexpensive
Area: Buckhead
Address: 360 Pharr Rd NE
Atlanta, GA 30305
Phone: (404) 237-3193

#88
H&M
Category: Men's Clothing, Women's Clothing, Children's Clothing
Average price: Inexpensive
Area: Atlantic Station
Address: 231 18th St NW
Atlanta, GA 30363
Phone: (404) 815-9430

#89
Phoenix & Dragon Bookstore
Category: Bookstore, Jewelry
Average price: Modest
Address: 5531 Roswell Rd NE
Atlanta, GA 30342
Phone: (404) 255-5207

#90
The Clothing Warehouse
Category: Used, Vintage, Men's Clothing, Women's Clothing
Average price: Modest
Area: Little Five Points
Address: 420 Moreland Ave NE
Atlanta, GA 30307
Phone: (404) 524-5070

#91
A Cappella Books
Category: Bookstore
Average price: Modest
Area: Inman Park
Address: 208 Haralson Ave NE
Atlanta, GA 30307
Phone: (404) 681-5128

#92
Antiques & Beyond
Category: Antiques, Interior Design
Average price: Expensive
Area: Morningside / Lenox Park
Address: 1853 Cheshire Bridge Rd
Atlanta, GA 30324
Phone: (404) 872-4342

#93
EyeHaven
Category: Eyewear, Opticians, Optometrists
Average price: Modest
Address: 1418 Dresden Dr
Atlanta, GA 30319
Phone: (404) 239-0272

#94
Apple Store
Category: Computers, Mobile Phones, Electronics
Average price: Expensive
Area: Buckhead
Address: 3393 Peachtree Rd NE
Atlanta, GA 30326
Phone: (404) 926-3085

#95
Lewis & Sheron Textiles
Category: Furniture Store, Fabric Store
Average price: Modest
Address: 912 Huff Rd NW
Atlanta, GA 30318
Phone: (404) 351-4833

#96
Rodica Lazarian Couture Bridal Design
Category: Bridal, Sewing, Alterations
Area: Buckhead
Address: 480 E Paces Ferry Rd
Atlanta, GA 30305
Phone: (678) 480-5629

#97
ULTA Cosmetics & Salon
Category: Cosmetics, Beauty Supply, Hair Salon
Average price: Modest
Area: Buckhead
Address: 3495 Buckhead Lp NE
Atlanta, GA 30326
Phone: (404) 266-3559

#98
High Country Outfitters
Category: Outdoor Gear, Sports Wear
Average price: Expensive
Area: Buckhead
Address: 3906 Roswell Rd NE
Atlanta, GA 30342
Phone: (404) 814-0999

#99
Mall At Peachtree Center
Category: Shopping Center
Average price: Inexpensive
Area: Downtown
Address: 231 Peachtree St NE
Atlanta, GA 30303
Phone: (404) 654-1296

#100
Rene Rene
Category: Women's Clothing
Average price: Expensive
Area: Little Five Points
Address: 1142 Euclid Ave NE
Atlanta, GA 30307
Phone: (404) 522-7363

#101
Fearless Weirdos
Category: Women's Clothing, Men's Clothing, Personal Shopping
Average price: Modest
Area: Little Five Points
Address: 426 Seminole Ave
Atlanta, GA 30307
Phone: (404) 941-8655

#102
Savvy Snoot
Category: Furniture Store, Interior Design, Home Decor
Average price: Modest
Area: Westside / Home Park
Address: 1080 Brady Ave
Atlanta, GA 30318
Phone: (404) 355-1399

#103
Colony Square
Category: Shopping Center
Average price: Modest
Area: Midtown
Address: 1175 Peachtree St NE
Atlanta, GA 30361
Phone: (404) 879-2250

#104
Norcostco Atlanta Costume
Category: Costumes, Cosmetics, Beauty Supply, Wigs
Average price: Modest
Address: 2089 Monroe Dr Ne
Atlanta, GA 30324
Phone: (404) 874-7511

#105
My Favorite Place
Category: Antiques, Flea Market
Average price: Inexpensive
Address: 5596 Peachtree Industrial
Atlanta, GA 30341
Phone: (770) 452-8397

#106
Crate and Barrel
Category: Furniture Store, Home Decor, Kitchen, Bath
Average price: Modest
Area: Buckhead
Address: 3400 Around Lenox Dr
Atlanta, GA 30326
Phone: (404) 239-0008

#107
Barnes & Noble Booksellers
Category: Bookstore
Average price: Modest
Area: Edgewood
Address: 1217 Caroline St NE
Atlanta, GA 30307
Phone: (404) 522-0212

#108
Bill Hallman Boutique
Category: Men's Clothing, Women's Clothing
Average price: Modest
Area: Virginia Highland
Address: 792 N Highland Ave NE
Atlanta, GA 30306
Phone: (404) 876-6055

#109
Sips n Strokes
Category: Art Gallery, Art School
Average price: Modest
Address: 3019 N Druid Hills Rd NE
Atlanta, GA 30329
Phone: (404) 901-1099

#110
LifeLine Repairs
Category: Electronics, Phone Repair
Average price: Modest
Address: 4505 Ashford Dunwoody Rd
Atlanta, GA 30346
Phone: (404) 989-4588

#111
Urban Cottage, Inc.
Category: Furniture Store, Home Decor
Average price: Modest
Area: Virginia Highland
Address: 998 N Highland Ave
Atlanta, GA 30306
Phone: (404) 815-9993

#112
Cultural Acc'nts
Category: Women's Clothing
Area: Little Five Points
Address: 1154 B Euclid Ave
Atlanta, GA 30307
Phone: (404) 414-9974

#113
Men's Wearhouse and Tux
Category: Men's Clothing, Formal Wear
Average price: Modest
Area: Buckhead
Address: 3393 Peachtree Rd NE
Atlanta, GA 30326
Phone: (404) 237-8340

#114
Apple Store Perimeter
Category: Computers
Address: 4400 Ashford Dunwoody Rd
Atlanta, GA 30346
Phone: (678) 459-9800

#115
Labels Resale Boutique
Category: Used, Vintage, Jewelry
Average price: Modest
Area: Buckhead
Address: 3202 Paces Ferry Pl
Atlanta, GA 30305
Phone: (404) 841-8444

#116
Room & Board
Category: Home Decor, Furniture Store
Average price: Expensive
Area: Westside / Home Park
Address: 1170 Howell Mill Rd NW
Atlanta, GA 30318
Phone: (404) 682-5900

#117
Fox's Designer Clothing
Category: Women's Clothing
Average price: Modest
Area: Buckhead
Address: 3804 Roswell Rd NE
Atlanta, GA 30342
Phone: (404) 814-9292

#118
Cooks Warehouse
Category: Kitchen, Bath
Average price: Expensive
Area: Brookhaven
Address: 4062 Peachtree Rd NE
Atlanta, GA 30319
Phone: (404) 949-9945

#119
Target
Category: Department Store
Average price: Modest
Address: 2400 N Druid Hills Rd NE
Atlanta, GA 30329
Phone: (404) 267-0060

#120
Dress Up Boutique
Category: Women's Clothing, Accessories
Average price: Modest
Address: 305 Brookhaven Ave, Bldg B, Ste 1190, Atlanta, GA 30319
Phone: (404) 812-7018

#121
Vape Atlanta
Category: Vape Shop
Average price: Modest
Area: Little Five Points
Address: 1083 Euclid Ave
Atlanta, GA 30307
Phone: (404) 207-4321

#122
Atlanta Contemporary Art Center
Category: Art Gallery
Average price: Inexpensive
Address: 535 Means St NW
Atlanta, GA 30318
Phone: (404) 688-1970

#123
Saks Fifth Avenue
Category: Department Store
Average price: Exclusive
Area: Buckhead
Address: 3500 Peachtree Road NE
Atlanta, GA 30326
Phone: (404) 261-7234

#124
Nearly New Shop
Category: Used, Vintage
Average price: Modest
Area: Westside / Home Park
Address: 1715 Howell Mill Road NW
Atlanta, GA 30318
Phone: (404) 355-3547

#125
Barnes & Noble Booksellers
Category: Bookstore, Toy Store, Music, DVDs
Average price: Modest
Address: 120 Perimeter Ctr W Ste 300
Atlanta, GA 30346
Phone: (770) 396-1200

#126
Tom Lowe Trap & Skeet Range
Category: Gun, Rifle
Average price: Inexpensive
Address: 3070 Merk Rd
Atlanta, GA 30349
Phone: (404) 346-8382

#127
Atlantis Eclectic Boutique
Category: Fashion, Jewelry
Average price: Modest
Area: Little Five Points
Address: 1164 Euclid Ave
Atlanta, GA 30307
Phone: (404) 276-6051

#128
Urban Outfitters
Category: Fashion, Home Decor
Average price: Modest
Area: Virginia Highland
Address: 1061 Ponce DeLeon Ave NE
Atlanta, GA 30306
Phone: (404) 541-9256

#129
Emory Point
Category: Shopping Center
Average price: Modest
Address: 1627 Clifton Rd NE
Atlanta, GA 30329
Phone: (866) 312-4782

#130
Ace Hardware
Category: Hardware Store
Average price: Modest
Address: 2983 N Druid Hills Rd NE
Atlanta, GA 30329
Phone: (404) 325-8000

#131
Beep Beep Gallery
Category: Art Gallery
Average price: Inexpensive
Area: Midtown, Old Fourth Ward
Address: 696 Charles Allen Dr
Atlanta, GA 30308
Phone: (404) 429-3320

#132
Toco Instant Printing
Category: Printing Services, Office Equipment, Cards, Stationery
Average price: Modest
Address: 2960 N Druid Hills Rd NE
Atlanta, GA 30329
Phone: (404) 321-5677

#133
Bombay Gal Boutique
Category: Women's Clothing
Average price: Modest
Area: Little Five Points
Address: 1130 Euclid Ave
Atlanta, GA 30307
Phone: (404) 668-4895

#134
Lowe's
Category: Hardware Store
Average price: Modest
Area: Edgewood
Address: 1280 Caroline St NE
Atlanta, GA 30307
Phone: (404) 658-8650

#135
Lifecycle Building Center
Category: Home, Garden, Building Supplies
Average price: Inexpensive
Address: 1116 Murphy Ave SW
Atlanta, GA 30310
Phone: (404) 997-3873

#136
Abbadabba's Buckhead
Category: Shoe Store
Average price: Modest
Area: Buckhead
Address: 4389 Roswell Rd NE
Atlanta, GA 30342
Phone: (404) 262-3356

#137
Festivity
Category: Women's Clothing
Average price: Modest
Area: Virginia Highland
Address: 1039 N Highland Ave NE
Atlanta, GA 30306
Phone: (404) 724-4883

#138
Sur La Table
Category: Kitchen, Bath, Specialty Food, Cooking School
Average price: Modest
Area: Buckhead
Address: 3500 Peachtree Rd
Atlanta, GA 30326
Phone: (404) 973-3371

#139
Richards Variety Store
Category: Toy Store, Party Supplies, Antiques
Average price: Modest
Area: Midtown
Address: 931 Monroe Dr
Atlanta, GA 30308
Phone: (404) 879-9877

#140
Woo Skincare & Cosmetics
Category: Cosmetics, Skin Care
Average price: Expensive
Area: Buckhead
Address: Peachtree Battle Shopping Ctr
Atlanta, GA 30305
Phone: (404) 477-5000

#141
Highland Runners
Category: Shoe Store, Sports Wear
Average price: Modest
Area: Morningside / Lenox Park
Address: 1393 N Highland Ave NE
Atlanta, GA 30306
Phone: (404) 549-3309

#142
Standard
Category: Women's Clothing, Accessories, Men's Clothing
Average price: Modest
Area: Buckhead
Address: 1841 Peachtree Rd NE
Atlanta, GA 30309
Phone: (404) 355-1410

#143
Madewell
Category: Women's Clothing, Accessories, Shoe Store
Average price: Modest
Area: Buckhead
Address: 3393 Peachtree Road
Atlanta, GA 30326
Phone: (404) 816-4178

#144
The North Face
Category: Sports Wear, Outdoor Gear
Average price: Expensive
Area: Buckhead
Address: 35 A West Paces Ferry Rd
Atlanta, GA 30305
Phone: (404) 467-0119

#145
Michal Evans Floral Design
Category: Florist
Average price: Exclusive
Area: Buckhead
Address: 3200 Cains Hill Place NW
Atlanta, GA 30305
Phone: (404) 365-0200

#146
Lush Handmade Cosmetics
Category: Cosmetics, Beauty Supply
Average price: Modest
Address: 4300 Ashford Dunwoody Rd NE,
Atlanta, GA 30346
Phone: (770) 396-5874

#147
Gallery1526
Category:
Average price: Art Gallery
Area: Candler Park
Address: 1526 Dekalb Ave NE
Atlanta, GA 30307
Phone: (404) 484-2871

#148
MarsHall
Category: Department Store
Average price: Modest
Address: 1131 Hammond Dr NE
Atlanta, GA 30346
Phone: (770) 396-8623

#149
Ace Hardware
Category: Hardware Store
Average price: Modest
Area: Buckhead
Address: 4405 Roswell Road NE
Atlanta, GA 30342
Phone: (404) 255-2411

#150
lululemon athletica
Category: Sports Wear, Women's Clothing, Yoga
Average price: Expensive
Area: Buckhead
Address: 3400 Around Lenox Rd NE, Ste 102A, Atlanta, GA 30326
Phone: (404) 816-7678

#151
Bed Bath & Beyond
Category: Kitchen, Bath
Average price: Modest
Area: Edgewood
Address: 1235 Caroline Street NE
Atlanta, GA 30307
Phone: (404) 522-3210

#152
Nandina Home & Design
Category: Home Decor, Furniture Store, Interior Design
Average price: Modest
Area: Old Fourth Ward, Inman Park
Address: 245 N Highland Ave
Atlanta, GA 30312
Phone: (404) 521-9303

#153
Bates Ace Hardware
Category: Hardware Store, Nursery, Gardening
Average price: Modest
Address: 1709 Howell Mill Rd NW
Atlanta, GA 30318
Phone: (404) 351-4240

#154
Baby Love
Category: Baby Gear, Furniture, Toy Store, Children's Clothing
Average price: Modest
Area: Grant Park
Address: 465 Boulevard SE
Atlanta, GA 30312
Phone: (404) 590-1380

#155
Gap
Category: Men's Clothing, Women's Clothing, Sports Wear
Average price: Modest
Area: Atlantic Station
Address: 260 18th Street
Atlanta, GA 30363
Phone: (404) 685-9492

#156
Intaglia Home Collection
Category: Furniture Store, Home Decor
Average price: Modest
Address: 1544 Piedmont Ave
Atlanta, GA 30324
Phone: (404) 607-9750

#157
Z Gallerie
Category: Furniture Store, Home Decor
Average price: Modest
Area: Atlantic Station
Address: Atlantic Station
Atlanta, GA 30363
Phone: (404) 870-8531

#158
MarsHall
Category: Department Store
Average price: Inexpensive
Area: Buckhead
Address: 3232 Peachtree Road NW
Atlanta, GA 30305
Phone: (404) 365-8155

#159
Fabricate Studio
Category: Arts, Crafts, Art School, Sewing, Alterations
Average price: Modest
Address: 1746-B Defoor Ave NW
Atlanta, GA 30318
Phone: (404) 981-4665

#160
Lui B
Category: Men's Clothing
Average price: Expensive
Area: Midtown
Address: 1116 W Peachtree St NW
Atlanta, GA 30309
Phone: (404) 810-0031

#161
Woodruff Arts Center
Category: Performing Arts, Art Gallery
Average price: Modest
Area: Midtown
Address: 1280 Peachtree St NE
Atlanta, GA 30309
Phone: (404) 733-4200

#162
Stanton Home Furnishings
Category: Home, Garden
Average price: Expensive
Area: Poncey-Highland
Address: 1050 N Highland Ave NE
Atlanta, GA 30306
Phone: (678) 973-0291

#163
Highland Woodworking
Category: Hobby Shop
Average price: Exclusive
Area: Virginia Highland
Address: 1045 N Highland Ave NE
Atlanta, GA 30306
Phone: (404) 872-4466

#164
Atlanta Salvage Outlet
Category: Hardware Store, Building Supplies
Average price: Inexpensive
Area: Westside / Home Park
Address: 1034 Howell Mill Rd NW
Atlanta, GA 30318
Phone: (404) 873-4416

#165
Candler Park Flower Mart
Category: Florist
Average price: Modest
Area: Candler Park
Address: 1395 McLendon Ave NE
Atlanta, GA 30307
Phone: (404) 522-0005

#166
Simplyput
Category: Cards, Stationery
Average price: Expensive
Area: Westside / Home Park
Address: 1170 Howell Mill Rd
Atlanta, GA 30318
Phone: (404) 881-8660

#167
Market
Category: Women's Clothing, Accessories
Average price: Modest
Address: 2770 Lenox Rd NE
Atlanta, GA 30324
Phone: (404) 814-0977

#168
Oxford Comics & Games
Category: Comic Books, Sporting Goods, Music, DVDs
Average price: Modest
Area: Buckhead
Address: 2855 Piedmont Rd NE
Atlanta, GA 30305
Phone: (404) 233-8682

#169
Best Buy
Category: Appliances, Computers
Average price: Modest
Area: Edgewood
Address: 1210 Caroline St NE
Atlanta, GA 30307
Phone: (404) 827-0137

#170
Veronica's Attic
Category: Women's Clothing
Address: 220 Sandy Springs Cir NE
Atlanta, GA 30328
Phone: (404) 257-1409

#171
Direct Furniture Atlanta
Category: Furniture Store, Home Decor
Average price: Expensive
Area: Westside / Home Park
Address: 1005 Howell Mill Rd NW
Atlanta, GA 30318
Phone: (404) 477-0038

#172
Town Brookhaven
Category: Shopping Center
Average price: Modest
Address: 4300 Peachtree Rd NE
Atlanta, GA 30319
Phone: (404) 281-3568

#173
Bombay Gal Boutique
Category: Women's Clothing, Jewelry
Average price: Modest
Area: Grant Park
Address: 674 A N Highlands Ave
Atlanta, GA 30312
Phone: (404) 941-8230

#174
The Impeccable Pig
Category: Shopping
Average price: Expensive
Area: Buckhead
Address: 3400 Around Lenox Dr NE
Atlanta, GA 30326
Phone: (404) 816-7337

#175
Pike Nursery
Category: Nursery, Gardening
Address: 2101 LaVista Rd
Atlanta, GA 30329
Phone: (404) 634-8604

#176
Jonathan Adler
Category: Accessories
Average price: Expensive
Area: Westside / Home Park
Address: 1198 Howell Mill Rd
Atlanta, GA 30318
Phone: (404) 367-0414

#177
Microsoft Store
Category: Electronics, Computers, Mobile Phones
Average price: Modest
Area: Buckhead
Address: 3393 Peachtree Road NE, Suite 3007A
Atlanta, GA 30326
Phone: (404) 942-6170

#178
Beverly Bremer Silver Shop
Category: Kitchen, Bath,
Metal Fabricator
Average price: Exclusive
Area: Buckhead
Address: 3164 Peachtree Rd NE
Atlanta, GA 30305
Phone: (404) 261-4009

#179
Boxwoods Gardens & Gifts
Category: Flowers, Gifts, Antiques
Average price: Exclusive
Area: Buckhead
Address: 100 E Andrews Dr NW
Atlanta, GA 30305
Phone: (404) 233-3400

#180
Mint Julep
Category: Women's Clothing, Children's Clothing, Accessories
Average price: Expensive
Area: Buckhead
Address: 2353 Peachtree Rd
Atlanta, GA 30305
Phone: (404) 814-9155

#181
Banana Republic
Category: Men's Clothing,
Women's Clothing
Average price: Modest
Area: Atlantic Station
Address: 1374 Atlantic Dr
Atlanta, GA 30363
Phone: (404) 249-9170

#182
Peachtree Petals
Category: Florist
Average price: Modest
Area: Midtown
Address: 1450 W Peachtree NW
Atlanta, GA 30309
Phone: (678) 336-1195

#183
Pollen
Category: Nursery, Gardening, Florist
Average price: Expensive
Area: Buckhead
Address: 432 E Paces Ferry Rd NE
Atlanta, GA 30305
Phone: (404) 262-2296

#184
Buckhead Crossing
Category: Shopping Center
Average price: Modest
Area: Lindbergh
Address: 740 Sidney Marcus Blvd NE
Atlanta, GA 31132
Phone: (404) 841-0883

#185
Just the Thing
Category: Jewelry, Accessories
Average price: Modest
Area: Buckhead
Address: 529 Pharr Rd NE
Atlanta, GA 30305
Phone: (404) 869-4100

#186
The Mercantile
Category: Home Decor
Average price: Expensive
Address: 1430 Dresden Dr
Atlanta, GA 30319
Phone: (404) 816-0060

#187
J's Cigar & Coffee House
Category:
Average price: Tobacco Shop
Address: 2072 Defoors Ferry Rd NW
Atlanta, GA 30318
Phone: (404) 355-2342

#188
Kroger
Category: Drugstore, Grocery
Average price: Modest
Address: 4498 Chamblee Dunwoody Rd
Atlanta, GA 30338
Phone: (770) 451-7408

#189
NV-U Boutique
Category: Women's Clothing
Average price: Modest
Area: Grant Park
Address: 465 Blvd SE
Atlanta, GA 30312
Phone: (404) 624-3737

#190
Liberator
Category: Adult, Lingerie
Average price: Expensive
Address: 2745 Bankers Industrial Dr
Atlanta, GA 30360
Phone: (770) 246-6422

#191
David Yurman
Category: Jewelry
Average price: Expensive
Area: Buckhead
Address: 3393 Peachtree Road NE
Atlanta, GA 30326
Phone: (404) 812-9225

#192
Mason Murer Fine Art
Category: Art Gallery, Venues
Average price: Exclusive
Area: Buckhead
Address: 199 Armour Dr NE
Atlanta, GA 30324
Phone: (404) 879-1500

#193
Dakota J's
Category: Fashion
Area: Virginia Highland
Address: 1030 N Highland Ave NE
Atlanta, GA 30306
Phone: (404) 870-0690

#194
Gucci
Category: Leather Goods, Men's Clothing, Women's Clothing
Average price: Exclusive
Area: Buckhead
Address: 3500 Peachtree Road
Atlanta, GA 30326
Phone: (404) 233-4899

#195
Pinkheart Accessories
Category: Women's Clothing
Average price: Modest
Area: Atlantic Station
Address: 1380 Atlantic Dr
Atlanta, GA 30363
Phone: (404) 347-2811

#196
Underground Atlanta
Category: Shopping Center, Amusement Park
Average price: Inexpensive
Area: Downtown
Address: 50 Upper Alabama St SW
Atlanta, GA 30303
Phone: (404) 523-2311

#197
Old Navy
Category: Fashion
Average price: Modest
Area: Atlantic Station
Address: 261 19th St
Atlanta, GA 30363
Phone: (404) 872-5138

#198
The District at Howell Mill
Category: Shopping Center
Average price: Modest
Area: Westside / Home Park
Address: 1801 Howell Mill Rd NW
Atlanta, GA 30318
Phone: (404) 355-1326

#199
Brooks Brothers
Category: Men's Clothing
Average price: Expensive
Area: Buckhead
Address: 3393 Peachtree Rd NE
Atlanta, GA 30326
Phone: (404) 237-7000

#200
TRIO Custom Clothiers
Category: Bespoke Clothing, Formal Wear, Men's Clothing
Average price: Modest
Area: Westside / Home Park
Address: 349 14th St
Atlanta, GA 30318
Phone: (404) 662-2263

#201
Urban Outfitters
Category: Department Store
Average price: Modest
Area: Buckhead
Address: 3393 Peachtree Rd NE
Atlanta, GA 30326
Phone: (404) 467-1615

#202
Mountain High Outfitters
Category: Outdoor Gear
Average price: Expensive
Area: West Paces Ferry / Northside
Address: 1248 B W Paces Ferry Rd
Atlanta, GA 30327
Phone: (404) 343-1764

#203
Reflections Eyecare
Category: Optometrists, Eyewear, Opticians
Average price: Modest
Address: 305 Brookhaven Ave
Atlanta, GA 30319
Phone: (404) 816-8889

#204
Teahouse Comics
Category: Comic Books
Average price: Inexpensive
Address: 5920 Roswell Rd NE
Atlanta, GA 30328
Phone: (404) 252-3994

#205
Rare Footage
Category: Shoe Store
Average price: Modest
Area: East Atlanta Village
Address: 493-C Flat Shoals Ave SE
Atlanta, GA 30316
Phone: (404) 215-2188

#206
Lilly Porter
Category: Jewelry, Antiques
Average price: Modest
Area: Buckhead
Address: 3121 Maple Dr
Atlanta, GA 30305
Phone: (404) 245-0586

#207
Bradley T Harris
Category: Jewelry, Jewelry Repairl
Average price: Modest
Address: 4360 Chamblee Dunwoody Rd
Atlanta, GA 30341
Phone: (770) 455-0822

#208
The Perfect Brows
Category: Hair Removal, Cosmetics, Beauty Supply
Average price: Modest
Area: Buckhead
Address: 56 E Andrews Dr
Atlanta, GA 30305
Phone: (404) 816-5392

#209
Laura Powers Jewelry
Category: Jewelry
Average price: Exclusive
Area: Buckhead
Address: 3344 Peachtree Rd
Atlanta, GA 30326
Phone: (404) 233-9841

#210
Free People
Category: Accessories, Women's Clothing
Average price: Expensive
Area: Buckhead
Address: 3393 Peachtree Rd NE
Atlanta, GA 30326
Phone: (404) 869-8101

#211
Alexis Suitcase
Category: Used, Vintage
Average price: Modest
Address: 7878 Roswell Rd
Atlanta, GA 30350
Phone: (770) 390-0010

#212
Atlantis Hydroponics
Category: Nursery, Gardening
Address: 1422 Woodmont Lane NW
Atlanta, GA 30318
Phone: (404) 367-0052

#213
Decades Antiques & Vintage
Category: Antiques
Average price: Modest
Area: Morningside / Lenox Park
Address: 1886 Cheshire Bridge Rd
Atlanta, GA 30324
Phone: (404) 888-0099

#214
Inserection
Category: Adult Entertainment, Adult
Average price: Modest
Area: Morningside / Lenox Park
Address: 1739 Cheshire Bridge Rd NE
Atlanta, GA 30324
Phone: (404) 875-9200

#215
Biggar Antiques
Category: Antiques
Average price: Expensive
Address: 5576 Peachtree Rd
Atlanta, GA 30341
Phone: (770) 451-2541

#216
No Mas! Hacienda
Category: Home Decor, Furniture Store
Average price: Modest
Area: Castleberry Hill
Address: 180 Walker St SW
Atlanta, GA 30313
Phone: (404) 215-9769

#217
Ross Dress For Less
Category: Women's Clothing, Men's Clothing, Shoe Store
Average price: Inexpensive
Area: Edgewood
Address: 1255 Caroline St
Atlanta, GA 30307
Phone: (404) 527-3769

#218
CVS/pharmacy
Category: Drugstore
Average price: Modest
Area: Old Fourth Ward
Address: 439 Highland Avenue NE
Atlanta, GA 30312
Phone: (404) 230-9385

#219
Pike Nursery
Category: Nursery, Gardening
Average price: Modest
Address: 4020 Roswell Rd NE
Atlanta, GA 30342
Phone: (404) 843-9578

#220
Atlanta Habitat for Humanity Restore
Category: Furniture Store, Kitchen, Bath
Average price: Modest
Area: Grant Park
Address: 519 Memorial Dr SE
Atlanta, GA 30312
Phone: (404) 525-2114

#221
Dollar Tree
Category: Home, Garden
Average price: Inexpensive
Address: 2036 M Johnson Ferry Rd
Atlanta, GA 30319
Phone: (770) 458-9397

#222
Engineer's Bookstore
Category: Bookstore
Average price: Modest
Address: 748 Marietta St NW
Atlanta, GA 30318
Phone: (404) 221-1669

#223
Art & Soul
Category: Art Supplies
Average price: Modest
Address: 4920 Roswell Rd NE
Atlanta, GA 30342
Phone: (404) 303-9959

#224
CVS/Pharmacy
Category: Drugstore
Average price: Inexpensive
Area: Midtown
Address: 842 Peachtree St NE
Atlanta, GA 30308
Phone: (404) 881-1605

#225
Baby Braithwaite
Category: Baby Gear, Furniture
Average price: Exclusive
Area: Buckhead
Address: 102 W Paces Ferry Rd NW
Atlanta, GA 30305
Phone: (404) 869-8665

#226
H&M
Category: Women's Clothing, Men's Clothing
Average price: Modest
Address: 1620 Cumberland Mall
Atlanta, GA 30339
Phone: (770) 801-2000

#227
MarsHall
Category: Department Store
Average price: Inexpensive
Address: 150 Brookhaven Ave NE
Atlanta, GA 30319
Phone: (404) 848-9447

#228
The Hookah Hook Up
Category: Tobacco Shop
Average price: Modest
Area: Little Five Points
Address: 421 Moreland Ave
Atlanta, GA 30307
Phone: (404) 589-4446

#229
Patagonia
Category: Sports Wear, Outdoor Gear
Average price: Expensive
Area: Buckhead
Address: 34 E Andrews Dr NW
Atlanta, GA 30305
Phone: (404) 266-8182

#230
Scarlett Loves Rhettro
Category: Antiques
Average price: Modest
Area: Midtown, Old Fourth Ward
Address: 436 Ponce De Leon AveNE
Atlanta, GA 30308
Phone: (404) 249-7699

#231
Bridal Couture by Ruby V
Category: Bridal
Average price: Exclusive
Area: Buckhead
Address: 110 E Andrews Dr NW
Atlanta, GA 30305
Phone: (404) 261-8866

#232
Goodwill of North Georgia
Category: Thrift Store
Average price: Inexpensive
Area: Buckhead
Address: 3906 Roswell Rd
Atlanta, GA 30342
Phone: (404) 869-3112

#233
Atlanta Activewear
Category: Sports Wear, Women's Clothing
Average price: Expensive
Area: Virginia Highland
Address: 996 Virginia Ave NE
Atlanta, GA 30306
Phone: (404) 532-1975

#234
Pike Nursery
Category: Nursery, Gardening
Average price: Modest
Area: Buckhead
Address: 2410 Camellia Ln NE
Atlanta, GA 30324
Phone: (404) 869-2875

#235
PB&J Gallery
Category: Art Gallery
Average price: Modest
Address: 35 Howard St SE
Atlanta, GA 30317
Phone: (404) 606-1856

#236
Williams-Sonoma
Category: Kitchen, Bath
Average price: Expensive
Address: 3393 Peachtree Rd NE
Atlanta, GA 30326
Phone: (404) 812-1703

#237
Wright's Buckhead
Wright's Florist
Category: Florist
Area: Buckhead
Address: 2393 Peachtree Road NE
Atlanta, GA 30305
Phone: (404) 233-4446

#238
Authentique
Category: Home Decor
Address: 312A N Highland Ave
Atlanta, GA 30307
Phone: (404) 428-6740

#239
Palas Jewelers
Category: Jewelry
Average price: Modest
Address: 3209 Paces Ferry Pl
Atlanta, GA 30305
Phone: (404) 846-8122

#240
Northlake Mall
Category: Shopping Center
Average price: Modest
Address: 4800 Briarcliff Rd NE
Atlanta, GA 30345
Phone: (770) 938-3565

#241
Polo Ralph Lauren Store
Category: Department Store
Area: Buckhead
Address: 3393 Peachtree Road NE
Atlanta, GA 30326
Phone: (404) 261-2663

#242
The Home Depot
Category: Hardware Store, Nursery, Gardening, Appliances
Average price: Modest
Area: Midtown
Address: 650 Ponce DE Leon
Atlanta, GA 30308
Phone: (404) 892-8042

#243
Blue Mark Studio
Category: Venues, Art Gallery
Average price: Modest
Address: 892 Jefferson St
Atlanta, GA 30318
Phone: (678) 786-9490

#244
Banana Republic
Category: Men's Clothing, Women's Clothing
Average price: Expensive
Address: Town Center Cobb
Atlanta, GA 30303
Phone: (678) 290-8405

#245
Spruill Center For the Arts
Category:
Average price: Art School, Art Gallery
Address: 5339 Chamblee Dunwoody Rd
Atlanta, GA 30338
Phone: (770) 394-3447

#246
J Crew
Category: Men's Clothing, Women's Clothing
Average price: Modest
Area: Buckhead
Address: 3393 Peachtree Rd NE
Atlanta, GA 30326
Phone: (404) 237-2739

#247
The Granite Room
Category: Venues, Art Gallery
Average price: Modest
Area: Castleberry Hill
Address: 211 Peters St
Atlanta, GA 30313
Phone: (404) 221-0201

#248
Francesca's Collections
Category: Women's Clothing
Average price: Modest
Address: 4300 Paces Ferry, Ste #257
Atlanta, GA 30339
Phone: (770) 431-9672

#249
BrandsMart USA
Category: Electronics, Appliances, Mobile Phones
Average price: Modest
Address: 5000 Motors Industrial Way
Atlanta, GA 30341
Phone: (770) 452-9500

#250
Rite Aid
Category: Drugstore, Convenience Store
Average price: Inexpensive
Address: 2498 Cumberland Parkway Se
Atlanta, GA 30339
Phone: (770) 432-1533

#251
Dillard's
Category: Women's Clothing
Average price: Expensive
Area: Atlantic Station
Address: 1371 Market St NW
Atlanta, GA 30363
Phone: (404) 879-0635

#252
East West Jewelers
Category: Watches, Art Gallery, Jewelry
Average price: Expensive
Address: 3005 Peachtree Rd Ne
Atlanta, GA 30305
Phone: (404) 869-9935

#253
Vision Source InSight Eyecare
Category: Optometrists, Eyewear
Average price: Modest
Address: 5380 Roswell Road NE
Atlanta, GA 30342
Phone: (404) 250-1680

#254
Office Depot
Category: Office Equipment
Average price: Modest
Area: Edgewood
Address: 1205 Caroline St NE
Atlanta, GA 30307
Phone: (404) 222-9611

#255
Buckhead Blooms
Category: Florist
Average price: Modest
Address: 3060 Peachtree Rd NE
Atlanta, GA 30305
Phone: (404) 266-2400

#256
Sports Authority
Category: Sporting Goods
Average price: Modest
Area: Buckhead
Address: 3221 Peachtree Rd NE
Atlanta, GA 30305
Phone: (404) 814-0710

#257
American Apparel
Category: Men's Clothing,
Women's Clothing, Accessories
Average price: Modest
Area: Little Five Points
Address: 1133 Euclid Avenue NE
Atlanta, GA 30307
Phone: (404) 880-8611

#258
MarsHall
Category: Department Store
Average price: Modest
Area: Lindbergh
Address: 2625 Piedmont Rd NE
Atlanta, GA 30324
Phone: (404) 233-3848

#259
The Cycle Of Style
Category: Women's Clothing, Vintage
Area: Westside / Home Park
Address: 216 14th St NW
Atlanta, GA 30318
Phone: (404) 565-0412

#260
Crown & Caliber
Category: Watches
Average price: Exclusive
Area: Buckhead
Address: 3565 Piedmont Rd
Atlanta, GA 30305
Phone: (800) 514-3750

#261
Bungalow Classic
Category: Home Decor, Furniture Store
Average price: Expensive
Area: Westside / Home Park
Address: 1197 Howell Mill Rd NW
Atlanta, GA 30318
Phone: (404) 351-9120

#262
Buckhead Spring Arts Festival
Category: Festival, Arts, Crafts, Jewelry
Average price: Modest
Address: 4001 Powers Ferry Rd NW
Atlanta, GA 30342
Phone: (404) 845-0793

#263
The Clothing Warehouse
Category: Used, Vintage
Area: Midtown
Address: 999 Peachtree St NE
Atlanta, GA 30309
Phone: (404) 669-9654

#264
Plush Boutique
Category: Women's Clothing, Accessories
Average price: Modest
Area: Buckhead
Address: 3060 Pharr Ct
Atlanta, GA 30305
Phone: (404) 671-8362

#265
Express
Category: Accessories, Men's Clothing, Women's Clothing
Average price: Expensive
Area: Atlantic Station
Address: 230 18th St NW
Atlanta, GA 30363
Phone: (404) 249-7763

#266
LensCrafters
Category: Eyewear, Opticians, Optometrists, Ophthalmologists
Average price: Expensive
Address: 1440 Cumberland Mall SE
Atlanta, GA 30339
Phone: (770) 434-9788

#267
Redefined Home Boutique
Category: Furniture Store
Average price: Expensive
Address: 887 Howell Mill Rd
Atlanta, GA 30318
Phone: (404) 815-7250

#268
Sam's Club
Category: Department Store
Average price: Modest
Address: 2901Clairmont Rd NE
Atlanta, GA 30353
Phone: (404) 325-4000

#269
CVS/Pharmacy
Category: Drugstore
Average price: Modest
Address: 2350 Cheshire Bridge Rd
Atlanta, GA 30324
Phone: (404) 486-7288

#270
Continental Styles
Category: Cosmetics, Beauty Supply
Average price: Modest
Area: Downtown
Address: 229 Peachtree St NE
Atlanta, GA 30303
Phone: (404) 577-6511

#271
T.J. Maxx
Category: Department Store
Average price: Modest
Address: 1801 Howell Mill Rd SW
Atlanta, GA 30318
Phone: (404) 355-2581

#272
Westside Provisions District
Category: Shopping Center
Average price: Expensive
Area: Westside / Home Park
Address: 1100-1210 Howell Mill Rd
Atlanta, GA 30318
Phone: (404) 835-8209

#273
Dick's Sporting Goods
Category: Sports Wear, Outdoor Gear
Average price: Modest
Area: Buckhead
Address: 3535 Peachtree Rd
Atlanta, GA 30326
Phone: (404) 267-0200

#274
Toys "R" Us
Category: Toy Store
Average price: Inexpensive
Area: Buckhead
Address: 1 Buckhead Lp Dr NE
Atlanta, GA 30326
Phone: (404) 467-8697

#275
Super Beauty
Category: Cosmetics, Beauty Supply
Average price: Modest
Address: 2841 Greenbriar Pkwy SW
Atlanta, GA 30331
Phone: (404) 344-8686

#276
The Container Store
Category: Kitchen, Bath
Average price: Modest
Area: Buckhead
Address: 3637 Peachtree Rd NE
Atlanta, GA 30319
Phone: (404) 963-9602

#277
Midtown Jewelers
Category: Watch Repair, Jewelry
Average price: Modest
Address: 1544 Piedmont Ave
Atlanta, GA 30324
Phone: (404) 724-9900

#278
Earthtone
Category: Men's Clothing, Women's Clothing
Area: Little Five Points
Address: 1139 Euclid Ave NE
Atlanta, GA 30307
Phone: (404) 748-4361

#279
LensCrafters
Category: Eyewear, Opticians, Optometrists, Ophthalmologists
Average price: Modest
Address: 2370 N Druid Hills Rd NE
Atlanta, GA 30329
Phone: (404) 321-2020

#280
Hermes of Paris
Category: Accessories
Area: Buckhead
Address: 273 Buckhead Ave NE
Atlanta, GA 30305
Phone: (404) 816-1179

#281
T-Mobile
Category: Mobile Phones
Average price: Modest
Area: Buckhead
Address: 3393 Peachtree Rd NE
Atlanta, GA 30326
Phone: (404) 848-9808

#282
Swank
Category: Accessories, Shoe Store, Women's Clothing
Average price: Expensive
Area: Buckhead
Address: 3400 Around Lenox Rd NE
Atlanta, GA 30326
Phone: (404) 231-4114

#283
K & G Men's Center
Category: Men's Clothing
Average price: Modest
Address: 1750-A Ellsworth Indstrial Blvd
Atlanta, GA 30318
Phone: (404) 352-3527

#284
Janke Studio
Category: Art Gallery, Arts, Crafts
Average price: Modest
Area: Old Fourth Ward
Address: 659 Auburn Ave NE
Atlanta, GA 30312
Phone: (404) 584-0305

#285
Brighton Collectibles
Category: Jewelry, Accessories
Average price: Expensive
Area: Buckhead
Address: 3500 Peachtree Rd NE
Atlanta, GA 30326
Phone: (404) 848-1032

#286
Pieces
Category: Furniture Store, Home Decor
Average price: Expensive
Area: Buckhead
Address: 3234 Roswell Road NW
Atlanta, GA 30305
Phone: (404) 869-2476

#287
Simmons World of Sleep Mattress Outlet
Category: Mattresses
Average price: Inexpensive
Address: 1335 Chattahoochee Ave NW
Atlanta, GA 30318
Phone: (404) 355-7606

#288
Party City
Category: Party Supplies, Cards, Stationery, Costumes
Average price: Expensive
Area: Buckhead
Address: 2900 Peachtree Rd
Atlanta, GA 30305
Phone: (404) 841-9170

#289
Achoo Allergy
Category: Health & Medical, Appliances
Average price: Modest
Address: 3411 Pierce Dr
Atlanta, GA 30341
Phone: (770) 455-9999

#290
The Salvation Army
Category: Thrift Store, Community Service/Non-Profit, Discount Store
Average price: Inexpensive
Address: 746 Marietta St NW
Atlanta, GA 30318
Phone: (404) 523-6214

#291
American Mountain
Category: Sports Wear, Outdoor Gear
Average price: Modest
Address: 4300 Paces Ferry Rd
Atlanta, GA 30339
Phone: (770) 432-1655

#292
Cummin Landscape Supply
Category: Nursery, Gardening
Average price: Modest
Area: Cabbagetown
Address: 724 Memorial Dr SE
Atlanta, GA 30316
Phone: (404) 221-9285

#293
Staples
Category: Office Equipment
Average price: Modest
Address: 5560 Roswell Rd
Atlanta, GA 30328
Phone: (404) 256-4602

#294
TK Designs
Category: Women's Clothing, Bridal, Sewing, Alterations
Average price: Modest
Address: 6333 Roswell Rd
Atlanta, GA 30328
Phone: (404) 943-0037

#295
Cabbagetown Clay & Glass Works
Category: Art Gallery
Average price: Modest
Address: 588 Woodward Avenue
Atlanta, GA 30312
Phone: (678) 778-7082

#296
Loose Nuts Cycles
Category: Bikes
Average price: Modest
Area: Grant Park
Address: 452 Cherokee Ave
Atlanta, GA 30312
Phone: (404) 228-5555

#297
Best Buy
Category: Electronics, Wholesale Store
Average price: Modest
Area: Lindbergh
Address: 2537 Piedmont Rd NE
Atlanta, GA 30324
Phone: (404) 842-0938

#298
The Home Depot
Category: Hardware Store, Gardening
Average price: Modest
Area: Lindbergh
Address: 2525 Piedmont Road NE
Atlanta, GA 30324
Phone: (404) 841-5608

#299
Walgreens
Category: Drugstore, Cosmetics, Beauty Supply, Convenience Store
Average price: Inexpensive
Address: 7530 Roswell Rd
Atlanta, GA 30350
Phone: (678) 731-9235

#300
Republic of Couture
Category: Men's Clothing, Women's Clothing
Average price: Expensive
Area: Midtown
Address: 1075 Peachtree St NE
Atlanta, GA 30309
Phone: (404) 872-0082

#301
iRepairit iPhone
Category: Electronics Repair, Mobile Phones, Phone Repair
Average price: Modest
Address: 2800 Spring Rd SE
Atlanta, GA 30339
Phone: (678) 575-1808

#302
Office Depot
Category: Office Equipment
Area: Midtown
Address: 859 Spring St NW
Atlanta, GA 30308
Phone: (404) 898-1804

#303
Fleet Feet Sports Atlanta Sandy Springs
Category: Sports Wear, Outdoor Gear
Average price: Expensive
Address: 224 Johnson Ferry Rd NE
Atlanta, GA 30328
Phone: (404) 255-3338

#304
Mitzi's Shoe Box
Category: Shoe Store
Average price: Expensive
Area: Virginia Highland
Address: 1004 Virginia Ave NE
Atlanta, GA 30306
Phone: (404) 873-4718

#305
Truly Living Well Center For Natural Urban Agriculture
Category: Farmer Market
Average price: Inexpensive
Address: 75 Hilliard St NE
Atlanta, GA 30312
Phone: (678) 973-0997

#306
Horizon Home
Category: Home Decor, Furniture Store
Average price: Modest
Address: 1611 Ellsworth Industrial
Atlanta, GA 30318
Phone: (404) 351-8090

#307
Edible Arrangements
Category: Florist
Average price: Expensive
Area: Buckhead
Address: 3655 Roswell Rd NE
Atlanta, GA 30342
Phone: (404) 814-0101

#308
LensCrafters
Category: Eyewear, Opticians, Optometrists, Ophthalmologists
Address: 4800 Briarcliff Rd NE
Atlanta, GA 30345
Phone: (770) 493-6553

#309
House Of Adrene
Category: Women's Clothing, Men's Clothing
Average price: Expensive
Area: Castleberry Hill
Address: 264 Peters St
Atlanta, GA 30313
Phone: (404) 688-8876

#310
Nihao Atlanta Bookstore
Category: Bookstore
Average price: Modest
Address: 5391-A New Peachtree Rd
Atlanta, GA 30341
Phone: (678) 918-4328

#311
Full Moon Records
Category: Music, DVDs
Average price: Inexpensive
Area: Candler Park
Address: 1653 NE McLendon Ave
Atlanta, GA 30307
Phone: (404) 377-1919

#312
Mall West End The
Category: Shopping Center
Average price: Inexpensive
Area: West End
Address: 850 Oak St SW
Atlanta, GA 30310
Phone: (404) 755-1001

#313
Chuck's Firearms
Category: Outdoor Gear, Guns, Ammo
Average price: Exclusive
Area: Buckhead
Address: 3099 Peachtree Rd NE
Atlanta, GA 30305
Phone: (404) 266-1250

#314
Highland Hardware
Category: Hardware Store
Average price: Expensive
Area: Virginia Highland
Address: 1045 N Highland Ave NE
Atlanta, GA 30306
Phone: (404) 872-4466

#315
Carols Daughter
Category: Cosmetics, Skin Care
Average price: Modest
Area: Buckhead
Address: 3393 Peachtree Rd NE
Atlanta, GA 30326
Phone: (404) 846-2663

#316
Sue Sandalon Jewelry Design
Category: Jewelry
Address: 5299 Roswell Road NE
Atlanta, GA 30342
Phone: (404) 257-0743

#317
Bare Escentuals
Category: Cosmetics, Beauty Supply
Average price: Expensive
Area: Buckhead
Address: 3393 Peachtree Rd.
Atlanta, GA 30326
Phone: (404) 814-1176

#318
Vinings Jubilee
Category: Shopping Center
Average price: Expensive
Area: Vinings
Address: 4300 Paces Ferry Rd
Atlanta, GA 30339
Phone: (770) 438-8080

#319
Ms. Tee's Furs
Category: Vintage, Local Flavor
Area: Grant Park
Address: Memorial Dr & Boulevard SE
Atlanta, GA 30312
Phone: (678) 698-1919

#320
Fallen Arrows
Category: T-Shirt Printing
Average price: Inexpensive
Address: 840 DeKalb Ave
Atlanta, GA 30307
Phone: (404) 635-6367

#321
MarsHall
Category: Department Store
Average price: Modest
Address: 6337 Roswell Rd NE
Atlanta, GA 30328
Phone: (404) 252-9679

#322
The Container Store
Category: Home Decor
Average price: Modest
Address: 120 Perimeter Ctr W
Atlanta, GA 30346
Phone: (770) 351-0065

#323
Target Store
Category: Department Store
Average price: Modest
Address: 3660 Marketplace Blvd
Atlanta, GA 30344
Phone: (404) 267-0063

#324
Cartridge World
Dunwoody Perimeter
Category: Office Equipment
Average price: Modest
Address: 1100 Hammond Dr NE
Atlanta, GA 30328
Phone: (770) 391-1100

#325
Flora Dora
Category: Home Decor, Florist
Area: Morningside / Lenox Park
Address: 1830 Cheshire Bridge Road
Atlanta, GA 30324
Phone: (404) 873-6787

#326
Taproot Hydroponics
Category: Nursery, Gardening
Address: 2111 Faulkner Road
Atlanta, GA 30324
Phone: (404) 464-8313

#327
Mickey Lynn
Category: Jewelry
Average price: Modest
Address: 75 Bennett St
Atlanta, GA 31136
Phone: (404) 214-6077

#328
Winnie Couture
Category: Bridal
Average price: Expensive
Area: Buckhead
Address: 3224 Peachtree Rd
Atlanta, GA 30305
Phone: (404) 835-0341

#329
C Lighting
Category: Lighting Fixtures, Equipment, Home Decor
Average price: Modest
Area: Buckhead
Address: 333 Buckhead Ave NE
Atlanta, GA 30305
Phone: (404) 760-1119

#330
Chelsea Floral Designs
Category: Florist
Average price: Expensive
Area: Buckhead
Address: 3094 East Shadowlawn Avenue
Atlanta, GA 30305
Phone: (678) 528-2987

#331
Unique Extensions
Category: Hair Extensions, Cosmetics, Beauty Supply
Average price: Modest
Area: Buckhead
Address: 3060 Pharr Ct N
Atlanta, GA 30305
Phone: (678) 755-3285

#332
Backstreet Boutique
Category: Women's Clothing
Average price: Exclusive
Area: Buckhead
Address: 3140 E Shadowlawn Ave NE
Atlanta, GA 30305
Phone: (404) 262-7783

#333
Epitome
Category: Shoe Store, Accessories
Average price: Expensive
Area: Buckhead
Address: 252 Pharr Rd NE
Atlanta, GA 30305
Phone: (404) 869-8700

#334
Staples
Category: Office Equipment
Average price: Modest
Area: Midtown, Old Fourth Ward
Address: 650 Ponce De Leon Ave
Atlanta, GA 30308
Phone: (404) 881-0354

#335
Maria Heckscher Salon
Category: Skin Care, Hair Stylists, Cosmetics, Beauty Supply
Average price: Expensive
Area: Buckhead
Address: 3210 Paces Ferry Pl NW
Atlanta, GA 30305
Phone: (404) 261-8036

#336
Skinchanted
Category: Cosmetics, Kitchen, Bath
Average price: Expensive
Area: Westside / Home Park
Address: 1700 Northside Dr Nw
Atlanta, GA 30318
Phone: (404) 439-0994

#337
Guffey's of Atlanta
Category: Men's Clothing, Sewing, Alterations, Formal Wear
Average price: Expensive
Area: Buckhead
Address: 3340 Peachtree Rd NE
Atlanta, GA 30326
Phone: (404) 231-0044

#338
All Saints
Category: Women's Clothing, Leather Goods, Accessories
Area: Buckhead
Address: 3393 Peachtree Rd NE, 2nd Fl
Atlanta, GA 30326
Phone: (404) 495-2838

#339
C. Wonder
Category: Accessories, Women's Clothing, Home Decor
Average price: Expensive
Area: Buckhead
Address: 3393 Peachtree Rd NE
Atlanta, GA 30326
Phone: (404) 816-3847

#340
Gold Traders
Category: Pawn Shop
Area: Buckhead
Address: 3372 Peachtree Rd NE
Atlanta, GA 30326
Phone: (404) 841-1200

#341
Georgia's Governor's Mansion
Category: Museum, Art Gallery
Address: 391 W Paces Ferry Rd NW
Atlanta, GA 30305
Phone: (404) 261-1776

#342
Publix Pharmacy
Category: Drugstore
Area: Buckhead
Address: 3535 Peachtree Rd NE
Atlanta, GA 30326
Phone: (404) 848-0929

#343
Lucky Brand Jeans
Category: Department Store
Average price: Expensive
Area: Buckhead
Address: 3500 Peachtree Road NE
Atlanta, GA 30326
Phone: (404) 842-0236

#344
Walmart
Category: Grocery, Drugstore, Discount Store
Average price: Inexpensive
Address: 4725 Ashford Dunwoody Rd
Atlanta, GA 30338
Phone: (770) 395-0199

#345
Arthur's Ladies Sportswear
Category: Women's Clothing
Average price: Modest
Address: 1710 Defoor Pl NW
Atlanta, GA 30318
Phone: (404) 355-2832

#346
Michaels
Category: Arts, Crafts, Knitting Supplies
Average price: Modest
Area: Lindbergh
Address: 2625 Piedmont Rd NE
Atlanta, GA 30324
Phone: (404) 266-8711

#347
Sephora
Category: Cosmetics, Beauty Supply
Average price: Expensive
Area: Buckhead
Address: 3393 Peachtree Rd NE
Atlanta, GA 30326
Phone: (404) 816-0123

#348
Kazoo Toys
Category: Toy Store
Average price: Expensive
Address: 3718 Roswell Rd NE
Atlanta, GA 30342
Phone: (404) 500-1027

#349
Fig & Flower
Category: Cosmetics, Beauty Supply
Average price: Modest
Area: Poncey-Highland
Address: 636 N Highland Ave
Atlanta, GA 30306
Phone: (404) 998-8198

#350
Atlanta Fabric
Category: Department Store
Average price: Modest
Address: 3267 Buford Hwy NE
Atlanta, GA 30329
Phone: (404) 633-3313

#351
Adore Furniture
Category: Furniture Store
Average price: Modest
Address: 1510 Ellsworth Industrial Blvd
Atlanta, GA 30318
Phone: (404) 355-9930

#352
Dollar Tree Store
Category: Discount Store
Average price: Inexpensive
Address: 3345 Buford Hwy NE
Atlanta, GA 30329
Phone: (404) 633-7793

#353
TWELVE
Category: Florist, Accessories
Average price: Expensive
Area: Virginia Highland
Address: 994 Virginia Ave NE
Atlanta, GA 30306
Phone: (404) 541-2357

#354
English Classics
Category: Antiques
Average price: Expensive
Address: 1442 Chattahoochee Avenue NW,
Atlanta, GA 30318
Phone: (404) 351-2252

#355
Powerhouse Skates
Category: Sporting Goods
Area: Old Fourth Ward, Poncey-Highland
Address: 331 Elizabeth St NE
Atlanta, GA 30307
Phone: (678) 705-4817

#356
Guy T Gunter
& Associates Appliances
Category: Appliances
Address: 1610 Southland Circle
Atlanta, GA 30318
Phone: (404) 874-7529

#357
Scott Antique Market
Category: Antiques
Average price: Expensive
Address: 3650 Jonesboro Rd SE
Atlanta, GA 30354
Phone: (404) 361-2000

#358
Haverty's Fine Furniture
Category: Furniture Store
Average price: Modest
Address: 132 Perimeter Ctr W
Atlanta, GA 30346
Phone: (770) 352-0901

#359
The Home Depot
Category: Hardware Store, Nursery,
Gardening, Appliances
Average price: Modest
Address: 6400 Pchtree-Dunwoody Rd
Atlanta, GA 30328
Phone: (770) 804-8065

#360
Hobby Lobby
Category: Art Supplies, Home Decor
Average price: Inexpensive
Address: 4715A Ashford Dunwoody Rd
Atlanta, GA 30338
Phone: (770) 677-1860

#361
Esperanza Atlanta
Category: Women's Clothing
Address: 1641 Duncan Dr
Atlanta, GA 30318
Phone: (404) 273-1082

#362
Walgreens
Category: Drugstore
Average price: Modest
Address: 4535 Roswell Rd NE
Atlanta, GA 30342
Phone: (404) 236-0838

#363
Bobbi Brown Cosmetics
Category: Cosmetics, Beauty Supply
Average price: Modest
Address: 3393 Peachtree Rd NE
Atlanta, GA 30327
Phone: (404) 495-2800

#364
Briggs Vision Group
Category: Optometrists, Medical Supplies, Eyewear, Opticians
Address: 1637 Mount Vernon Rd
Atlanta, GA 30338
Phone: (770) 396-3460

#365
BigHouse Gallery
Category: Art Gallery, Venues
Area: Castleberry Hill
Address: 211 Peters St
Atlanta, GA 30313
Phone: (404) 221-0201

#366
Goodwill
Category: Thrift Store
Average price: Inexpensive
Address: 1165 Perimeter Ctr W
Atlanta, GA 30338
Phone: (770) 350-7895

#367
Kaboodle
Category: Furniture Store
Average price: Modest
Area: East Atlanta Village
Address: 485 Flat Shoals Ave SE
Atlanta, GA 30316
Phone: (404) 522-3006

#368
Range Clothing Boutique
Category: Women's Clothing
Average price: Modest
Area: Buckhead
Address: 3231- A Cains Hill Pl
Atlanta, GA 30305
Phone: (404) 816-8230

#369
B & R Thrift Store
Category: Thrift Store
Average price: Inexpensive
Address: 6650 Roswell Rd
Atlanta, GA 30328
Phone: (404) 303-3023

#370
The Seed Factory
Category: Baby Gear, Furniture
Average price: Expensive
Area: Westside / Home Park
Address: 1170 Howell Mill Rd
Atlanta, GA 30318
Phone: (404) 355-2043

#371
Macy's
Category: Department Store, Men's Clothing, Women's Clothing
Average price: Modest
Address: 2841 Greenbriar Parkway
Atlanta, GA 30331
Phone: (404) 346-2690

#372
RadioShack
Category: Mobile Phones, Hobby Shop, Electronics
Average price: Modest
Address: 1544 Peidmont Rd
Atlanta, GA 30324
Phone: (404) 873-6488

#373
Mitchell Gold + Bob Williams
Category: Furniture Store
Average price: Expensive
Area: Buckhead
Address: 3081 Peachtree Rd NE
Atlanta, GA 30305
Phone: (404) 869-1770

#374
Charlotte Russe
Category: Women's Clothing
Average price: Inexpensive
Address: 4400 Ashford Dunwoody Rd
Atlanta, GA 30346
Phone: (770) 668-0004

#375
Lowe's
Category: Home, Garden
Average price: Expensive
Address: 3625 N Commerce Dr
Atlanta, GA 30344
Phone: (404) 838-2000

#376
Kroger
Category: Drugstore
Address: 3030 Headland Drive SW
Atlanta, GA 30311
Phone: (404) 344-5383

#377
Amy's Hallmark #723
Category: Cards, Stationery
Average price: Modest
Address: 1000 Cumberland Mall SE
Atlanta, GA 30339
Phone: (770) 436-2806

#378
Demure Boutique
Category: Women's Clothing
Average price: Modest
Area: Edgewood
Address: 1230 Caroline St
Atlanta, GA 30307
Phone: (404) 856-0930

#379
Steven R Warstadt & Associates
Category: Optometrists, Eyewear
Average price: Inexpensive
Address: 4800 Briarcliff Rd NE
Atlanta, GA 30345
Phone: (770) 493-9171

#380
Kmkitrentals
Category: Cosmetics, Beauty Supply
Address: 1151 Hammond Dr NE
Atlanta, GA 30346
Phone: (404) 281-7855

#381
Rhubarb & Custard
Category: Children's Clothing,
Baby Gear, Furniture
Average price: Modest
Area: Buckhead
Address: 3265 Roswell Rd
Atlanta, GA 30305
Phone: (404) 474-9860

#382
Big John's Christmas Trees
Category: Home, Garden
Average price: Expensive
Area: Buckhead
Address: 2963 Piedmont Rd NE
Atlanta, GA 30305
Phone: (404) 261-4497

#383
Peachtree Computers
Category: Computer Repair, Computers
Average price: Inexpensive
Address: 2022 Powers Ferry Rd SE
Atlanta, GA 30339
Phone: (770) 575-2029

#384
Boomerang
Category: Antiques
Average price: Modest
Area: Virginia Highland
Address: 1101 Ponce De Leon Ave
Atlanta, GA 30306
Phone: (404) 736-6533

#385
Ack Radio & Electronics Supply
Category: Electronics
Average price: Modest
Address: 554 Deering Rd NW
Atlanta, GA 30309
Phone: (404) 351-6340

#386
Salon 11 Studio + 11 Boutique
Category: Hair Salon, Women's Clothing,
Spray Tanning
Average price: Expensive
Address: 4520 Olde Perimeter Way
Atlanta, GA 30346
Phone: (770) 395-1153

#387
Tall Tales Book Shop
Category: Bookstore
Average price: Modest
Address: 2105 Lavista Rd NE
Atlanta, GA 30329
Phone: (404) 636-2498

#388
Ginstar Computer Inc.
Category: Computers, Electronics
Average price: Inexpensive
Area: Westside / Home Park
Address: 1046 Northside Dr NW
Atlanta, GA 30318
Phone: (404) 876-1224

#389
The Museum of Contemporary Art of Georgia
Category: Museum, Art Gallery
Average price: Inexpensive
Address: 75 Bennett St NW
Atlanta, GA 30309
Phone: (404) 367-8700

#390
Desu Couture Consignment
Category: Used, Vintage
Average price: Modest
Area: Morningside / Lenox Park
Address: 1403 N Highland Ave NE
Atlanta, GA 30306
Phone: (404) 885-1101

#391
Savvi Formalwear
Category: Men's Clothing
Average price: Modest
Address: 4511 Olde Perimeter Way
Atlanta, GA 30346
Phone: (770) 394-2860

#392
Eye Gallery the
Category: Eyewear, Opticians
Average price: Modest
Address: 4520 Olde Perimeter Way Ste 110, Atlanta, GA 30346
Phone: (770) 500-3937

#393
Dollar Tree
Category: Department Store
Average price: Inexpensive
Address: 2480 Briarcliff Rd NE
Atlanta, GA 30329
Phone: (404) 486-7714

#394
Salle Opticians
Category: Eyewear, Opticians
Average price: Expensive
Area: Buckhead
Address: 3500 Peachtree Rd NE
Atlanta, GA 30326
Phone: (404) 816-6266

#395
Greenbriar Mall
Category: Shopping Center
Average price: Modest
Address: 2841 Greenbriar Pkwy SW
Atlanta, GA 30331
Phone: (404) 344-6611

#396
Ham Radio Outlet
Category: Hobby Shop
Average price: Expensive
Address: 6071 Buford Hwy NE
Atlanta, GA 30340
Phone: (770) 263-0700

#397
Desperate Housewares
Category: Antiques
Average price: Modest
Address: 241 Blvd NE
Atlanta, GA 30312
Phone: (404) 522-0404

#398
The Home Depot
Category: Nursery, Gardening, Appliances, Hardware Store
Average price: Modest
Address: 4343 Tilly Mill Rd
Atlanta, GA 30360
Phone: (770) 452-8858

#399
Wax 'N' Facts
Category: Music, DVDs, Vinyl Records
Average price: Inexpensive
Area: Little Five Points
Address: 432 Moreland Ave NE
Atlanta, GA 30307
Phone: (404) 525-2275

#400
Inserection
Category: Adult
Average price: Expensive
Area: Midtown
Address: 1023 W Peachtree St NW
Atlanta, GA 30309
Phone: (404) 249-9281

#401
Goodwill
Category: Used, Vintage
Average price: Inexpensive
Area: West End
Address: 888 Ralph David Abernathy SW, Atlanta, GA 31132
Phone: (404) 755-6440

#402
Victoria's Secret
Category: Lingerie
Average price: Modest
Address: 1417 Cumberland Mall SE
Atlanta, GA 30339
Phone: (770) 319-0344

#403
Vaperite
Category: Vape Shop
Average price: Modest
Address: 2350 Cheshire Bridge Rd
Atlanta, GA 30324
Phone: (404) 500-5826

#404
Cosign Resale Boutique
Category: Used, Vintage
Area: Westside / Home Park
Address: 1016 Howell Mill Rd
Atlanta, GA 30318
Phone: (404) 390-3994

#405
Atlanta Vision Optical
Category: Eyewear, Opticians
Average price: Expensive
Area: Edgewood
Address: 1215 Caroline St
Atlanta, GA 30307
Phone: (404) 522-8886

#406
Dunwoody Photo
Category: Photography Store
Average price: Modest
Address: 5588 Chamblee Dunwoody Rd
Atlanta, GA 30338
Phone: (678) 320-0202

#407
Strivers Row USA
Category: Shopping
Area: Virginia Highland
Address: 774 North Highland Ave NE
Atlanta, GA 30306
Phone: (678) 973-0045

#408
Suitsupply
Category: Men's Clothing
Average price: Expensive
Area: Buckhead
Address: 3400 Around Lenox Rd NE
Atlanta, GA 30326
Phone: (404) 857-2800

#409
Jared the Galleria of Jewelry
Category: Jewelry
Average price: Modest
Address: 4503 Ashford Dunwoody Road
Atlanta, GA 30346
Phone: (770) 393-4599

#410
Shoe Land
Category: Shoe Store
Average price: Inexpensive
Address: 3267 Buford Hwy NE
Atlanta, GA 30329
Phone: (404) 486-7566

#411
The Defoor Centre
Category: Venues, Art Gallery
Average price: Expensive
Address: 1710 Defoor Ave NW
Atlanta, GA 30318
Phone: (404) 591-3900

#412
Bennie's Shoes
Category: Shoe Store, Shoe Repair
Average price: Modest
Area: Lindbergh
Address: 2625 Piedmont Rd NE
Atlanta, GA 30324
Phone: (404) 262-1966

#413
By Design Furniture
Category: Furniture Store
Average price: Modest
Area: Morningside / Lenox Park
Address: 1747 Cheshire Bridge Rd
Atlanta, GA 30324
Phone: (404) 607-9098

#414
Izzy Maternity
Category: Maternity Wear
Average price: Expensive
Address: 2385 Peachtree Rd NE
Atlanta, GA 30305
Phone: (404) 949-0222

#415
Showcase School of Photography
Category: Photography Store
Average price: Modest
Address: 1135 Sheridan Rd NE
Atlanta, GA 30324
Phone: (404) 965-2205

#416
The Trading Post
Category: Cards, Stationery
Area: Midtown
Address: 1375 Peachtree Street NE
Atlanta, GA 30309
Phone: (404) 733-6490

#417
H&A International Jewelry
Category: Jewelry
Average price: Expensive
Address: 1820 Independence Sq. Suite C, Atlanta, GA 30338
Phone: (770) 396-3456

#418
Sephora
Category: Cosmetics, Beauty Supply
Average price: Modest
Address: 4400 Ashford Dunwoody Rd Atlanta, GA 30346
Phone: (678) 731-9950

#419
Stardust
Category: Adult, Lingerie
Average price: Modest
Address: 3007 Buford Hwy Atlanta, GA 30329
Phone: (404) 633-7733

#420
Strings and Strands
Category: Arts, Crafts
Average price: Modest
Address: 5299 Roswell Rd Atlanta, GA 30342
Phone: (404) 252-9662

#421
Fab'rik
Category: Women's Clothing
Average price: Modest
Address: 4520 Olde Perimeter Way Atlanta, GA 30346
Phone: (770) 391-0219

#422
Angie's Beauty Supply
Category: Cosmetics, Beauty Supply
Average price: Modest
Area: West End
Address: 1145 Ralph David Abernathy Blvd, Atlanta, GA 30310
Phone: (404) 755-0546

#423
Pinkheart Accessories
Category: Cosmetics, Jewelry
Average price: Inexpensive
Area: Atlantic Station
Address: 231 18th St Atlanta, GA 30363
Phone: (404) 347-2811

#424
Tuesday Morning
Category: Furniture Store
Average price: Modest
Area: Buckhead
Address: 3145 Piedmont Road NE Atlanta, GA 30305
Phone: (404) 814-9169

#425
MAC Cosmetics
Category: Cosmetics, Makeup Artists
Average price: Expensive
Area: Buckhead
Address: 3393 Peachtree Road N.E. Atlanta, GA 30326
Phone: (404) 231-2800

#426
Kiehls
Category: Cosmetics, Beauty Supply
Average price: Expensive
Address: Unnamed Rd Atlanta, GA
Phone: (800) 543-4572

#427
Ace Hardware
Category: Hardware Store
Average price: Modest
Area: Buckhead
Address: 2365 Peachtree Road NE Atlanta, GA 30305
Phone: (404) 841-9525

#428
Swoozie's
Category: Cards, Stationery
Average price: Modest
Area: Buckhead
Address: 4285 Roswell Rd Atlanta, GA 30342
Phone: (404) 252-7979

#429
Kohl's Department Store
Category: Home Decor, Swimwear, Children's Clothing
Average price: Modest
Address: 4820 Briarcliff Rd NE Atlanta, GA 30345
Phone: (770) 270-1201

#430
CVS/Pharmacy
Category: Drugstore
Address: 3401 Northside Pkwy Atlanta, GA 30327
Phone: (404) 261-7123

#431
Office Depot
Category: Office Equipment
Average price: Modest
Area: Buckhead
Address: 2284 Peachtree Road NW
Atlanta, GA 30309
Phone: (404) 355-4667

#432
Georgia Eye Associates
Category: Optometrists
Area: Buckhead
Address: 3120 Maple Dr NE
Atlanta, GA 30305
Phone: (404) 233-3267

#433
Papyrus
Category: Cards, Stationery
Average price: Expensive
Area: Buckhead
Address: 3393 Peachtree Rd NE, Ste 4001,
Atlanta, GA 30326
Phone: (404) 233-1292

#434
Tuesday Morning
Category: Home Decor, Furniture Store
Average price: Modest
Area: Midtown
Address: 931 Monroe Dr NE
Atlanta, GA 30308
Phone: (404) 541-0621

#435
American Eagle Outfitters
Category: Sports Wear
Average price: Modest
Area: Buckhead
Address: 3393 Peachtree Rd NE
Atlanta, GA 30326
Phone: (404) 812-1768

#436
Vera Bradley At Phipps Plaza
Category: Luggage
Average price: Expensive
Area: Buckhead
Address: 3500 Peachtree Rd NE
Atlanta, GA 30326
Phone: (404) 467-8345

#437
Kroger
Category: Drugstore, Grocery
Average price: Modest
Address: 2685 Metropolitan Pkwy SW
Atlanta, GA 30315
Phone: (404) 761-7409

#438
Dabberdoo
Category: Toy Store, Accessories, Cards, Stationery
Average price: Modest
Area: Virginia Highland
Address: 1048 N Highland Ave
Atlanta, GA 30306
Phone: (404) 815-6700

#439 ..
CVS/Pharmacy
Category: Drugstore
Average price: Inexpensive
Area: Midtown, Old Fourth Ward
Address: 680 Ponce De Leon Ave
Atlanta, GA 30308
Phone: (404) 892-1164

#440
LEGOLAND Discovery Center
Category: Toy Store
Average price: Modest
Area: Buckhead
Address: 3500 Lenox Rd NE
Atlanta, GA 30326
Phone: (404) 848-9252

#441
Batteries Plus Bulbs
Category: Mobile Phones, Electronics
Average price: Modest
Address: 4418 Roswell Rd NE
Atlanta, GA 30342
Phone: (404) 256-0310

#442
European Alterations & Tailoring
Category: Sewing, Alterations, Fashion
Average price: Modest
Address: 2341A Peachtree Rd NE
Atlanta, GA 30305
Phone: (404) 231-0352

#443
Toni Neal
Category: Cosmetics, Beauty Supply, Hair Extensions, Hair Stylists
Average price: Modest
Address: 290 Martin Luther King Dr, Ste 101 SE, Atlanta, GA 30312
Phone: (404) 856-0254

#444
Jackson Fine Art Gallery
Category: Art Gallery
Average price: Exclusive
Area: Buckhead
Address: 3115 E Shadowlawn Ave NE
Atlanta, GA 30305
Phone: (404) 233-3739

#445
Elements of Style
Category: Women's Clothing
Area: Buckhead
Address: 258 Pharr Rd NE
Atlanta, GA 30305
Phone: (404) 846-2182

#446
Orvis Atlanta
Category: Women's Clothing, Outdoor Gear, Men's Clothing
Average price: Exclusive
Area: Buckhead
Address: 3275 Peachtree Rd
Atlanta, GA 30305
Phone: (404) 841-0093

#447
Cantoni Furniture
Category: Furniture Store, Home Decor
Area: Virginia Highland
Address: 1011 Monroe Drive NE
Atlanta, GA 30306
Phone: (404) 881-8111

#448
Solstice Sunglasses
Category: Eyewear, Opticians, Accessories
Area: Buckhead
Address: 3393 Peachtree RD NE, Space 4038
Atlanta, GA 30326
Phone: (404) 869-8102

#449
L'occitane
Category: Cosmetics, Beauty Supply
Area: Buckhead
Address: 3393 Peachtree Road NE
Atlanta, GA 30326
Phone: (404) 841-6213

#450
Clarks
Category: Shoe Store
Average price: Modest
Area: Buckhead
Address: 3393 Peachtree Rd NE
Atlanta, GA 30326
Phone: (404) 816-2175

#451
GameStop
Category: Videos, Video Game Rental
Average price: Modest
Area: Buckhead
Address: 3393 Peachtree Rd NE
Atlanta, GA 30326
Phone: (404) 261-7944

#452
Lovesac
Category: Furniture Store
Average price: Expensive
Area: Buckhead
Address: 3393 Peachtree Road NE
Atlanta, GA 30326
Phone: (404) 816-0070

#453
Zara
Category: Men's Clothing, Women's Clothing
Average price: Modest
Address: 4400 Ashford Dunwoody Rd
Atlanta, GA 30346
Phone: (770) 698-5256

#454
Robin Stiles Hair Face Body
Category: Hair Salon, Cosmetics, Beauty Supply
Average price: Expensive
Area: Buckhead
Address: 56 E Andrews Dr
Atlanta, GA 30305
Phone: (404) 264-9932

#455
Lagerquist Gallery
Category: Art Gallery
Average price: Exclusive
Area: Buckhead
Address: 3235 Paces Ferry Pl NW
Atlanta, GA 30305
Phone: (404) 261-8273

#456
Kuhlman
Category: Men's Clothing, Women's Clothing
Area: Buckhead
Address: 3500 Peachtree Road NE
Atlanta, GA 30326
Phone: (404) 869-4097

#457
Tory by Trb Retail
Category: Women's Clothing, Accessories
Average price: Expensive
Area: Buckhead
Address: 3500 Peachtree Road NE
Atlanta, GA 30326
Phone: (404) 816-3261

#458
Sprout
Category: Children's Clothing
Average price: Expensive
Area: Westside / Home Park
Address: 1198 Howell Mill Rd NW
Atlanta, GA 30318
Phone: (404) 352-0864

#459
Williams-Sonoma
Category: Kitchen, Bath
Average price: Expensive
Area: Buckhead
Address: 3500 Peachtree Rd NE
Atlanta, GA 30326
Phone: (404) 237-0912

#460
American Period Furniture
Category: Antiques
Average price: Modest
Area: Virginia Highland
Address: 1097 Ponce De Leon Ave NE
Atlanta, GA 30306
Phone: (404) 892-8576

#461
Tuxedo Frame Gallery
Category: Art Gallery, Framing, Interior Design
Average price: Expensive
Address: 3800 Roswell Rd NE
Atlanta, GA 30342
Phone: (404) 261-5570

#462
TWEEDS
Category: Men's Clothing
Average price: Expensive
Address: 1009-A Marietta St NW
Atlanta, GA 30318
Phone: (404) 892-0302

#463
Foglio Press
Category: Cards, Stationery
Average price: Expensive
Address: 1000 Marietta St NW
Atlanta, GA 30318
Phone: (404) 401-4760

#464
Men's Wearhouse
Category: Men's Clothing, Formal Wear
Average price: Expensive
Area: Buckhead
Address: 3500 Peachtree Rd. Ne #E-24
Atlanta, GA 30326
Phone: (404) 266-1275

#465
Westside Market
Category: Interior Design, Furniture Store
Average price: Expensive
Address: 1530 Ellsworth Industrial Blvd
Atlanta, GA 30318
Phone: (404) 941-3466

#466
Brookhaven Home
Category: Home Decor
Average price: Expensive
Area: Brookhaven
Address: 4060 Peachtree Rd
Atlanta, GA 30319
Phone: (404) 231-1887

#467
CVS/Pharmacy
Category: Drugstore
Average price: Modest
Area: Buckhead
Address: 1943 Peachtree Rd NE
Atlanta, GA 30309
Phone: (404) 351-7629

#468
Florist Atlanta
Category: Florist
Average price: Modest
Address: 1750 Howell Mill Rd NW
Atlanta, GA 30318
Phone: (404) 355-4898

#469
Claire's
Category: Cosmetics, Beauty Supply, Piercing, Jewelry
Average price: Inexpensive
Address: 4400 Ashford Dunwoody Rd
Atlanta, GA 30346
Phone: (770) 677-0313

#470
ABV Creative Agency & Gallery
Category: Art Gallery
Average price: Inexpensive
Area: Old Fourth Ward
Address: 659 Auburn Ave
Atlanta, GA 30312
Phone: (213) 915-6448

#471
Big Lots
Category: Department Store
Average price: Inexpensive
Address: 3358 Chamblee Tucker Rd
Atlanta, GA 30341
Phone: (770) 457-5176

#472
Kiang Projects
Category: Art Gallery
Average price: Inexpensive
Address: 1011A Marietta St
Atlanta, GA 30318
Phone: (404) 892-5477

#473
Spanx
Category: Women's Clothing
Average price: Expensive
Area: Buckhead
Address: 3391 Peachtree Rd NE
Atlanta, GA 30326
Phone: (404) 321-1608

#474
Huria Boutique
Category: Women's Clothing
Area: Castleberry Hill
Address: 132 Walker St SW
Atlanta, GA 30313
Phone: (678) 515-7501

#475
Bookhaus
Category: Bookstore, Cards, Stationery, Newspapers & Magazines
Average price: Modest
Area: Downtown
Address: 227 Sandy Springs Pl NE
Atlanta, GA 31136
Phone: (404) 257-2221

#476
Walmart Historic Westside Village
Category: Department Store
Average price: Modest
Address: 825 Martin Luther King Jr Dr SW, Atlanta, GA 30314
Phone: (404) 460-2703

#477
MAC Cosmetics
Category: Cosmetics, Beauty Supply
Area: Atlantic Station
Address: 1371 Market Street
Atlanta, GA 30363
Phone: (404) 541-9599

#478
CVS/Pharmacy
Category: Drugstore
Average price: Modest
Address: 2830 N Druid Hills Rd NE
Atlanta, GA 30329
Phone: (404) 679-4666

#479
Sports Authority
Category: Sporting Goods
Average price: Modest
Address: 1155 Mount Vernon Hwy, Ste 500, Atlanta, GA 30338
Phone: (770) 390-3095

#480
Hancock Fabrics
Category: Fabric Store
Average price: Modest
Area: Lindbergh
Address: 2625 Piedmont Rd NE
Atlanta, GA 30324
Phone: (404) 266-0517

#481
Victoria's Secret
Category: Lingerie
Average price: Modest
Area: Buckhead
Address: 3393 Peachtree Rd NE
Atlanta, GA 30326
Phone: (404) 365-8860

#482
Polished And Primped
Category: Nail Salon, Women's Clothing, Gift Shop
Average price: Modest
Area: Midtown
Address: 950 W Peachtree St NW
Atlanta, GA 30309
Phone: (404) 879-0500

#483
Poppy's of Atlanta
Category: Women's Clothing
Average price: Expensive
Area: Buckhead
Address: 56 E Andrews Dr NW
Atlanta, GA 30305
Phone: (404) 237-7015

#484
Walmart
Category: Drugstore, Discount Store
Average price: Inexpensive
Address: 835 Martin Luther King Jr Drive Nw, Atlanta, GA 30314
Phone: (404) 460-2703

#485
Schneider's Jewelry-Midtown
Category: Jewelry
Average price: Modest
Area: Midtown
Address: 1197 Peachtree Street NE
Atlanta, GA 30361
Phone: (404) 874-8459

#486
The Merchant At Howell Mill
Category: Antiques, Gift Shop
Average price: Modest
Address: 993 Marietta St NW
Atlanta, GA 30318
Phone: (404) 347-8200

#487
Urbanbella
Category: Hair Salon, Cosmetics, Beauty Supply
Average price: Expensive
Address: 141 W Wieuca Rd NE
Atlanta, GA 30342
Phone: (404) 255-5022

#488
Sugar Britches
Category: Women's Clothing, Accessories
Area: East Atlanta Village
Address: 491 Flat Shoals Ave SE
Atlanta, GA 30316
Phone: (404) 522-9098

#489
Hand In Pocket Denim Boutique
Category: Women's Clothing
Average price: Expensive
Address: 1675 Cumberland Pkwy
Atlanta, GA 30080
Phone: (678) 309-9550

#490
Office Depot
Category: Office Equipment, Computers
Area: Lindbergh
Address: 2625 Piedmont Rd NE
Atlanta, GA 30324
Phone: (404) 467-7554

#491
RadioShack
Category: Mobile Phones, Electronics
Average price: Modest
Area: Lindbergh
Address: 2625 Piedmont Rd Ne #58A
Atlanta, GA 30324
Phone: (404) 841-8776

#492
AT&T
Category: Mobile Phones
Average price: Expensive
Area: Atlantic Station
Address: 1380 Atlantic Drive
Atlanta, GA 30363
Phone: (404) 249-9052

#493
StickFigure Distribution
Category: Music, DVDs, Vinyl Records
Address: 712 Shelton Ave SW
Atlanta, GA 30310
Phone: (404) 752-7399

#494
Peachtree Flowers
Category: Florist
Average price: Modest
Address: 4280 Peachtree Rd. NE
Atlanta, GA 30319
Phone: (404) 266-8800

#495
Gems of Africa Gallery
Category: Art Gallery, Home Decor
Average price: Expensive
Area: Poncey-Highland
Address: 630 N Highland Ave NE
Atlanta, GA 30306
Phone: (404) 876-8200

#496
Ichiyo Art
Category: Art School, Florist
Address: 1224 Converse Dr NE
Atlanta, GA 30324
Phone: (404) 233-1846

#497
Washi Accents
Category: Art Supplies, Cards
Address: 1224 Converse Dr NE
Atlanta, GA 30324
Phone: (404) 233-1846

#498
Hill Street Warehouse
Category: Furniture Store, Home Decor
Address: 1357 Collier Rd NW
Atlanta, GA 30318
Phone: (404) 352-5001

#499
Gamestop
Category: Videos, Video Game Rental
Average price: Modest
Area: Edgewood
Address: 1250 Caroline St NE
Atlanta, GA 30307
Phone: (404) 586-9393

#500
Things Remembered
Category: Women's Clothing, Gift Shop
Address: 1430 Cumberland Mall SE
Atlanta, GA 30339
Phone: (770) 432-9446

TOP 500 RESTAURANTS

The Most Recommended by Locals & Trevelers

(From #1 to #500)

#1
Aviva by Kameel
Cuisines: Mediterranean, Juice Bar
Average price: Under $10
Area: Downtown
Address: 225 Peachtree St
Atlanta, GA 30303
Phone: (404) 698-3600

#2
Canoe
Cuisines: American, Seafood
Average price: $31-$60
Area: Vinings
Address: 4199 Paces Ferry Rd NW
Atlanta, GA 30339
Phone: (770) 432-2663

#3
Better Half
Cuisines: American
Average price: $31-$60
Area: Westside / Home Park
Address: 349 14th St
Atlanta, GA 30318
Phone: (404) 695-4547

#4
Heirloom Market BBQ
Cuisines: Barbeque
Average price: $11-$30
Address: 2243 Akers Mill Rd SE
Atlanta, GA 30339
Phone: (770) 612-2502

#5
Holeman & Finch Public House
Cuisines: American, Gastropub
Average price: $11-$30
Area: Buckhead
Address: 2277 Peachtree Rd NE
Atlanta, GA 30309
Phone: (404) 948-1175

#6
Poor Calvin's
Cuisines: American, Thai, Asian Fusion
Average price: $11-$30
Area: Downtown
Address: 510 Piedmont Ave NE
Atlanta, GA 30308
Phone: (404) 254-4051

#7
Local Three
Cuisines: American, Burgers
Average price: $31-$60
Area: West Paces Ferry / Northside
Address: 3290 Northside Pkwy
Atlanta, GA 30327
Phone: (404) 968-2700

#8
Woodfire Grill
Cuisines: American
Average price: $31-$60
Area: Morningside / Lenox Park
Address: 1782 Cheshire Bridge Rd NE
Atlanta, GA 30324
Phone: (404) 347-9055

#9
Antico Pizza
Cuisines: Pizza
Average price: $11-$30
Area: Westside / Home Park
Address: 1093 Hemphill Ave NW
Atlanta, GA 30318
Phone: (404) 724-2333

#10
Ssam Burger
Cuisines: Bubble Tea, Burgers, Asian Fusion
Average price: Under $10
Address: 2072 Defoors Ferry Rd NW
Atlanta, GA 30318
Phone: (404) 609-5533

#11
Bacchanalia
Cuisines: American
Average price: Above $61
Area: Westside / Home Park
Address: 1198 Howell Mill Rd Nw
Atlanta, GA 30318
Phone: (404) 365-0410

#12
Seven Lamps
Cuisines: American
Average price: $11-$30
Area: Buckhead
Address: 3400 Around Lenox Rd
Atlanta, GA 30326
Phone: (404) 467-8950

#13
Lunacy Black Market
Cuisines: American, Wine Bar
Average price: $11-$30
Address: 231 Mitchell St SW
Atlanta, GA 30303
Phone: (404) 688-0806

#14
Caf' Agora
Cuisines: Turkish, Mediterranean
Average price: $11-$30
Area: Buckhead
Address: 318 E Paces Ferry Rd NE
Atlanta, GA 30305
Phone: (404) 949-0900

#15
Arepa Mia
Cuisines: Gluten-Free, Venezuelan
Average price: Under $10
Area: Downtown
Address: 209 Edgewood Ave SE
Atlanta, GA 30303
Phone: (404) 880-8575

#16
Urban Cannibals Bodega & Bites
Cuisines: Deli, Grocery, Sandwiches
Average price: $11-$30
Area: East Atlanta Village
Address: 477 Flat Shoals Ave SE
Atlanta, GA 30316
Phone: (404) 230-9865

#17
South City Kitchen
Cuisines: Southern, Breakfast & Brunch
Average price: $11-$30
Area: Midtown
Address: 1144 Cresent Ave NE
Atlanta, GA 30309
Phone: (404) 873-7358

#18
Couscous Atlanta
Cuisines: Mediterranean, American, Beer, Wine, Spirits
Average price: $11-$30
Area: Morningside / Lenox Park
Address: 560 Dutch Valley Rd NE
Atlanta, GA 30324
Phone: (404) 685-3111

#19
Le Petit March'
Cuisines: Specialty Food, Breakfast & Brunch
Average price: Under $10
Area: Kirkwood
Address: 1986 Hosea L Williams Dr
Atlanta, GA 30317
Phone: (404) 371-9888

#20
Home Grown
Cuisines: Southern
Average price: Under $10
Area: Reynoldstown
Address: 968 Memorial Dr
Atlanta, GA 30316
Phone: (404) 222-0455

#21
Bantam Pub
Cuisines: American, Pub
Average price: $11-$30
Area: Old Fourth Ward
Address: 737 Ralph McGill Blvd NE
Atlanta, GA 30312
Phone: (404) 223-1500

#22
Hankook Taqueria
Cuisines: Korean
Average price: Under $10
Address: 1341 Collier Rd NW
Atlanta, GA 30318
Phone: (404) 352-8881

#23
Wrecking Bar Brewpub
Cuisines: Gastropub, Pub, Brewery
Average price: $11-$30
Area: Little Five Points
Address: 292 Moreland Ave NE
Atlanta, GA 30307
Phone: (404) 221-2600

#24
Illegal Food
Cuisines: Diner
Average price: $11-$30
Address: 427 Edgewood Ave
Atlanta, GA 30312
Phone: (404) 525-3002

#25
Rosebud
Cuisines: Southern, American
Average price: $11-$30
Area: Morningside / Lenox Park
Address: 1397 N Highland Ave NE
Atlanta, GA 30306
Phone: (404) 347-9747

#26
Fox Bros.
Cuisines: Barbeque
Average price: $11-$30
Address: 1238 Dekalb Ave NE
Atlanta, GA 30307
Phone: (404) 577-4030

#27
The Food Shoppe
Cuisines: Cajun/Creole
Average price: Under $10
Area: Downtown
Address: 123 Luckie St NW
Atlanta, GA 30303
Phone: (404) 600-8443

#28
Sweet Georgia's Juke Joint
Cuisines: Southern, Venues
Average price: $11-$30
Area: Downtown
Address: 200 Peachtree St NE
Atlanta, GA 30303
Phone: (404) 230-5853

#29
Bocado
Cuisines: American
Average price: $11-$30
Address: 887 Howell Mill Rd
Atlanta, GA 30318
Phone: (404) 815-1399

#30
Star Provisions
Cuisines: Cheese Shop,
Meat Shop, Sandwiches
Average price: $11-$30
Area: Westside / Home Park
Address: 1198 Howell Mill Rd NW
Atlanta, GA 30318
Phone: (404) 365-0410

#31
The Porter Beer Bar
Cuisines: American, Pub
Average price: $11-$30
Area: Little Five Points
Address: 1156 Euclid Ave NE
Atlanta, GA 30307
Phone: (404) 223-0393

#33
Desta Ethiopian Kitchen
Cuisines: Ethiopian, Sandwiches
Average price: $11-$30
Address: 3086 Briarcliff Rd NE
Atlanta, GA 30329
Phone: (404) 929-0011

#32
Two Urban Licks
Cuisines: Bar, American
Average price: $31-$60
Area: Old Fourth Ward, Poncey-Highland
Address: 820 Ralph McGill Blvd NE
Atlanta, GA 30306
Phone: (404) 522-4622

#34
Casseroles
Cuisines: American
Average price: Under $10
Area: Morningside / Lenox Park
Address: 1393 N Highland Ave
Atlanta, GA 30306
Phone: (404) 228-3260

#35
Fat Matt's Rib Shack
Cuisines: Barbeque
Average price: $11-$30
Area: Morningside / Lenox Park
Address: 1811 Piedmont Ave NE
Atlanta, GA 30324
Phone: (404) 607-1622

#36
Joy Cafe
Cuisines: Breakfast & Brunch, Sandwiches, Cafe
Average price: $11-$30
Area: Buckhead
Address: 316 Pharr Rd NE
Atlanta, GA 30305
Phone: (404) 816-0306

#37
Gunshow
Cuisines: American, Southern
Average price: $31-$60
Area: Ormewood Park
Address: 924 Garrett St SE
Atlanta, GA 30316
Phone: (404) 380-1886

#38
Alma Cocina
Cuisines: Latin American
Average price: $11-$30
Area: Downtown
Address: Peachtree Tower, 191 Peachtree Street NE
Atlanta, GA 30303
Phone: (404) 968-9662

#39
BoccaLupo
Cuisines: Italian
Average price: $31-$60
Area: Inman Park
Address: 753 Edgewood Ave NE
Atlanta, GA 30307
Phone: (404) 577-2332

#40
Crooked Tree Cafe
Cuisines: Barbeque, Southern, Breakfast & Brunch
Average price: Under $10
Address: 2355 Cumberland Pkwy SE
Atlanta, GA 30339
Phone: (770) 333-9119

#41
Murphy's
Cuisines: American, Breakfast & Brunch, Desserts
Average price: $11-$30
Area: Virginia Highland
Address: 997 Virginia Ave NE
Atlanta, GA 30306
Phone: (404) 872-0904

#42
Ecco
Cuisines: European, Cocktail Bar
Average price: $31-$60
Area: Midtown
Address: 40 7th Street NE
Atlanta, GA 30308
Phone: (404) 347-9555

#43
Ink & Elm
Cuisines: American, Lounge, Gastropub
Average price: $31-$60
Address: 1577 N Decatur Rd NE
Atlanta, GA 30307
Phone: (678) 244-7050

#44
The Optimist
Cuisines: Seafood
Average price: $31-$60
Area: Westside / Home Park
Address: 914 Howell Mill Rd
Atlanta, GA 30318
Phone: (404) 477-6260

#45
JCT Kitchen & Bar
Cuisines: Southern
Average price: $11-$30
Area: Westside / Home Park
Address: 1198 Howell Mill Rd
Atlanta, GA 30318
Phone: (404) 355-2252

#46
Agave Restaurant
Cuisines: Tex-Mex
Average price: $11-$30
Address: 242 Blvd SE
Atlanta, GA 30312
Phone: (404) 588-0006

#47
The General Muir
Cuisines: Deli, American
Average price: $11-$30
Address: 1540 Ave Place, Ste B-230
Atlanta, GA 30329
Phone: (678) 927-9131

#48
Sway
Cuisines: Southern
Average price: $11-$30
Address: 265 Peachtree St NE
Atlanta, GA 30308
Phone: (404) 577-1234

#49
Sushi House Hayakawa
Cuisines: Japanese, Sushi Bar
Average price: $31-$60
Address: 5979 Buford Hwy
Atlanta, GA 30340
Phone: (770) 986-0010

#50
Rumi's Kitchen
Cuisines: Persian/Iranian
Average price: $11-$30
Address: 6112 Roswell Rd NE
Atlanta, GA 30328
Phone: (404) 477-2100

#51
Bone's Restaurant
Cuisines: Steakhouse
Average price: Above $61
Area: Buckhead
Address: 3130 Piedmont Rd NE
Atlanta, GA 30305
Phone: (404) 237-2663

#52
Gio's Chicken Amalfitano
Cuisines: Italian, Chicken Wings, Pizza
Average price: $11-$30
Area: Westside / Home Park
Address: 1099 Hemphill Ave
Atlanta, GA 30318
Phone: (404) 347-3874

#53
Vortex Bar & Grill
Cuisines: American
Average price: $11-$30
Area: Little Five Points
Address: 438 Moreland Ave NE
Atlanta, GA 30307
Phone: (404) 688-1828

#54
The Vortex Bar And Grill
Cuisines: Burgers, American
Average price: $11-$30
Area: Midtown
Address: 878 Peachtree St NE
Atlanta, GA 30309
Phone: (404) 875-1667

#55
Buttermilk Kitchen
Cuisines: American, Breakfast & Brunch
Average price: $11-$30
Area: Buckhead
Address: 4225 Roswell Rd NE
Atlanta, GA 30342
Phone: (678) 732-3274

#56
Cypress Street Pint & Plate
Cuisines: American, Chicken Wings
Average price: $11-$30
Area: Midtown
Address: 817 W Peachtree St NW
Atlanta, GA 30308
Phone: (404) 815-9243

#57
endive Publik house
Cuisines: American
Average price: $11-$30
Area: Atlantic Station
Address: 1468 Mecaslin St NW
Atlanta, GA 30309
Phone: (404) 504-9044

#58
Ammazza
Cuisines: Pizza, Italian
Average price: $11-$30
Area: Old Fourth Ward
Address: 591 Edgewood Ave
Atlanta, GA 30312
Phone: (404) 228-1036

#59
Gato
Cuisines: Tex-Mex, Japanese
Average price: Under $10
Area: Candler Park
Address: 1660 McLendon Ave NE
Atlanta, GA 30307
Phone: (404) 371-0889

#60
King+Duke
Cuisines: American
Average price: $31-$60
Area: Buckhead
Address: 3060 Peachtree Rd NW
Atlanta, GA 30305
Phone: (404) 477-3500

#61
Nick's Food To Go
Cuisines: Greek, Mediterranean
Average price: Under $10
Address: 240 Martin Luther King Jr Dr SE,
Atlanta, GA 30312
Phone: (404) 521-2220

#62
One Eared Stag
Cuisines: Tapas, American
Average price: $31-$60
Area: Inman Park
Address: 1029 Edgewood Ave
Atlanta, GA 30307
Phone: (404) 525-4479

#63
Babs
Cuisines: Breakfast & Brunch
Average price: $11-$30
Area: Midtown
Address: 814 Juniper St
Atlanta, GA 30308
Phone: (404) 541-0888

#64
Purnima
Cuisines: Indian
Average price: $11-$30
Address: 4646-A Buford Hwy
Atlanta, GA 30341
Phone: (770) 609-8587

#65
Yeah! Burger
Cuisines: Burgers
Average price: $11-$30
Area: Westside / Home Park
Address: 1168 Howell Mill Rd
Atlanta, GA 30318
Phone: (404) 496-4393

#66
Highland Bakery
Cuisines: Bakery, Breakfast & Brunch, Sandwiches
Average price: $11-$30
Area: Old Fourth Ward
Address: 655 Highland Ave NE
Atlanta, GA 30312
Phone: (404) 586-0772

#67
Shujaa's BBQ
Cuisines: Barbeque, Halal
Average price: $11-$30
Area: Little Five Points
Address: 1087 Euclid Ave NE
Atlanta, GA 30307
Phone: (404) 254-2097

#68
Crawfish Shack Seafood
Cuisines: Seafood, Cajun/Creole
Average price: $11-$30
Address: 4337 Buford Hwy
Atlanta, GA 30341
Phone: (404) 329-1610

#69
Blossom Tree
Cuisines: Korean
Average price: Under $10
Area: Downtown
Address: 64 Peachtree St NW
Atlanta, GA 30303
Phone: (404) 223-7500

#70
Mary Mac's Tea Room
Cuisines: Southern
Average price: $11-$30
Area: Midtown, Old Fourth Ward
Address: 224 Ponce de Leon Ave
Atlanta, GA 30308
Phone: (404) 876-1800

#71
Sun In My Belly
Cuisines: Breakfast & Brunch, Cafe, Bagels
Average price: $11-$30
Address: 2161 College Ave NE
Atlanta, GA 30317
Phone: (404) 370-1088

#72
Doggy Dogg
Cuisines: Street Vendor, Hot Dogs
Average price: Under $10
Area: Old Fourth Ward
Address: 154 Randolph St NE
Atlanta, GA 30312

#73
La Tavola Trattoria
Cuisines: Italian, Breakfast & Brunch
Average price: $11-$30
Area: Virginia Highland
Address: 992 Virginia Ave. NE
Atlanta, GA 30306
Phone: (404) 873-5430

#74
We Suki Suki
Cuisines: Vietnamese
Average price: Under $10
Area: East Atlanta Village
Address: 479-B Flat Shoals Ave SE
Atlanta, GA 30316
Phone: (404) 430-7613

#75
Seasons 52
Cuisines: Vegetarian, Wine Bar
Average price: $11-$30
Area: Buckhead
Address: 3050 Peachtree Rd NW
Atlanta, GA 30305
Phone: (404) 846-1552

#76
Flip Burger Boutique
Cuisines: Burgers
Average price: $11-$30
Address: 1587 Howell Mill Rd
Atlanta, GA 30318
Phone: (404) 352-3547

#77
The Hungry Peach
Cuisines: Southern, Salad, Sandwiches
Average price: $11-$30
Address: 351 Peachtree Hills Ave NE
Atlanta, GA 30305
Phone: (404) 816-9009

#78
Newk's Eatery
Cuisines: Cafe, Sandwiches, American
Average price: Under $10
Address: 305 Brookhaven Ave
Atlanta, GA 30319
Phone: (678) 365-4410

#79
Lee's Bakery
Cuisines: Bakery, Vietnamese
Average price: Under $10
Address: 4005 Buford Hwy NE
Atlanta, GA 30345
Phone: (404) 728-1008

#80
Park Bar
Cuisines: Bar, Burgers
Average price: $11-$30
Address: 150 Walton St
Atlanta, GA 30303
Phone: (404) 524-0444

#81
Houston's Restaurant
Cuisines: American
Average price: $11-$30
Area: Buckhead
Address: 3321 Lenox Rd NE
Atlanta, GA 30326
Phone: (404) 237-7534

#82
Little Bangkok
Cuisines: Chinese, Thai
Average price: $11-$30
Address: 2225 Cheshire Bridge Rd NE
Atlanta, GA 30324
Phone: (404) 315-1530

#83
Umi
Cuisines: Sushi Bar
Average price: Above $61
Area: Buckhead
Address: 3050 Peachtree Rd
Atlanta, GA 30305
Phone: (404) 841-0040

#84
Papi's Cuban & Caribbean Grill
Cuisines: Caribbean
Average price: Under $10
Area: Midtown, Old Fourth Ward
Address: 216 Ponce de Leon Ave Ne
Atlanta, GA 30308
Phone: (404) 607-1525

#85
Barcelona Atlanta
Cuisines: Spanish, Tapas, Tapas Bar
Average price: $31-$60
Area: Inman Park
Address: 240 N Highland Ave
Atlanta, GA 30307
Phone: (404) 589-1010

#86
Busy Bee Cafe
Cuisines: Soul Food
Average price: $11-$30
Address: 810 Martin Luther King Jr Dr
Atlanta, GA 30314
Phone: (404) 525-9212

#87
Ameer's Mediterranean Grill
Cuisines: Mediterranean,
Middle Eastern
Average price: $11-$30
Address: 2168 Briarcliff Rd
Atlanta, GA 30329
Phone: (404) 982-0666

#88
Taqueria Del Sol
Cuisines: Tex-Mex
Average price: Under $10
Area: Westside / Home Park
Address: 1200 Howell Mill Rd NW
Atlanta, GA 30318
Phone: (404) 352-5811

#89
Sweet Auburn BBQ
Cuisines: Barbeque, Sandwiches
Average price: $11-$30
Area: Poncey-Highland
Address: 656 N Highland Ave NE
Atlanta, GA 30306
Phone: (678) 515-3550

#90
Bottle Rocket
Cuisines: Sushi Bar, Japanese
Average price: $11-$30
Area: Castleberry Hill
Address: 180 Walker St SW
Atlanta, GA 30313
Phone: (404) 574-5680

#91
Farm Burger
Cuisines: Burgers
Average price: $11-$30
Area: Buckhead
Address: 3365 Piedmont Rd
Atlanta, GA 30305
Phone: (404) 816-0603

#92
Quinones
Cuisines: Southern
Average price: Above $61
Area: Westside / Home Park
Address: 1198 Howell Mill Rd
Atlanta, GA 30318
Phone: (404) 365-0410

#93
Noni's Bar & Deli
Cuisines: Italian, Sandwiches, Lounge
Average price: $11-$30
Address: 357 Edgewood Ave
Atlanta, GA 30312
Phone: (404) 343-1808

#94
Haven
Cuisines: Southern
Average price: $31-$60
Area: Brookhaven
Address: 1441 Dresden Dr NE
Atlanta, GA 30319
Phone: (404) 969-0700

#95
1KEPT Kitchen & Bar
Cuisines: American
Average price: $11-$30
Area: Buckhead
Address: 2293 Peachtree Rd NE
Atlanta, GA 30309
Phone: (404) 254-1973

#96
Grindhouse Killer Burgers
Cuisines: Burgers
Average price: Under $10
Area: Downtown
Address: 209 Edgewood Ave SE
Atlanta, GA 30303
Phone: (404) 522-3444

#97
The Earl
Cuisines: Dive Bar, American
Average price: Under $10
Area: East Atlanta Village
Address: 488 Flat Shoals Ave SE
Atlanta, GA 30316
Phone: (404) 522-3950

#98
Co'm Vietnamese Grill
Cuisines: Vietnamese, Seafood
Average price: $11-$30
Address: 4005 Buford Hwy
Atlanta, GA 30345
Phone: (404) 320-0405

#99
The Greater Good BBQ
Cuisines: Barbeque
Average price: $11-$30
Area: Buckhead
Address: 4441 Roswell Rd
Atlanta, GA 30342
Phone: (404) 303-8525

#100
Avellino's
Cuisines: Pizza, Italian
Average price: $11-$30
Address: 1328 Windsor Pkwy
Atlanta, GA 30319
Phone: (404) 500-3841

#101
Taqueria Del Sol
Cuisines: Tex-Mex
Average price: Under $10
Address: 2165 Cheshire Bridge Rd
Atlanta, GA 30324
Phone: (404) 321-1118

#102
YEAH! Burger
Cuisines: Burgers, Gluten-Free
Average price: $11-$30
Area: Virginia Highland
Address: 1017 N Highland Ave
Atlanta, GA 30306
Phone: (404) 437-7845

#103
Double Zero Napoletana
Cuisines: Italian, Pizza
Average price: $11-$30
Address: 5825 Roswell Rd NE
Atlanta, GA 30328
Phone: (404) 991-3666

#104
Varuni Napoli
Cuisines: Pizza
Average price: $11-$30
Area: Morningside / Lenox Park
Address: 1540 Monroe Dr NE
Atlanta, GA 30324
Phone: (404) 709-2690

#105
Saltyard
Cuisines: Tapas
Average price: $11-$30
Address: 1820 Peachtree Rd NW
Atlanta, GA 30309
Phone: (404) 382-8088

#106
Goin' Coastal
Cuisines: Seafood
Average price: $11-$30
Area: Virginia Highland
Address: 1021 Virginia Ave NE
Atlanta, GA 30306
Phone: (404) 941-9117

#107
Folk Art
Cuisines: American, Breakfast & Brunch, Diner
Average price: $11-$30
Area: Little Five Points
Address: 465 N Highland Ave
Atlanta, GA 30307
Phone: (404) 537-4493

#108
Ann's Snack Bar
Cuisines: Burgers, Hot Dogs
Average price: Under $10
Area: Kirkwood
Address: 1615 Memorial Dr
Atlanta, GA 30317
Phone: (404) 687-9207

#109
Nicky's Seafood
Cuisines: Seafood
Average price: $11-$30
Address: 609 Whitehall St SW
Atlanta, GA 30303
Phone: (404) 588-3474

#110
Rise-N-Dine
Cuisines: Breakfast & Brunch
Average price: Under $10
Area: Emory Village
Address: 1565 N Decatur Rd NE
Atlanta, GA 30307
Phone: (404) 377-4407

#111
Pho Dai Loi
Cuisines: Vietnamese
Average price: Under $10
Address: 4186 Buford Hwy NE
Atlanta, GA 30345
Phone: (404) 633-2111

#112
Hovan Gourmet
Cuisines: Mediterranean, Greek
Average price: Under $10
Address: 2148 Johnson Ferry Rd
Atlanta, GA 30319
Phone: (770) 396-1770

#113
So Kong Dong Tofu House
Cuisines: Korean
Average price: $11-$30
Address: 5280 Buford Hwy NE
Atlanta, GA 30340
Phone: (678) 205-0555

#114
Egg Harbor Caf'
Cuisines: Breakfast & Brunch, Gluten-Free, Sandwiches
Average price: $11-$30
Area: Buckhead
Address: 1820 Peachtree Road NW
Atlanta, GA 30309
Phone: (470) 225-1901

#115
Yebo
Cuisines: South African, Lounge
Average price: $11-$30
Area: Buckhead
Address: 3500 Peachtree Rd NE
Atlanta, GA 30326
Phone: (404) 467-4988

#116
Dua Vietnamese
Cuisines: Vietnamese
Average price: Under $10
Area: Downtown
Address: 53 Broad St NW
Atlanta, GA 30303
Phone: (404) 589-8889

#117
Argosy
Cuisines: American, Gastropub, Burgers
Average price: $11-$30
Area: East Atlanta Village
Address: 470 Flat Shoals Ave SE
Atlanta, GA 30316
Phone: (404) 577-0407

#118
Delia's Chicken Sausage Stand
Cuisines: Food Stands, Hot Dogs
Average price: Under $10
Address: 489 Moreland Ave SE
Atlanta, GA 30316
Phone: (404) 474-9651

#119
The Lawrence
Cuisines: American
Average price: $11-$30
Area: Midtown
Address: 905 Juniper St
Atlanta, GA 30309
Phone: (404) 961-7177

#120
Nuevo Laredo Cantina
Cuisines: Mexican
Average price: $11-$30
Address: 1495 Chattahoochee Ave NW
Atlanta, GA 30318
Phone: (404) 352-9009

#121
Proof and Provision
Cuisines: American, Gastropub
Average price: $11-$30
Area: Midtown
Address: 659 Peachtree St NE
Atlanta, GA 30308
Phone: (404) 897-1991

#122
Sushi Huku Japanese Restaurant
Cuisines: Japanese, Sushi Bar
Average price: $11-$30
Address: 6300 Powers Ferry Rd NW
Atlanta, GA 30339
Phone: (770) 956-9559

#123
Serpas
Cuisines: American
Average price: $31-$60
Area: Old Fourth Ward
Address: 659 Auburn Ave NE
Atlanta, GA 30312
Phone: (404) 688-0040

#124
R Thomas Deluxe Grill
Cuisines: Vegetarian, Vegan, American
Average price: $11-$30
Address: 1812 Peachtree St NW
Atlanta, GA 30309
Phone: (404) 872-2942

#125
Gladys Knight's Signature Chicken & Waffles
Cuisines: Southern, Soul Food
Average price: $11-$30
Address: 529 Peachtree St NE
Atlanta, GA 30308
Phone: (404) 874-9393

#126
Yard House
Cuisines: American
Average price: $11-$30
Area: Atlantic Station
Address: 261 19th Street NW
Atlanta, GA 30363
Phone: (404) 815-8990

#127
Nicola's Restaurant
Cuisines: Middle Eastern
Average price: $11-$30
Address: 1602 Lavista Rd NE
Atlanta, GA 30329
Phone: (404) 325-2524

#128
Georgia Grille
Cuisines: American
Average price: $31-$60
Area: Buckhead
Address: 2290 Peachtree Rd NW
Atlanta, GA 30309
Phone: (404) 352-3517

#129
Ria's Bluebird
Cuisines: Southern, Breakfast & Brunch
Average price: $11-$30
Area: Grant Park
Address: 421 Memorial Dr SE
Atlanta, GA 30312
Phone: (404) 521-3737

#130
Fritti
Cuisines: Italian, Pizza
Average price: $11-$30
Area: Inman Park
Address: 309 N Highland Ave NE
Atlanta, GA 30307
Phone: (404) 880-9559

#131
Aria
Cuisines: American
Average price: Above $61
Area: Buckhead
Address: 490 E Paces Ferry Rd NE
Atlanta, GA 30305
Phone: (404) 233-7673

#132
Empire State South
Cuisines: Southern, Breakfast & Brunch
Average price: $31-$60
Area: Midtown
Address: 999 Peachtree St
Atlanta, GA 30309
Phone: (404) 541-1105

#133
Wisteria
Cuisines: American, Southern
Average price: $31-$60
Area: Inman Park
Address: 471 N Highland Ave
Atlanta, GA 30307
Phone: (404) 525-3363

#134
Little's Food Store and Grill
Cuisines: Grocery, Beer, Burgers
Average price: Under $10
Area: Cabbagetown
Address: 198 Carroll St
Atlanta, GA 30312
Phone: (404) 963-7012

#135
Chong Qing Hot Pot
Cuisines: Szechuan
Average price: Under $10
Address: 5385 New Peachtree Rd
Atlanta, GA 30341
Phone: (770) 936-1379

#136
Vine & Tap
Cuisines: Wine Bar, Tapas
Average price: $11-$30
Address: 2770 Lenox Rd NE
Atlanta, GA 30324
Phone: (404) 600-5820

#137
The Flying Biscuit Cafe
Cuisines: Breakfast & Brunch, American
Average price: $11-$30
Area: Midtown
Address: 1001 Piedmont Ave NE
Atlanta, GA 30309
Phone: (404) 874-8887

#138
Elmyriachi
Cuisines: Mexican
Average price: $11-$30
Area: Kirkwood
Address: 1950 Hosea L Williams Dr NE
Atlanta, GA 30317
Phone: (678) 705-9902

#139
Urban pL8
Cuisines: Gluten-Free, Breakfast & Brunch, American
Average price: $11-$30
Address: 1082 Huff Rd
Atlanta, GA 30318
Phone: (404) 367-0312

#140
Lure
Cuisines: Seafood, Breakfast & Brunch
Average price: $31-$60
Area: Midtown
Address: 1106 Crescent Avenue NE
Atlanta, GA 30309
Phone: (404) 817-3650

#141
Bone Garden Cantina
Cuisines: Mexican
Average price: $11-$30
Address: 1425 Ellsworth Industrial Blvd
Atlanta, GA 30318
Phone: (404) 418-9072

#142
Daddy D'z BBQ Joynt
Cuisines: Barbeque
Average price: $11-$30
Address: 264 Memorial Dr SE
Atlanta, GA 30312
Phone: (404) 222-0206

#143
Smoke Ring
Cuisines: Barbeque
Average price: $11-$30
Area: Castleberry Hill
Address: 309 Nelson St
Atlanta, GA 30313
Phone: (404) 228-6377

#144
10 Degrees South
Cuisines: African
Average price: $31-$60
Area: Buckhead
Address: 4183 Roswell Rd NE
Atlanta, GA 30342
Phone: (404) 705-8870

#145
Quoc Huong Banh Mi Fast Food
Cuisines: Vietnamese, Fast Food
Average price: Under $10
Address: 5150 Buford Hwy NE
Atlanta, GA 30340
Phone: (770) 936-0605

#146
Mediterranean Grill
Cuisines: Middle Eastern
Average price: Under $10
Area: Virginia Highland
Address: 985 Monroe Dr NE
Atlanta, GA 30308
Phone: (404) 917-1100

#147
Ziba's Bistro
Cuisines: Tapas, Sandwiches, Beer, Wine, Spirits
Average price: $11-$30
Area: Grant Park
Address: 560 Blvd SE
Atlanta, GA 30312
Phone: (404) 622-4440

#148
Fresh To Order
Cuisines: Sandwiches
Average price: $11-$30
Area: Midtown
Address: 860 Peachtree St NE
Atlanta, GA 30308
Phone: (404) 593-2333

#149
Elliott Street Deli & Pub
Cuisines: Deli, Sandwiches, Pub
Average price: $11-$30
Area: Castleberry Hill
Address: 51 Elliott St SW
Atlanta, GA 30313
Phone: (404) 523-2174

#150
Valenza
Cuisines: Italian
Average price: $31-$60
Area: Brookhaven
Address: 1441 Dresden Dr NE
Atlanta, GA 30319
Phone: (404) 969-3233

#151
Thumbs Up Diner
Cuisines: Breakfast & Brunch
Average price: Under $10
Address: 826 Marietta St
Atlanta, GA 30318
Phone: (404) 745-4233

#152
Dough Bakery
Cuisines: Vegan, Bakery, Deli
Average price: Under $10
Address: 100 Hurt St
Atlanta, GA 30307
Phone: (404) 380-1400

#153
Fellini's Pizza Buckhead
Cuisines: Pizza
Average price: Under $10
Area: Buckhead
Address: 2809 Peachtree Rd NE
Atlanta, GA 30305
Phone: (404) 266-0082

#154
West Egg Caf'
Cuisines: Breakfast & Brunch, Bakery, American
Average price: $11-$30
Area: Westside / Home Park
Address: 1100 Howell Mill Rd NW
Atlanta, GA 30318
Phone: (404) 872-3973

#155
Manuel's Tavern
Cuisines: American
Average price: $11-$30
Area: Poncey-Highland
Address: 602 N Highland Ave NE
Atlanta, GA 30307
Phone: (404) 525-3447

#156
St. Cecilia
Cuisines: Seafood, Italian
Average price: $31-$60
Area: Buckhead
Address: 3455 Peachtree Rd NE
Atlanta, GA 30326
Phone: (404) 554-9995

#157
Thumbs Up Diner
Cuisines: Breakfast & Brunch
Average price: Under $10
Area: Old Fourth Ward
Address: 573 Edgewood Ave NE
Atlanta, GA 30312
Phone: (404) 223-0690

#158
Ted's Montana Grill
Cuisines: Burgers, American
Average price: $11-$30
Area: Downtown
Address: 133 Luckie St NW
Atlanta, GA 30303
Phone: (404) 521-9796

#159
Kana Ethiopian Bistro
Cuisines: Ethiopian
Average price: $11-$30
Address: 3667 Clairmont Rd
Atlanta, GA 30341
Phone: (678) 381-1333

#160
Krog Bar
Cuisines: Tapas Bar, Wine Bar
Average price: $11-$30
Area: Old Fourth Ward, Inman Park
Address: 112 Krog St
Atlanta, GA 30307
Phone: (404) 524-1618

#161
The One Sushi
Cuisines: Asian Fusion
Average price: $11-$30
Area: Brookhaven
Address: 2523 Caldwell Rd NE
Atlanta, GA 30319
Phone: (404) 869-6988

#162
Falafel King
Cuisines: Falafel
Average price: Under $10
Area: Emory Village
Address: 1405 Oxford Rd NE
Atlanta, GA 30307
Phone: (404) 377-1716

#163
Osteria del FIGO
Cuisines: Italian
Average price: $11-$30
Area: Westside / Home Park
Address: 1210 Howell Mill Road
Atlanta, GA 30318
Phone: (404) 351-3700

#164
Marlow's Tavern
Cuisines: Pub, American
Average price: $11-$30
Address: 2355 Cumberland Pkwy
Atlanta, GA 30339
Phone: (770) 432-2526

#165
Max Lager's Wood Fired Grill & Brewery
Cuisines: American, Brewery
Average price: $11-$30
Area: Downtown
Address: 320 Peachtree St NE
Atlanta, GA 30308
Phone: (404) 525-4400

#166
ADios Cafe
Cuisines: Coffee, Tea, Breakfast & Brunch
Average price: Under $10
Area: Castleberry Hill
Address: 180 Walker St SW
Atlanta, GA 30313
Phone: (404) 574-5678

#167
Sausalito West Coast Grill
Cuisines: Latin American
Average price: Under $10
Area: Midtown
Address: 1389 Peachtree St NE
Atlanta, GA 30309
Phone: (404) 875-5005

#168
Grindhouse Killer Burgers
Cuisines: Burgers
Average price: $11-$30
Address: 1842 Piedmont Rd
Atlanta, GA 30324
Phone: (404) 254-2273

#169
Tuk Tuk Thai Food Loft
Cuisines: Thai
Average price: $11-$30
Area: Buckhead
Address: 1745 Peachtree St
Atlanta, GA 30309
Phone: (678) 539-6181

#170
Elmyr
Cuisines: Mexican, Dive Bar
Average price: Under $10
Area: Little Five Points
Address: 1091 Euclid Ave NE
Atlanta, GA 30307
Phone: (404) 588-0250

#171
Hoki Japanese Restaurant
Cuisines: Sushi Bar, Japanese
Average price: $11-$30
Address: 3300 Cobb Pkwy SE
Atlanta, GA 30339
Phone: (770) 690-0555

#172
Carroll Street Caf'
Cuisines: Bar, Breakfast & Brunch
Average price: $11-$30
Area: Cabbagetown
Address: 208 Carroll St SE
Atlanta, GA 30312
Phone: (404) 577-2700

#173
Babette's Caf'
Cuisines: Breakfast & Brunch, French, Tapas
Average price: $11-$30
Area: Poncey-Highland
Address: 573 N Highland Ave NE
Atlanta, GA 30307
Phone: (404) 523-9121

#174
Acapulco Mexican Taqueria
Cuisines: Mexican
Average price: Under $10
Address: 2102 Hollywood Rd
Atlanta, GA 30318
Phone: (404) 941-7865

#175
Jack's New Yorker Deli
Cuisines: Deli, Sandwiches, Breakfast & Brunch
Average price: Under $10
Area: Buckhead
Address: 3333 Piedmont Rd NE
Atlanta, GA 30305
Phone: (404) 869-7776

#176
Alon's Bakery & Market
Cuisines: Bakery, Sandwiches
Average price: $11-$30
Address: 4505 Ashford Dunwoody Rd
Atlanta, GA 30346
Phone: (678) 397-1781

#177
Jack's Pizza & Wings
Cuisines: Pizza, Pub, Chicken Wings
Average price: Under $10
Area: Old Fourth Ward
Address: 676 Highland Ave NE
Atlanta, GA 30312
Phone: (404) 525-4444

#178
Tropical Smoothie Cafe
Cuisines: Juice Bar, Cafe
Average price: Under $10
Address: 1155 Mt Vernon Hwy
Atlanta, GA 30338
Phone: (770) 522-8866

#179
Mali Restaurant
Cuisines: Thai, Sushi Bar
Average price: $11-$30
Area: Virginia Highland
Address: 961 Amsterdam Ave NE
Atlanta, GA 30306
Phone: (404) 874-1411

#180
Roasters
Cuisines: Southern
Average price: $11-$30
Address: 2770 Lenox Rd NE
Atlanta, GA 30324
Phone: (404) 237-1122

#181
Street Food Thursdays
Cuisines: Food Stands, Street Vendor
Average price: Under $10
Area: Midtown
Address: 12th & Peachtree St
Atlanta, GA 30309

#182
Alon's
Cuisines: Bakery, Sandwiches
Average price: $11-$30
Area: Morningside / Lenox Park
Address: 1394 N Highland Ave NE
Atlanta, GA 30306
Phone: (404) 872-6000

#183
Righteous Room
Cuisines: American, Bar
Average price: $11-$30
Area: Virginia Highland
Address: 1051 Ponce De Leon Ave NE
Atlanta, GA 30306
Phone: (404) 874-0939

#184
ParkGrounds
Cuisines: Coffee, Tea, Sandwiches
Average price: Under $10
Area: Reynoldstown
Address: 142 Flat Shoals Ave SE
Atlanta, GA 30316
Phone: (678) 528-9901

#185
The Shed at Glenwood
Cuisines: American, Bar
Average price: $11-$30
Address: 475 Bill Kennedy Way
Atlanta, GA 30316
Phone: (404) 835-4363

#186
Colonnade Restaurant
Cuisines: Southern, American
Average price: $11-$30
Area: Morningside / Lenox Park
Address: 1879 Cheshire Bridge Rd NE
Atlanta, GA 30324
Phone: (404) 874-5642

#187
4th & Swift
Cuisines: American
Average price: $31-$60
Area: Old Fourth Ward
Address: 621 N Ave NE
Atlanta, GA 30308
Phone: (678) 904-0160

#188
Gutenfleischers
Cuisines: Vegan
Average price: Under $10
Address: 100 Hurt St
Atlanta, GA 30307
Phone: (404) 380-1400

#189
MetroFresh
Cuisines: Soup, Sandwiches
Average price: $11-$30
Area: Midtown
Address: 931 Monroe Dr
Atlanta, GA 30308
Phone: (404) 724-0151

#190
Campagnolo
Cuisines: Italian
Average price: $11-$30
Area: Midtown
Address: 980 Piedmont Ave NE
Atlanta, GA 30309
Phone: (404) 343-2446

#191
Cook-Out
Cuisines: Hot Dogs, Burgers, Fast Food
Average price: Under $10
Address: 403 Moreland Ave SE
Atlanta, GA 30316
Phone: (404) 865-4909

#192
Souper Jenny
Cuisines: Sandwiches, Soup
Average price: $11-$30
Area: Buckhead
Address: 56 E Andrews Dr NW
Atlanta, GA 30305
Phone: (404) 239-9023

#193
Cafe Agora Midtown
Cuisines: Mediterranean
Average price: $11-$30
Area: Midtown
Address: 92 Peachtree Pl NE
Atlanta, GA 30309
Phone: (404) 253-2997

#194
Bistro Niko
Cuisines: French
Average price: $31-$60
Area: Buckhead
Address: 3344 Peachtree Rd
Atlanta, GA 30326
Phone: (404) 261-6456

#195
Senor Patron Midtown
Cuisines: Mexican
Average price: $11-$30
Area: Midtown
Address: 860 Peachtree St
Atlanta, GA 30308
Phone: (404) 645-7987

#196
Radial Cafe
Cuisines: American
Average price: $11-$30
Area: Candler Park
Address: 1530 Dekalb Ave
Atlanta, GA 30307
Phone: (404) 659-6594

#197
Sufi's
Cuisines: Persian/Iranian
Average price: $11-$30
Address: 1814 Peachtree St
Atlanta, GA 30309
Phone: (404) 888-9699

#198
Marlow's Tavern
Cuisines: Pub, American
Average price: $11-$30
Area: Midtown
Address: 950 W Peachtree St NE
Atlanta, GA 30309
Phone: (404) 815-0323

#199
Max's Coal Oven Pizzeria
Cuisines: Pizza, Salad, Italian
Average price: $11-$30
Area: Downtown
Address: 300 Marietta St NW
Atlanta, GA 30313
Phone: (404) 974-2941

#200
Sotto Sotto
Cuisines: Italian
Average price: $31-$60
Area: Inman Park
Address: 309 N Highland Ave NE
Atlanta, GA 30307
Phone: (404) 523-6678

#201
Kat's Cafe
Cuisines: American, Music Venues
Average price: $11-$30
Area: Midtown
Address: 970 Piedmont Ave
Atlanta, GA 30306
Phone: (404) 347-2263

#202
Fellini's Pizza
Cuisines: Pizza
Average price: Under $10
Address: 1991 Howell Mill Rd NW
Atlanta, GA 30318
Phone: (404) 352-0799

#203
Miller Union
Cuisines: Southern, American
Average price: $31-$60
Area: Westside / Home Park
Address: 999 Brady Ave
Atlanta, GA 30318
Phone: (678) 733-8550

#204
Verde Taqueria
Cuisines: Mexican
Average price: Under $10
Address: 1193 Collier Rd
Atlanta, GA 30318
Phone: (404) 963-5362

#205
Cafe Bombay
Cuisines: Indian
Average price: $11-$30
Address: 2615 Briarcliff Rd
Atlanta, GA 30329
Phone: (404) 320-0229

#206
The Nook On Piedmont Park
Cuisines: American
Average price: $11-$30
Area: Midtown
Address: 1144 Piedmont Ave NE
Atlanta, GA 30309
Phone: (404) 745-9222

#207
Houston's Restaurant
Cuisines: American
Average price: $11-$30
Address: 2166 Peachtree Rd NW
Atlanta, GA 30309
Phone: (404) 351-2442

#208
Top Spice Thai & Malaysian Cuisine
Cuisines: Thai, Malaysian
Average price: $11-$30
Address: 3007 N Druid Hills Rd NE
Atlanta, GA 30329
Phone: (404) 728-0588

#209
Sophie's Uptown
Cuisines: Bakery, Deli
Average price: Under $10
Area: Buckhead
Address: 54 Pharr Rd NW
Atlanta, GA 30305
Phone: (404) 812-0477

#210
Floataway Caf'
Cuisines: Cafe, French
Average price: $31-$60
Address: 1123 Zonolite Rd NE
Atlanta, GA 30306
Phone: (404) 892-1414

#211
Anis Bistro
Cuisines: French
Average price: $11-$30
Area: Buckhead
Address: 2974 Grandview Ave NE
Atlanta, GA 30305
Phone: (404) 233-9889

#212
The Spence
Cuisines: American, Diner
Average price: $31-$60
Area: Midtown
Address: 75 5th St NW
Atlanta, GA 30308
Phone: (404) 892-9111

#213
Nakato Japanese Restaurant
Cuisines: Japanese, Sushi Bar
Average price: $11-$30
Area: Morningside / Lenox Park
Address: 1776 Cheshire Bridge Rd NE
Atlanta, GA 30324
Phone: (404) 873-6582

#214
Ok Cafe
Cuisines: Cafe
Average price: $11-$30
Area: West Paces Ferry / Northside
Address: 1284 W Paces Ferry Rd Nw
Atlanta, GA 30327
Phone: (404) 233-2888

#215
Cibo e Beve
Cuisines: Italian, Pizza
Average price: $11-$30
Address: 4969 Roswell Rd
Atlanta, GA 30342
Phone: (404) 250-8988

#216
Caf' 640
Cuisines: American, Breakfast & Brunch
Average price: $11-$30
Area: Poncey-Highland
Address: 640 N Highland Ave
Atlanta, GA 30306
Phone: (404) 724-0711

#217
Woo Nam Jeong Stone Bowl House
Cuisines: Korean
Average price: $11-$30
Address: 5953 Buford Hwy
Atlanta, GA 30340
Phone: (678) 530-0844

#218
Anatolia Cafe & Hookah Lounge
Cuisines: Turkish, Hookah Bar
Average price: $11-$30
Area: Downtown
Address: 52 Peachtree St NW
Atlanta, GA 30303
Phone: (404) 589-8008

#219
Mellow Mushroom
Cuisines: Pizza, Sandwiches
Average price: $11-$30
Address: 1679 Lavista Rd
Atlanta, GA 30329
Phone: (404) 325-0330

#220
Healthful Essence
Cuisines: Caribbean, Vegan, Vegetarian
Average price: Under $10
Area: West End
Address: 875 York Ave
Atlanta, GA 30310
Phone: (404) 806-0830

#221
La Pastorcita
Cuisines: Mexican
Average price: Under $10
Address: 3304 Buford Hwy
Atlanta, GA 30329
Phone: (404) 325-5925

#222
Eats
Cuisines: Southern, Italian, Caribbean
Average price: Under $10
Area: Midtown, Old Fourth Ward
Address: 600 Ponce De Leon Ave
Atlanta, GA 30308
Phone: (404) 888-9149

#223
Fado Irish Pub & Restaurant
Cuisines: Pub, Irish
Average price: $11-$30
Area: Buckhead
Address: 273 Buckhead Ave
Atlanta, GA 30305
Phone: (404) 841-0066

#224
Abattoir
Cuisines: American
Average price: $31-$60
Area: Westside / Home Park
Address: 1170 Howell Mill Rd
Atlanta, GA 30318
Phone: (404) 892-3335

#225
Kaleidoscope Bistro & Pub
Cuisines: Gastropub, American
Average price: $11-$30
Area: Brookhaven
Address: 1410 Dresden Dr
Atlanta, GA 30319
Phone: (404) 474-9600

#226
Bantam + Biddy
Cuisines: Breakfast & Brunch, Southern, Gluten-Free
Average price: $11-$30
Address: 1544 Piedmont Ave
Atlanta, GA 30324
Phone: (404) 907-3469

#227
Kwan's Deli and Korean Kitchen
Cuisines: Deli, Sandwiches, Diner
Average price: Under $10
Area: Downtown
Address: 267 Marietta St NW
Atlanta, GA 30313
Phone: (404) 522-9796

#228
Panbury's Double Crust Pies
Cuisines: British, Australian, Bakery
Average price: Under $10
Address: 209 Edgewood Ave SE
Atlanta, GA 30303
Phone: (404) 500-1279

#229
Mediterranean Bakery & Sandwich
Cuisines: Mediterranean, Middle Eastern
Average price: Under $10
Address: 3362 Chamblee Tucker Rd
Atlanta, GA 30341
Phone: (770) 220-0706

#230
Caf' 458 Brunch
Cuisines: Breakfast & Brunch, American, Diner
Average price: Under $10
Address: 458 Edgewood Ave NE
Atlanta, GA 30312
Phone: (404) 446-4688

#231
Pasta Da Pulcinella
Cuisines: Italian
Average price: $11-$30
Area: Midtown
Address: 1123 Peachtree Walk NE
Atlanta, GA 30309
Phone: (404) 876-1114

#232
Southern Art
Cuisines: Southern
Average price: $31-$60
Area: Buckhead
Address: 3315 Peachtree Rd NE
Atlanta, GA 30326
Phone: (404) 946-9070

#233
Cafe Sunflower Sandy Springs
Cuisines: Vegetarian
Average price: $11-$30
Address: 5975 Roswell Rd NE
Atlanta, GA 30328
Phone: (404) 256-1675

#234
Der Biergarten
Cuisines: German
Average price: $11-$30
Address: 300 Marietta St NW
Atlanta, GA 30313
Phone: (404) 521-2728

#235
Harry & Sons
Cuisines: Sushi Bar, Thai
Average price: $11-$30
Area: Virginia Highland
Address: 820 N Highland Ave NE
Atlanta, GA 30306
Phone: (404) 873-2009

#236
Le French Quarter Cafe
Cuisines: French
Average price: Under $10
Area: Downtown
Address: 57 Forsyth St NW
Atlanta, GA 30303
Phone: (404) 645-7963

#237
Julianna's Crepes
Cuisines: Crepes, Desserts
Average price: Under $10
Area: Inman Park
Address: 775 Lake Ave
Atlanta, GA 30307
Phone: (404) 436-1825

#238
Am'lie's
Cuisines: Bakery, Cafe
Average price: Under $10
Address: 840 Marietta St NW
Atlanta, GA 30318
Phone: (404) 921-0276

#239
Shorty's
Cuisines: Pizza, Salad, Italian
Average price: $11-$30
Address: 2884 N Druid Hills Rd NE
Atlanta, GA 30329
Phone: (404) 315-6262

#240
Chow Bing
Cuisines: Chinese, Taiwanese
Average price: Under $10
Address: 349 Decatur St
Atlanta, GA 30312
Phone: (404) 614-6199

#241
Savage Pizza
Cuisines: Pizza
Average price: Under $10
Area: Little Five Points
Address: 484 Moreland Ave NE
Atlanta, GA 30307
Phone: (404) 523-0500

#242
Stone Soup Kitchen
Cuisines: Breakfast & Brunch
Average price: Under $10
Area: Grant Park
Address: 584 Woodward Ave
Atlanta, GA 30312
Phone: (404) 524-1222

#243
NaanStop
Cuisines: Indian, Halal, Vegetarian
Average price: Under $10
Area: Downtown
Address: 64 Broad St Nw
Atlanta, GA 30303
Phone: (404) 522-6226

#244
The Mad Italian
Cuisines: Italian, Sandwiches
Average price: Under $10
Address: 2197 Savoy Dr
Atlanta, GA 30341
Phone: (770) 451-8048

#245
Waikikie Hawaiian BBQ
Cuisines: Barbeque, Hawaiian
Average price: Under $10
Address: 2160 Briarcliff Rd
Atlanta, GA 30329
Phone: (404) 638-1115

#246
Grant Park Coffeehouse
Cuisines: Coffee, Tea, Bakery, Sandwiches
Average price: Under $10
Area: Grant Park
Address: 753-A Cherokee Ave SE
Atlanta, GA 30315
Phone: (404) 856-0433

#247
Bartaco
Cuisines: Mexican, Tapas Bar
Average price: $11-$30
Address: 969 Marietta St NW
Atlanta, GA 30318
Phone: (404) 607-8226

#248
Terra Terroir
Cuisines: Wine Bar, American
Average price: $11-$30
Area: Brookhaven
Address: 3974 Peachtree Rd
Atlanta, GA 30319
Phone: (404) 841-1032

#249
Moon Indian Cuisine
Cuisines: Indian
Average price: $11-$30
Address: 2144 Johnson Ferry Rd
Atlanta, GA 30319
Phone: (770) 817-1097

#250
Miso Izakaya
Cuisines: Japanese, Sushi Bar
Average price: $11-$30
Area: Old Fourth Ward
Address: 619 Edgewood Ave
Atlanta, GA 30312
Phone: (678) 701-0128

#251
Sub-Base Sandwich Shoppe
Cuisines: Sandwiches, Donuts
Average price: Under $10
Address: 3665 Chamblee Dunwoody Rd
Atlanta, GA 30341
Phone: (770) 457-6953

#252
Blue Ridge Grill
Cuisines: Seafood, Steakhouse
Average price: $31-$60
Area: West Paces Ferry / Northside
Address: 1261 W Paces Ferry Rd NW
Atlanta, GA 30327
Phone: (404) 233-5030

#253
Tin Lizzy's Cantina
Cuisines: Mexican, Bar, Tex-Mex
Average price: $11-$30
Area: Buckhead
Address: 3639 Piedmont Rd NE
Atlanta, GA 30305
Phone: (404) 846-6000

#254
Tacos and Tequilas Mexican Grill
Cuisines: Mexican
Average price: $11-$30
Area: Buckhead
Address: 4279 Roswell Rd
Atlanta, GA 30342
Phone: (404) 705-8225

#255
The Pullman
Cuisines: Gastropub,
Breakfast & Brunch
Average price: $11-$30
Area: Kirkwood
Address: 1992 Hosea Williams Dr
Atlanta, GA 30317
Phone: (404) 371-1115

#256
Himalayan Spice
Cuisines: Indian, Himalayan/Nepalese
Average price: $11-$30
Address: 2773 Clairmont Rd
Atlanta, GA 30329
Phone: (404) 549-7602

#257
Atlanta Food Truck Park
Cuisines: Street Vendor, Food Stands
Average price: Under $10
Address: 1850 Howell Mill Rd
Atlanta, GA 30318

#258
J Alexander's
Cuisines: American
Average price: $11-$30
Address: 4701 Ashford Dunwoody Rd
Atlanta, GA 30338
Phone: (770) 512-0153

#259
BrickTop's
Cuisines: American
Average price: $11-$30
Area: Buckhead
Address: 3280 Peachtree Rd NE
Atlanta, GA 30305
Phone: (404) 841-2212

#260
The Original Pancake House
Cuisines: Breakfast & Brunch
Average price: $11-$30
Address: 2321 Lavista Rd NE
Atlanta, GA 30324
Phone: (404) 633-5677

#261
S Teamshouse Lounge
Cuisines: Seafood, Dive Bar
Average price: $11-$30
Area: Midtown
Address: 1051 W Peachtree St NW
Atlanta, GA 30309
Phone: (404) 233-7980

#262
International Cafe
Cuisines: American, Cafe, Sandwiches
Average price: Under $10
Address: 3066 Buford Hwy NE
Atlanta, GA 30329
Phone: (404) 633-2428

#263
Noche
Cuisines: Tapas Bar, Bar
Average price: $11-$30
Area: Virginia Highland
Address: 1000 Virginia Ave NE
Atlanta, GA 30306
Phone: (404) 815-9155

#264
Clay's Sports Cafe
Cuisines: Dive Bar, Chicken Wings
Average price: Under $10
Address: 6518 Roswell Rd NE
Atlanta, GA 30328
Phone: (404) 843-1233

#265
Treehouse Restaurant and Pub
Cuisines: Restaurant, Pub
Average price: $11-$30
Area: Buckhead
Address: 7 Kings Cir NE
Atlanta, GA 30305
Phone: (404) 266-2732

#266
Gyro Gyro
Cuisines: Greek
Average price: Under $10
Address: 5000 Winters Chapel Rd
Atlanta, GA 30360
Phone: (770) 352-4976

#267
Six Feet Under Pub & Fish House
Cuisines: Seafood, Tex-Mex
Average price: $11-$30
Area: Grant Park
Address: 437 Memorial Drive SE
Atlanta, GA 30312
Phone: (404) 523-6664

#268
Fellini's Pizza
Cuisines: Pizza
Average price: Under $10
Area: Candler Park
Address: 1634 McLendon Ave NE
Atlanta, GA 30307
Phone: (404) 687-9190

#269
Vin Vie Bistro
Cuisines: French, Steakhouse
Average price: $31-$60
Area: Buckhead
Address: 2285 Peachtree Rd. NE
Atlanta, GA 30309
Phone: (404) 317-7020

#270
El Mexicano
Cuisines: Mexican
Average price: Under $10
Address: 1341 Moreland Ave SE
Atlanta, GA 30316
Phone: (404) 622-3501

#271
Breadwinner Cafe and Bakery
Cuisines: Bakery, Sandwiches
Average price: $11-$30
Address: 220 Sandy Springs Cir
Atlanta, GA 30328
Phone: (404) 843-0224

#272
Six Feet Under Pub & Fish House
Cuisines: Seafood, Pub
Average price: $11-$30
Area: Westside / Home Park
Address: 685 11th St
Atlanta, GA 30318
Phone: (404) 810-0040

#273
White Oak Kitchen & Cocktails
Cuisines: Southern, American, Venues
Average price: $31-$60
Area: Downtown
Address: 270 Peachtree St
Atlanta, GA 30303
Phone: (404) 524-7200

#274
Reuben's Deli
Cuisines: Sandwiches, Deli, Burgers
Average price: Under $10
Area: Downtown
Address: 57 Broad St NW
Atlanta, GA 30303
Phone: (404) 589-9800

#275
Bone Lick BBQ
Cuisines: Barbeque, Bar
Average price: $11-$30
Address: 1133 Huff Rd NW
Atlanta, GA 30318
Phone: (404) 343-6574

#276
Al-Amin Restaurant
Cuisines: Bangladeshi, Grocery
Average price: Under $10
Address: 5466 Buford Hwy NE
Atlanta, GA 30340
Phone: (470) 375-4078

#277
The Red Snapper Seafood Restaurant
Cuisines: American, Seafood
Average price: $11-$30
Address: 2100 Cheshire Bridge Rd N
Atlanta, GA 30324
Phone: (404) 634-8947

#278
Bangkok Thyme
Cuisines: Thai, Sushi Bar
Average price: $11-$30
Address: 4969 Roswell Rd NE
Atlanta, GA 30342
Phone: (404) 389-0909

#279
The Fry Guy
Cuisines: Food Stands
Average price: Under $10
Area: Virginia Highland
Address: Highland Ave
Atlanta, GA 30306
Phone:

#280
Atkins Park Restaurant
Cuisines: American, Salad, Soup
Average price: $11-$30
Area: Virginia Highland
Address: 794 N Highland Ave NE
Atlanta, GA 30306
Phone: (404) 876-7249

#281
Malaya
Cuisines: Chinese, Malaysian
Average price: $11-$30
Address: 857 Collier Rd NW
Atlanta, GA 30318
Phone: (404) 609-9991

#282
Woody's CheeseSteaks
Cuisines: Sandwiches, Cheesesteaks, Hot Dogs
Average price: Under $10
Area: Midtown
Address: 981 Monroe Dr NE
Atlanta, GA 30308
Phone: (404) 876-1939

#283
Pita Palace
Cuisines: Middle Eastern, Kosher
Average price: Under $10
Address: 1658 La Vista Rd
Atlanta, GA 30329
Phone: (404) 781-7482

#284
The Downwind Restaurant and Lounge
Cuisines: American, Burgers
Average price: $11-$30
Address: 2000 Airport Rd
Atlanta, GA 30341
Phone: (770) 452-0973

#285
Meehan's Public House
Cuisines: Pub, Irish
Average price: $11-$30
Address: 2810 Paces Ferry Rd SE
Atlanta, GA 30339
Phone: (770) 433-1920

#286
The Highlander
Cuisines: Dive Bar, American
Average price: $11-$30
Area: Midtown
Address: 931 Monroe Dr NE
Atlanta, GA 30308
Phone: (404) 872-0060

#287
The Flying Biscuit Cafe
Cuisines: Breakfast & Brunch, Coffee, Tea, American
Average price: $11-$30
Area: Candler Park
Address: 1655 McLendon Ave NE
Atlanta, GA 30307
Phone: (404) 687-8888

#288
Canton Cooks
Cuisines: Chinese
Average price: $11-$30
Address: 5984 Roswell Rd NE
Atlanta, GA 30328
Phone: (404) 250-0515

#289
The Rusty Nail Pub
Cuisines: Burgers, American, Dive Bar
Average price: $11-$30
Address: 2900 Buford Hwy NE
Atlanta, GA 30329
Phone: (404) 634-6306

#290
10th & Piedmont
Cuisines: American, Breakfast & Brunch
Average price: $11-$30
Area: Midtown
Address: 991 Piedmont Ave NE
Atlanta, GA 30309
Phone: (404) 602-5510

#291
Tin Lizzy's Cantina
Cuisines: Bar, Tex-Mex
Average price: $11-$30
Area: Midtown
Address: 1136 Crescent Ave NE
Atlanta, GA 30309
Phone: (404) 537-5060

#292
SIP The Experience
Cuisines: Coffee, Tea, Desserts, Sandwiches
Average price: Under $10
Area: Lindbergh
Address: 528 Main St
Atlanta, GA 30324
Phone: (404) 816-3001

#293
Olde Blind Dog
Cuisines: Irish, Pub
Average price: $11-$30
Address: 705 Town Blvd
Atlanta, GA 30319
Phone: (404) 816-5739

#294
Top Flr
Cuisines: American, Wine Bar
Average price: $11-$30
Area: Midtown
Address: 674 Myrtle St NE
Atlanta, GA 30308
Phone: (404) 685-3110

#295
Ghion Cultural Hall
Cuisines: Ethiopian
Average price: $11-$30
Address: 2080 Cheshire Bridge Rd
Atlanta, GA 30324
Phone: (704) 449-8991

#296
Cafe Sunflower Buckhead
Cuisines: Vegetarian
Average price: $11-$30
Address: 2140 Peachtree Rd Nw
Atlanta, GA 30309
Phone: (404) 352-8859

#297
HOBNOB
Cuisines: American, Pub
Average price: $11-$30
Area: Morningside / Lenox Park
Address: 1551 Piedmont Ave NE
Atlanta, GA 30324
Phone: (404) 968-2288

#298
Verde Taqueria
Cuisines: Mexican, Tex-Mex
Average price: $11-$30
Area: Brookhaven
Address: 1426 Dresden Dr
Atlanta, GA 30319
Phone: (404) 254-5319

#299
Article 14
Cuisines: American
Average price: $11-$30
Area: Midtown
Address: 1180 Peachtree St
Atlanta, GA 30309
Phone: (404) 443-8432

#300
57th Fighter Group Restaurant
Cuisines: American
Average price: $11-$30
Address: 3829 Clairmont Rd
Atlanta, GA 30341
Phone: (770) 234-0057

#301
The Euclid Avenue Yacht Club
Cuisines: Dive Bar
Average price: Under $10
Area: Little Five Points
Address: 1136 Euclid Ave NE
Atlanta, GA 30307
Phone: (404) 688-2582

#302
Cafe Vena At Vinings
Cuisines: American
Average price: $11-$30
Address: 3300 Cobb Pkwy
Atlanta, GA 30339
Phone: (770) 937-9089

#303
Flip Burger Boutique
Cuisines: Burgers, American, Wine Bar
Average price: $11-$30
Area: Buckhead
Address: 3655 Roswell Rd NE
Atlanta, GA 30305
Phone: (404) 549-3298

#304
Ocean Prime
Cuisines: Steakhouse, Seafood
Average price: $31-$60
Area: Buckhead
Address: 3102 Piedmont Rd NE
Atlanta, GA 30305
Phone: (404) 846-0505

#305
Fresh 4 U Mediterranean Cafe
Cuisines: Mediterranean
Average price: Under $10
Area: Buckhead
Address: 1937 Peachtree St
Atlanta, GA 30309
Phone: (404) 603-8883

#306
Little Thai Cuisine
Cuisines: Thai
Average price: $11-$30
Address: 220 Sandy Springs Cir
Atlanta, GA 30328
Phone: (404) 943-9189

#307
Buckhead Diner
Cuisines: American, Ethnic Food, Diner
Average price: $11-$30
Address: 3073 Piedmont Rd NE
Atlanta, GA 30305
Phone: (404) 262-3336

#308
Gekko Sushi
Cuisines: Japanese, Sushi Bar
Average price: $11-$30
Area: Old Fourth Ward
Address: 620 Glen Iris Dr NE
Atlanta, GA 30308
Phone: (404) 249-4300

#309
The Original El Taco
Cuisines: Mexican
Average price: $11-$30
Area: Virginia Highland
Address: 1186 N. Highland Avenue NE
Atlanta, GA 30306
Phone: (404) 873-4656

#310
Sweet Cheats
Cuisines: Desserts, Cafe,
Food Delivery Services
Average price: Under $10
Area: Cabbagetown
Address: 692-B Kirkwood Ave
Atlanta, GA 30316
Phone: (404) 590-6086

#311
Gordon Biersch Brewery
Cuisines: American, Brewery
Average price: $11-$30
Area: Buckhead
Address: 3242 Peachtree Rd NE
Atlanta, GA 30305
Phone: (404) 264-0253

#312
Tabla
Cuisines: Indian
Average price: $11-$30
Area: Midtown
Address: 77th 12th St
Atlanta, GA 30309
Phone: (404) 464-8571

#313
Parish Foods and Goods
Cuisines: American
Average price: $11-$30
Area: Old Fourth Ward, Poncey-Highland
Address: 240 N Highland Ave
Atlanta, GA 30307
Phone: (404) 681-4434

#314
H Harper Station
Cuisines: American, Bar
Average price: $11-$30
Area: Reynoldstown
Address: 904 Memorial Dr SE
Atlanta, GA 30316
Phone: (678) 732-0415

#315
Augustine's
Cuisines: Gastropub, American
Average price: $11-$30
Area: Grant Park
Address: 327 Memorial Dr
Atlanta, GA 30312
Phone: (404) 681-3344

#316
Takorea
Cuisines: Bar, Korean, Mexican
Average price: $11-$30
Area: Midtown
Address: 818 Juniper St
Atlanta, GA 30308
Phone: (404) 532-1944

#317
Trader Vic's
Cuisines: Hawaiian, Asian Fusion
Average price: $31-$60
Address: 255 Courtland St NE
Atlanta, GA 30303
Phone: (404) 221-6339

#318
D.B.A.
Cuisines: Barbeque
Average price: $11-$30
Area: Virginia Highland
Address: 1190 N Highland Ave NE
Atlanta, GA 30306
Phone: (404) 249-5000

#319
Piu Bello Pizzeria Restaurant
Cuisines: Pizza, Italian
Average price: Under $10
Area: Buckhead
Address: 3330 Piedmont Rd NE
Atlanta, GA 30305
Phone: (404) 814-0304

#320
One Midtown Kitchen
Cuisines: American
Average price: $31-$60
Area: Morningside / Lenox Park
Address: 559 Dutch Valley Rd NE
Atlanta, GA 30324
Phone: (404) 892-4111

#321
Fortune Cookie
Cuisines: Chinese
Average price: $11-$30
Address: 2480 Briarcliff Rd NE
Atlanta, GA 30329
Phone: (404) 636-8899

#322
Babylon Cafe
Cuisines: Coffee, Tea, Middle Eastern
Average price: $11-$30
Address: 2257 Lenox Rd NE
Atlanta, GA 30324
Phone: (404) 329-1007

#323
Grant Central Pizza & Pasta
Cuisines: Pizza
Average price: Under $10
Area: Grant Park
Address: 451 Cherokee Ave SE
Atlanta, GA 30312
Phone: (404) 523-8900

#324
Man Chun Hong
Cuisines: Chinese, Korean
Average price: $11-$30
Address: 5953 Buford Hwy NE
Atlanta, GA 30340
Phone: (770) 454-5640

#325
Yoi Yoi Japanese Steakhouse & Sushi
Cuisines: Japanese, Sushi Bar, Steakhouse
Average price: $11-$30
Address: 857 Collier Rd
Atlanta, GA 30318
Phone: (404) 351-1788

#326
Lips Atlanta
Cuisines: Bar, American
Average price: $11-$30
Address: 3011 Buford Hwy NE
Atlanta, GA 30329
Phone: (404) 315-7711

#327
Top Spice Thai & Malaysian Cuisine
Cuisines: Thai
Average price: $11-$30
Area: Morningside / Lenox Park
Address: 1529 Piedmont Ave NE
Atlanta, GA 30324
Phone: (404) 685-9333

#328
Zo's Kitchen
Cuisines: Sandwiches
Average price: Under $10
Area: Emory Village
Address: 1385 Oxford Rd NE
Atlanta, GA 30322
Phone: (404) 377-9048

#329
5 Seasons Westside
Cuisines: American, Brewery
Average price: $11-$30
Address: 1000 Marietta St NW
Atlanta, GA 30318
Phone: (404) 875-3232

#330
Houstons
Cuisines: American, Steakhouse
Average price: $31-$60
Area: West Paces Ferry / Northside
Address: 3539 Northside Pkwy NW
Atlanta, GA 30327
Phone: (404) 262-7130

#331
Kang Nam
Cuisines: Korean, Japanese
Average price: $11-$30
Address: 5715 Buford Hwy NE
Atlanta, GA 30340
Phone: (770) 455-3464

#332
Bhojanic
Cuisines: Ethnic Food, Indian
Average price: $11-$30
Area: Buckhead
Address: 3400 Around Lenox Rd
Atlanta, GA 30326
Phone: (404) 841-8472

#333
Las Tortas Locas
Cuisines: Mexican
Average price: Under $10
Address: 5841 Roswell Rd. NE
Atlanta, GA 30328
Phone: (404) 844-4445

#334
Cafe Momo
Cuisines: Buffets
Average price: Under $10
Area: Downtown
Address: 235 Peachtree St NE
Atlanta, GA 30303
Phone: (404) 254-5885

#335
The Brooklyn Cafe
Cuisines: American
Average price: $11-$30
Address: 220 Sandy Springs Cir NE
Atlanta, GA 30328
Phone: (404) 843-8377

#336
Sushi Matsuya
Cuisines: Japanese, Sushi Bar
Average price: $11-$30
Address: 2899 N Druid Hills Rd
Atlanta, GA 30329
Phone: (404) 321-1605

#337
Edgewood Corner Tavern
Cuisines: American
Average price: $11-$30
Address: 464 Edgewood Ave
Atlanta, GA 30312
Phone: (404) 577-2310

#338
Fellini's Pizza
Cuisines: Pizza
Average price: Under $10
Area: Poncey-Highland
Address: 909 Ponce de Leon Ave NE
Atlanta, GA 30306
Phone: (404) 873-3088

#339
Get Fruity Cafe
Cuisines: Juice Bar, Salad, Sandwiches
Average price: Under $10
Area: Downtown
Address: 79 Marietta St NW
Atlanta, GA 30303
Phone: (404) 521-0109

#340
Mr Everything Cafe
Cuisines: Fast Food, Sandwiches
Average price: Under $10
Address: 870 Martin Luther King Jr Dr NW,
Atlanta, GA 30314
Phone: (404) 521-9903

#341
The Brickery Grill & Bar
Cuisines: American
Average price: $11-$30
Address: 6125 Roswell Rd NE
Atlanta, GA 30328
Phone: (404) 843-8002

#342
Scotch Bonnet Jamaican Eatery
Cuisines: Caribbean
Average price: $11-$30
Address: 4454 Campbellton Rd SW
Atlanta, GA 30331
Phone: (404) 344-3359

#343
La Fonda Latina
Cuisines: Spanish, Mexican
Average price: Under $10
Area: Westside / Home Park
Address: 1025 Howell Mill Rd
Atlanta, GA 30318
Phone: (404) 249-2272

#344
Willy's Mexicana Grill
Cuisines: Mexican
Average price: Under $10
Area: Midtown
Address: 1071 Piedmont Ave NE
Atlanta, GA 30309
Phone: (404) 249-9054

#345
STEEL Restaurant & Lounge
Cuisines: Asian Fusion, Sushi Bar, Thai
Average price: $11-$30
Area: Midtown
Address: 950 W Peachtree St
Atlanta, GA 30309
Phone: (404) 477-6111

#346
Publik Draft House
Cuisines: Pub, American
Average price: $11-$30
Area: Midtown
Address: 654 Peachtree St
Atlanta, GA 30308
Phone: (404) 885-7505

#347
Flying Biscuit
Cuisines: American, Coffee, Tea, Breakfast & Brunch
Average price: $11-$30
Area: Buckhead
Address: 3280 Peachtree Rd NE
Atlanta, GA 30305
Phone: (404) 477-0013

#348
Havana Restaurant
Cuisines: Cuban
Average price: Under $10
Address: 3979 Buford Hwy
Atlanta, GA 30319
Phone: (404) 633-7549

#349
Stoney River Legendary Steaks
Cuisines: Steakhouse, Seafood
Average price: $31-$60
Address: 1640 Cumberland Mall SE
Atlanta, GA 30339
Phone: (678) 305-9229

#350
Fontaine's Oyster House
Cuisines: Seafood, Bar
Average price: $11-$30
Area: Virginia Highland
Address: 1026 N Highland Ave NE
Atlanta, GA 30306
Phone: (404) 872-0869

#351
Thai Chili
Cuisines: Thai
Average price: $11-$30
Address: 2169 Briarcliff Rd NE
Atlanta, GA 30329
Phone: (404) 315-6750

#352
Newk's Express Cafe
Cuisines: Salad, Pizza, Sandwiches
Average price: $11-$30
Area: Midtown
Address: 933 Peachtree St
Atlanta, GA 30309
Phone: (404) 853-2555

#353
Eclectic Bistro & Bar
Cuisines: American
Average price: $11-$30
Address: 1425 Piedmont Ave
Atlanta, GA 30309
Phone: (404) 426-7728

#354
North Highland Pub
Cuisines: American
Average price: Under $10
Area: Inman Park
Address: 469 N Highland Ave NE
Atlanta, GA 30307
Phone: (404) 522-4600

#355
La Fonda Latina
Cuisines: Latin American, Mexican
Average price: Under $10
Area: Poncey-Highland
Address: 923 Ponce De Leon Ave NE
Atlanta, GA 30306
Phone: (404) 607-0665

#356
Osteria 832
Cuisines: Pizza, Italian, Salad
Average price: $11-$30
Area: Virginia Highland
Address: 832 N Highland Ave NE
Atlanta, GA 30306
Phone: (404) 897-1414

#357
Le Triskell
Cuisines: Crepes
Average price: Under $10
Area: Buckhead
Address: 3833 Roswell Rd
Atlanta, GA 30342
Phone: (404) 814-8208

#358
MAX's Wine Dive
Cuisines: American, Comfort Food
Average price: $11-$30
Area: Midtown
Address: 77 12th St. NE,
Atlanta, GA 30309
Phone: (404) 249-0445

#359
Sushi Bar Yu-ka
Cuisines: Sushi Bar
Average price: $11-$30
Area: Buckhead
Address: 3330 Piedmont Rd NE
Atlanta, GA 30305
Phone: (404) 233-6700

#360
Dantanna's
Cuisines: Steakhouse, Seafood
Average price: $11-$30
Address: 3400 Around Lenox Rd NE
Atlanta, GA 30326
Phone: (404) 760-8873

#361
Eclipse Di Luna
Cuisines: Tapas Bar, Spanish
Average price: $11-$30
Area: Lindbergh
Address: 764 Miami Cir NE
Atlanta, GA 30324
Phone: (404) 846-0449

#362
Grub Burger Bar
Cuisines: Burgers
Average price: $11-$30
Address: 2955 Cobb Pkwy SE
Atlanta, GA 30339
Phone: (678) 573-9030

#363
Apache Caf'
Cuisines: Music Venues, Southern
Average price: $11-$30
Area: Midtown
Address: 64 3rd St NW
Atlanta, GA 30308
Phone: (404) 876-5436

#364
Drink Art
Cuisines: Thai, Vegan
Average price: $11-$30
Area: Castleberry Hill
Address: 199 Walker St
Atlanta, GA 30313
Phone: (404) 592-5275

#365
Ray's On the River
Cuisines: Seafood, Venues, Breakfast & Brunch
Average price: $31-$60
Address: 6700 Powers Ferry Rd
Atlanta, GA 30339
Phone: (770) 955-1187

#366
Fresh To Order
Cuisines: Fruits & Veggies, Sandwiches
Average price: Under $10
Address: 1260 Cumberland Mall
Atlanta, GA 30339
Phone: (678) 564-1400

#367
Octopus Bar
Cuisines: American
Average price: $11-$30
Area: East Atlanta Village
Address: 561 Gresham Ave
Atlanta, GA 30316
Phone: (404) 627-9911

#368
Heart of India
Cuisines: Indian
Average price: $11-$30
Address: 3362 Chamblee Tucker Rd
Atlanta, GA 30341
Phone: (470) 246-4317

#369
Spoon Eastside
Cuisines: Thai
Average price: $11-$30
Area: Ormewood Park
Address: 749 Moreland Ave SE
Atlanta, GA 30316
Phone: (404) 624-4713

#370
Taqueria Los Rayos
Cuisines: Mexican
Average price: Under $10
Address: 3473 Clairmont Rd
Atlanta, GA 30319
Phone: (404) 634-0100

#371
MOTHER
Cuisines: Bar, American, Dance Club
Average price: $11-$30
Address: 447 Edgewood Ave SE
Atlanta, GA 30312
Phone: (404) 524-4605

#372
Noodle Cafe
Cuisines: Thai
Average price: Under $10
Area: Downtown
Address: 233 Peachtree St NE
Atlanta, GA 30303
Phone: (404) 880-9884

#373
Pig-N-Chik BBQ
Cuisines: Barbeque
Average price: Under $10
Address: 5071 Peachtree Industrial Blvd
Atlanta, GA 30341
Phone: (770) 451-1112

#374
Moe's and Joe's
Cuisines: Dive Bar, American
Average price: Under $10
Area: Virginia Highland
Address: 1033 N Highland Ave NE
Atlanta, GA 30306
Phone: (404) 873-6090

#375
Tin Lizzy's Cantina
Cuisines: Mexican, Sports Bar
Average price: $11-$30
Area: Grant Park
Address: 415 Memorial Dr
Atlanta, GA 30312
Phone: (404) 554-8220

#376
Chef Liu
Cuisines: Chinese
Average price: Under $10
Address: 5283 Buford Hwy NE
Atlanta, GA 30340
Phone: (770) 936-0532

#377
The Big Ketch Saltwater Grill
Cuisines: Seafood
Average price: $11-$30
Area: Buckhead
Address: 3279 Roswell Rd
Atlanta, GA 30305
Phone: (404) 474-9508

#378
Taqueria El Rey Del Taco
Cuisines: Mexican
Average price: Under $10
Address: 5288 Buford Hwy NE
Atlanta, GA 30340
Phone: (770) 986-0032

#379
Horseradish Grill
Cuisines: Breakfast & Brunch, American, Desserts
Average price: $31-$60
Address: 4320 Powers Ferry Rd NW
Atlanta, GA 30342
Phone: (404) 255-7277

#380
Holy Taco
Cuisines: Mexican
Average price: $11-$30
Area: East Atlanta Village
Address: 1314 Glenwood Ave SE
Atlanta, GA 30316
Phone: (404) 230-6177

#381
Ah-Ma's Taiwanese Kitchen
Cuisines: Taiwanese, Chinese, Tapas
Average price: Under $10
Area: Midtown
Address: 931 Monroe Dr
Atlanta, GA 30308
Phone: (404) 549-9848

#382
Burger Win
Cuisines: Chinese, Burgers
Average price: Under $10
Area: East Atlanta Village
Address: 1181 McPherson Ave
Atlanta, GA 30316
Phone: (404) 525-2255

#383
Ali Baba Mediterranean Delites
Cuisines: Mediterranean, Turkish
Average price: Under $10
Area: Downtown
Address: 60 Broad St NW
Atlanta, GA 30303
Phone: (404) 681-3997

#384
Highland Tap
Cuisines: Steakhouse, Bar
Average price: $11-$30
Area: Virginia Highland
Address: 1026 N Highland Ave NE
Atlanta, GA 30306
Phone: (404) 875-3673

#385
Shucks Oyster and Wine Bar
Cuisines: Seafood
Average price: $11-$30
Address: 705 Town Brookhaven
Atlanta, GA 30319
Phone: (404) 846-1777

#386
Chat Patti
Cuisines: Indian, Vegetarian
Average price: Under $10
Address: 1594 Woodcliff Dr NE
Atlanta, GA 30329
Phone: (404) 633-5595

#387
The Flying Biscuit Cafe
Cuisines: Southern, Breakfast & Brunch
Average price: $11-$30
Address: 5975 Roswell Rd
Atlanta, GA 30328
Phone: (404) 252-1182

#388
Red Pepper Taqueria
Cuisines: Sports Bar, Mexican
Average price: $11-$30
Area: Buckhead
Address: 3135 Piedmont Rd
Atlanta, GA 30305
Phone: (404) 869-2773

#389
Blue Moon Pizza
Cuisines: Pizza
Average price: $11-$30
Area: Buckhead
Address: 325 E Paces Ferry Rd
Atlanta, GA 30305
Phone: (404) 814-1515

#390
East Point Corner Tavern
Cuisines: Bar, American
Average price: $11-$30
Address: 2783 Main St
Atlanta, GA 30344
Phone: (404) 768-0007

#391
The Flying Biscuit Cafe
Cuisines: American, Breakfast & Brunch
Average price: $11-$30
Area: West Paces Ferry / Northside
Address: 3515 Northside Pkwy NW
Atlanta, GA 30327
Phone: (404) 816-3152

#392
Taco Mac
Cuisines: Burgers, Bar, American
Average price: $11-$30
Address: 1211 Ashford Crossing
Atlanta, GA 30346
Phone: (678) 336-1381

#393
Fellini's Pizza
Cuisines: Pizza
Average price: Under $10
Area: Buckhead
Address: 4429 Roswell Rd NE
Atlanta, GA 30342
Phone: (404) 303-8248

#394
Stillhouse Craft Burgers & Moonshine
Cuisines: Cocktail Bar, Burgers
Average price: $11-$30
Area: Buckhead
Address: 56 E Andrews Dr NW
Atlanta, GA 30305
Phone: (678) 244-3601

#395
The Albert
Cuisines: Bar, American
Average price: $11-$30
Area: Inman Park
Address: 918 Austin Ave
Atlanta, GA 30307
Phone: (404) 872-4990

#396
Apres Diem
Cuisines: American, Bar
Average price: $11-$30
Area: Midtown
Address: 931 Monroe Dr NE
Atlanta, GA 30308
Phone: (404) 872-3333

#397
DaVinci's Pizzeria
Cuisines: Pizza, Italian
Average price: $11-$30
Area: Midtown
Address: 1270 W Peachtree St NW
Atlanta, GA 30309
Phone: (404) 249-7800

#398
The Mercantile
Cuisines: Grocery, Sandwiches
Average price: $11-$30
Area: Candler Park
Address: 1660 Dekalb Ave
Atlanta, GA 30307
Phone: (404) 378-0096

#399
Nam Phuong
Cuisines: Vietnamese
Average price: $11-$30
Address: 4051 Buford Hwy NE
Atlanta, GA 30345
Phone: (404) 633-2400

#400
Baraonda Italian Restaurant
Cuisines: Italian, Pizza
Average price: $11-$30
Area: Midtown
Address: 710 Peachtree St NE
Atlanta, GA 30308
Phone: (404) 879-9962

#401
Pizzeria Vesuvius
Cuisines: Pizza
Average price: $11-$30
Address: 327 Edgewood Ave
Atlanta, GA 30312
Phone: (404) 343-4404

#402
Truva
Cuisines: Mediterranean
Average price: $11-$30
Area: Downtown
Address: 60 Andrew Young International Blvd NE, Atlanta, GA 30303
Phone: (404) 577-8788

#403
Chinese Buddha
Cuisines: Chinese
Average price: $11-$30
Area: Midtown
Address: 100 10th St NW
Atlanta, GA 30309
Phone: (404) 874-5158

#404
Fresh To Order
Cuisines: Sandwiches, Vegetarian, Salad
Average price: $11-$30
Area: Buckhead
Address: 3344 Peachtree Rd
Atlanta, GA 30326
Phone: (404) 503-9999

#405
Dakota Blue
Cuisines: Breakfast & Brunch, Tex-Mex
Average price: Under $10
Area: Grant Park
Address: 454 Cherokee Ave SE
Atlanta, GA 30312
Phone: (404) 589-8002

#406
Del Frisco's Grille
Cuisines: American, Wine Bar
Average price: $31-$60
Area: Buckhead
Address: 3376 Peachtree Rd NE
Atlanta, GA 30326
Phone: (404) 537-2828

#407
Rosa's Pizza
Cuisines: Pizza
Average price: Under $10
Address: 62 Broad St NW
Atlanta, GA 30303
Phone: (404) 521-2596

#408
Flatiron Restaurant & Bar
Cuisines: American, Bar
Average price: $11-$30
Area: East Atlanta Village
Address: 520 Flat Shoals Ave SE
Atlanta, GA 30316
Phone: (404) 688-8864

#409
Meehan's Public House
Cuisines: Irish, Pub
Average price: $11-$30
Area: Downtown
Address: 200 Peachtree St
Atlanta, GA 30303
Phone: (404) 214-9821

#410
FuegoMundo
Cuisines: Latin American
Average price: $11-$30
Address: 5590 Roswell Rd, Ste 120
Atlanta, GA 30342
Phone: (404) 256-4330

#411
Loving Hut
Cuisines: Vegan, Vegetarian
Average price: Under $10
Address: 220 Hammond Dr NE
Atlanta, GA 30328
Phone: (404) 941-7992

#412
Gato Arigato
Cuisines: Japanese
Average price: $11-$30
Area: Candler Park
Address: 1660 McLendon Ave NE
Atlanta, GA 30307
Phone: (404) 371-0889

#413
Baci
Cuisines: American
Average price: $11-$30
Address: 705 Town Blvd
Atlanta, GA 30319
Phone: (678) 705-7628

#414
Front Page News
Cuisines: American, Breakfast & Brunch
Average price: $11-$30
Area: Midtown
Address: 1104 Crescent Ave NE
Atlanta, GA 30309
Phone: (404) 897-3500

#415
So Ba East Atlanta Village
Cuisines: Vietnamese
Average price: $11-$30
Area: East Atlanta Village
Address: 560 Gresham Ave
Atlanta, GA 30316
Phone: (404) 627-9911

#416
La Petite Maison
Cuisines: French
Average price: $31-$60
Address: 6510 Roswell Rd NE
Atlanta, GA 30328
Phone: (404) 303-6600

#417
Raku
Cuisines: Japanese
Average price: $11-$30
Address: 810 Marietta St NW
Atlanta, GA 30318
Phone: (404) 500-1908

#418
Zinburger Wine & Burger Bar
Cuisines: Salad, Burgers
Average price: $11-$30
Area: Buckhead
Address: 3393 Peachtree Rd NE
Atlanta, GA 30326
Phone: (404) 963-9611

#419
Penn Station
Cuisines: Sandwiches
Average price: Under $10
Address: 2566 Briarcliff Rd NE
Atlanta, GA 30329
Phone: (404) 500-4294

#420
Eclipse di Luna
Cuisines: Tapas Bar, Ethnic Food
Average price: $11-$30
Address: 4505 Ashford Dunwoody Rd NE,
Atlanta, GA 30346
Phone: (678) 205-5862

#421
Thaicoon & Sushi Bar
Cuisines: Sushi Bar, Thai
Average price: $11-$30
Address: 1799 Briarcliff Rd NE
Atlanta, GA 30306
Phone: (404) 817-9805

#422
There
Cuisines: Gastropub, American
Average price: $11-$30
Address: 305 Brookhaven Ave
Atlanta, GA 30319
Phone: (404) 949-9677

#423
Ration & Dram
Cuisines: Southern
Average price: $11-$30
Area: Edgewood
Address: 130 Arizona Ave NE
Atlanta, GA 30307
Phone: (678) 974-8380

#424
The Pickle
Cuisines: Food Stands, Caterers
Average price: Under $10
Area: Grant Park
Address: The Pickle in Atlanta,
Atlanta, GA 30312
Phone: (404) 421-9080

#425
285 West Soul Food Restaurant
Cuisines: Soul Food
Average price: Under $10
Address: 2636 Martin Luther King Jr Dr
Atlanta, GA 30311
Phone: (404) 691-5968

#426
The Wing Ranch
Cuisines: Chicken Wings
Average price: Under $10
Address: 2146 Johnson Ferry Rd NE
Atlanta, GA 30319
Phone: (770) 455-4233

#427
Com Dunwoody Vietnamese Grill
Cuisines: Vietnamese, Asian Fusion
Average price: $11-$30
Address: 5486 Chamblee Dunwoody Rd
Atlanta, GA 30338
Phone: (770) 512-7410

#428
Legal Sea Foods
Cuisines: Seafood
Average price: $31-$60
Area: Downtown
Address: 275 Baker St NW
Atlanta, GA 30313
Phone: (678) 500-3700

#429
Loca Luna
Cuisines: Tapas Bar
Average price: $11-$30
Area: Morningside / Lenox Park
Address: 550 Amsterdam Ave NE
Atlanta, GA 30306
Phone: (404) 875-4494

#430
Coast Seafood and Raw Bar
Cuisines: Seafood
Average price: $11-$30
Area: Buckhead
Address: 111 W Paces Ferry Rd
Atlanta, GA 30305
Phone: (404) 869-0777

#431
Elder Tree Public House
Cuisines: Irish, Sports Bar, Gastropub
Average price: $11-$30
Area: East Atlanta Village
Address: 469 Flat Shoals Ave
Atlanta, GA 30316
Phone: (404) 658-6108

#432
Cook Hall
Cuisines: American, Gastropub
Average price: $31-$60
Area: Buckhead
Address: 3377 Peachtree Rd NE
Atlanta, GA 30326
Phone: (404) 523-3600

#433
Jamal's Buffalo Wings
Cuisines: Chicken Wings
Average price: Under $10
Address: 10 Northside Dr NW
Atlanta, GA 30314
Phone: (404) 221-0088

#434
Good Food Truck
Cuisines: Food Stands, Food Truck
Average price: Under $10
Address: Food Truck, Atlanta, GA 30312
Phone: (678) 481-8182

#435
Willy's Mexicana Grill
Cuisines: Mexican
Average price: Under $10
Address: 1100 Hammond Dr NE
Atlanta, GA 30328
Phone: (770) 512-0555

#436
Food 101
Cuisines: American
Average price: $11-$30
Address: 4969 Roswell Rd NE
Atlanta, GA 30342
Phone: (404) 497-9700

#437
SOHO Restaurant
Cuisines: American, Wine Bar
Average price: $31-$60
Area: Vinings
Address: 4300 Paces Ferry Road
Atlanta, GA 30339
Phone: (770) 801-0069

#438
Veni Vidi Vici
Cuisines: Italian
Average price: $31-$60
Area: Midtown
Address: 41 14th St NW
Atlanta, GA 30309
Phone: (404) 875-8424

#439
Hal's On Old Ivy Buckhead
Cuisines: American, Steakhouse
Average price: $31-$60
Area: Buckhead
Address: 30 Old Ivy Rd NE
Atlanta, GA 30342
Phone: (404) 261-0025

#440
Spondivits
Cuisines: Seafood
Average price: $11-$30
Address: 1219 Virginia Ave
Atlanta, GA 30344
Phone: (404) 767-1569

#441
Cuts Steakhouse
Cuisines: Steakhouse, American
Average price: $31-$60
Area: Downtown
Address: 60 Andrew Young International Blvd NE, Atlanta, GA 30349
Phone: (404) 525-3399

#442
Cameli's Pizza
Cuisines: Pizza
Average price: Under $10
Area: Old Fourth Ward, Poncey-Highland
Address: 699 Ponce De Leon Ave NE
Atlanta, GA 30308
Phone: (404) 249-9020

#443
Sushi Itto
Cuisines: Sushi Bar
Average price: $11-$30
Address: 2173 Briarcliff Rd
Atlanta, GA 30329
Phone: (404) 633-3400

#444
El Taco Veloz
Cuisines: Mexican
Average price: Under $10
Address: 5670 Roswell Rd NE
Atlanta, GA 30342
Phone: (404) 252-5100

#445
Another Broken Egg
Cuisines: Breakfast & Brunch
Average price: $11-$30
Area: Buckhead
Address: 2355 Peachtree Rd NE
Atlanta, GA 30321
Phone: (404) 254-0219

#446
Simply Thai
Cuisines: Thai
Average price: $11-$30
Address: 4639 N Shallowford Rd
Atlanta, GA 30338
Phone: (770) 458-9977

#447
Osteria Cibo Rustico
Cuisines: Italian
Average price: $11-$30
Address: 2945 N Druid Hills Rd NE
Atlanta, GA 30329
Phone: (678) 704-2700

#448
KR SteakBar
Cuisines: Steakhouse, Italian
Average price: $31-$60
Area: Buckhead
Address: 349 Peachtree Hills Ave NE
Atlanta, GA 30305
Phone: (404) 841-8820

#449
Vickery's Glenwood Park
Cuisines: American
Average price: $11-$30
Area: Ormewood Park
Address: 933 Garrett St
Atlanta, GA 30316
Phone: (404) 627-8818

#450
Portofino
Cuisines: Italian
Average price: $31-$60
Area: Buckhead
Address: 3199 Paces Ferry Pl NW
Atlanta, GA 30305
Phone: (404) 231-1136

#451
Marlow's Tavern
Cuisines: American, Gastropub
Average price: $11-$30
Address: 1627 Clifton Rd
Atlanta, GA 30329
Phone: (404) 343-3283

#452
Fred's Place
Cuisines: American
Average price: Under $10
Area: Downtown
Address: 132 Mitchell St
Atlanta, GA 30303
Phone: (404) 524-5665

#453
Rose and Crown Tavern
Cuisines: Pub, American, British
Average price: $11-$30
Address: 1931 Powers Ferry Rd SE
Atlanta, GA 30339
Phone: (770) 933-5595

#454
The Cheesecake Factory
Cuisines: Desserts, American
Average price: $11-$30
Address: 4400 Ashford-Dunwoody Road
Atlanta, GA 30346
Phone: (678) 320-0201

#455
Noodle
Cuisines: Vietnamese, Thai
Average price: $11-$30
Area: Midtown
Address: 903 Peachtree St
Atlanta, GA 30309
Phone: (404) 685-3010

#456
Pho 24
Cuisines: Vietnamese
Average price: Under $10
Address: 4646 Buford Hwy NE
Atlanta, GA 30341
Phone: (770) 710-0178

#457
Tap
Cuisines: Pub, Sandwiches, Gastropub
Average price: $11-$30
Area: Midtown
Address: 1180 Peachtree St NE
Atlanta, GA 30309
Phone: (404) 347-2220

#458
Googie Burger
Cuisines: Burgers
Average price: Under $10
Area: Downtown
Address: 190 Marietta St
Atlanta, GA 30303
Phone: (404) 223-4664

#459
Tacos & Tequilas Mexican Grill
Cuisines: Mexican
Average price: $11-$30
Area: Midtown
Address: 650 Ponce De Leon Ave NE
Atlanta, GA 30308
Phone: (678) 705-5955

#460
Donnie's Country Cookin'
Cuisines: Southern
Average price: Under $10
Address: 3300 Clairmont Rd NE
Atlanta, GA 30329
Phone: (404) 728-1188

#461
Basil's Restaurant & Bar
Cuisines: Greek, American, Mediterranean
Average price: $11-$30
Area: Buckhead
Address: 2985 Grandview Ave NE
Atlanta, GA 30305
Phone: (404) 233-9755

#462
Dave's Cosmic Subs
Cuisines: Sandwiches, Fast Food
Average price: Under $10
Area: Emory Village
Address: 1540 N Decatur Rd NE
Atlanta, GA 30307
Phone: (404) 373-6250

#463
Kiri
Cuisines: Asian Fusion,
Japanese, Korean
Average price: $11-$30
Area: Midtown
Address: 931 Monroe Dr
Atlanta, GA 30308
Phone: (404) 875-0800

#464
El Potro Mexican Restaurant
Cuisines: Mexican
Average price: Under $10
Address: 3396 Buford Hwy NE
Atlanta, GA 30329
Phone: (404) 325-9312

#465
Sea Bass Kitchen
Cuisines: Seafood, Mediterranean
Average price: $11-$30
Address: 6152 Roswell Rd
Atlanta, GA 30328
Phone: (404) 705-8880

#466
Villains
Cuisines: Sandwiches, American
Average price: $11-$30
Area: Midtown
Address: 903 Peachtree St
Atlanta, GA 30309
Phone: (404) 347-3335

#467
The Glenwood
Cuisines: Pub, American
Average price: $11-$30
Area: East Atlanta Village
Address: 1263 Glenwood Ave SE
Atlanta, GA 30316
Phone: (404) 748-1984

#468
Cafe Mezo
Cuisines: Mediterranean, Greek
Average price: $11-$30
Area: Midtown
Address: 794 Juniper St NE
Atlanta, GA 30308
Phone: (404) 343-6783

#469
Watershed on Peachtree
Cuisines: American, Cajun/Creole
Average price: $31-$60
Area: Buckhead
Address: 1820 Peachtree Rd NW
Atlanta, GA 30309
Phone: (404) 809-3561

#470
Taco Mac
Cuisines: American, Mexican
Average price: $11-$30
Area: Midtown
Address: 933 Peachtree St NE
Atlanta, GA 30309
Phone: (678) 904-7211

#471
La Fonda Latina
Cuisines: Latin American
Average price: $11-$30
Area: Buckhead
Address: 4427 Roswell Rd NE
Atlanta, GA 30342
Phone: (404) 303-8201

#472
Fresh To Order
Cuisines: Sandwiches, American, Beer
Average price: Under $10
Address: 1520 Ave Pl
Atlanta, GA 30329
Phone: (404) 844-2020

#473
Escorpi'n
Cuisines: Latin American, Bar
Average price: $11-$30
Area: Midtown
Address: 800 Peachtree St NE
Atlanta, GA 30308
Phone: (678) 666-5198

#474
The Real Chow Baby
Cuisines: Buffets, Mongolian
Average price: $11-$30
Area: Westside / Home Park
Address: 1016 Howell Mill Rd
Atlanta, GA 30318
Phone: (404) 815-4900

#475
Casa Vieja Restaurant
Cuisines: Colombian
Average price: Under $10
Address: 3652 Shallowford Rd NE
Atlanta, GA 30340
Phone: (770) 454-8557

#476
Urban Pie
Cuisines: Pizza
Average price: $11-$30
Area: Kirkwood
Address: 2012 Hosea L Williams Dr SE
Atlanta, GA 30317
Phone: (404) 373-2778

#477
El Norteno Mexican Restaurant
Cuisines: Mexican
Average price: Under $10
Address: 4929 Buford Hwy
Atlanta, GA 30341
Phone: (678) 209-4601

#478
Tex's Tacos
Cuisines: Tex-Mex, Food Truck
Average price: Under $10
Address: Food Truck, Atlanta, GA 30318
Phone: (678) 379-8397

#479
FIGO Pasta
Cuisines: Italian
Average price: $11-$30
Address: 1170 Collier Rd NW
Atlanta, GA 30318
Phone: (404) 351-9667

#480
Anna's BBQ
Cuisines: Barbeque
Average price: $11-$30
Area: Kirkwood
Address: 1976 Hosea L Williams Dr NE
Atlanta, GA 30317
Phone: (404) 963-6976

#481
Rain
Cuisines: Japanese, Thai, Sushi Bar
Average price: $11-$30
Address: 2345 Cheshire Bridge Rd NE
Atlanta, GA 30324
Phone: (404) 325-6963

#482
Pacific Grill
Cuisines: Asian Fusion
Average price: Under $10
Area: Midtown
Address: 675 W Peachtree St NW
Atlanta, GA 30308
Phone: (404) 876-1122

#483
Pour Bistro
Cuisines: Wine Bar, American
Average price: $31-$60
Area: Brookhaven
Address: 1418 Dresden Ave
Atlanta, GA 30319
Phone: (404) 254-5277

#484
Varasano's Pizzeria
Cuisines: Pizza
Average price: $11-$30
Area: Buckhead
Address: 2171 Peachtree Rd NE
Atlanta, GA 30309
Phone: (404) 352-8216

#485
Henry's Midtown Tavern
Cuisines: Burgers, American, Sandwiches
Average price: $11-$30
Area: Midtown
Address: 132 10th St
Atlanta, GA 30309
Phone: (404) 537-4477

#486
Thelma's Kitchen
Cuisines: Soul Food
Average price: Under $10
Address: 302 Auburn Ave
Atlanta, GA 30303
Phone: (404) 688-5855

#487
West Midtown Corner Tavern
Cuisines: American
Average price: $11-$30
Address: 1133 Huff Rd
Atlanta, GA 30318
Phone: (404) 228-5164

#488
ROXX Tavern
Cuisines: American, Burgers, Gastropub
Average price: $11-$30
Area: Morningside / Lenox Park
Address: 1824 Cheshire Bridge Rd NE
Atlanta, GA 30324
Phone: (404) 892-4541

#489
Wild Ginger
Cuisines: Thai, Sushi Bar
Average price: $11-$30
Address: 2201 Savoy Dr
Atlanta, GA 30341
Phone: (770) 450-9950

#490
Sage Woodfire Tavern
Cuisines: American, Bar
Average price: $11-$30
Address: 4505 Ashford Dunwoody
Atlanta, GA 30346
Phone: (770) 804-8880

#491
Newk's Eatery
Cuisines: Pizza
Average price: Under $10
Area: Midtown
Address: 933 Peachtree St
Atlanta, GA 30309
Phone: (404) 853-2555

#492
Zoes Kitchen
Cuisines: Mediterranean, Greek
Average price: Under $10
Area: Buckhead
Address: 2333 Peachtree Rd NE
Atlanta, GA 30305
Phone: (404) 233-9637

#493
Cafe At Pharr
Cuisines: Cafe
Average price: Under $10
Area: Buckhead
Address: 3145 Peachtree Rd
Atlanta, GA 30305
Phone: (404) 238-9288

#494
Goldberg's Bagel Company & Deli
Cuisines: Deli, Bagels, Sandwiches
Average price: $11-$30
Area: West Paces Ferry / Northside
Address: 1272 W Paces Ferry Rd NW
Atlanta, GA 30327
Phone: (404) 266-0123

#495
Amsterdam Cafe
Cuisines: European
Average price: $11-$30
Area: Virginia Highland
Address: 502 Amsterdam Ave NE
Atlanta, GA 30306
Phone: (404) 892-2227

#496
Lusca
Cuisines: American
Average price: $31-$60
Area: Buckhead
Address: 1829 Peachtree Rd NE
Atlanta, GA 30309
Phone: (678) 705-1486

#497
Taco Mac
Cuisines: Sports Bar, Tex-Mex, Mexican
Average price: $11-$30
Area: Virginia Highland
Address: 1006 N Highland Ave NE
Atlanta, GA 30306
Phone: (404) 873-6529

#498
The Family Dog
Cuisines: Bar, American
Average price: $11-$30
Area: Morningside / Lenox Park
Address: 1402 N Highland Ave
Atlanta, GA 30306
Phone: (404) 249-0180

#499
Corner Pizza
Cuisines: Pizza
Average price: Under $10
Address: 2163 Johnson Ferry Rd
Atlanta, GA 30319
Phone: (770) 216-8404

#500
Red Pepper Taquer'a
Cuisines: Mexican, Latin American
Average price: $11-$30
Address: 2149 Briarcliff Rd
Atlanta, GA 30329
Phone: (404) 325-8151

TOP 500
ARTS & ENTERTAINMENT

The Most Recommended by Locals & Trevelers

(From #1 to #500)

#1
Historic Oakland Cemetery
Category: Attraction
Address: 248 Oakland Ave SE
Atlanta, GA 30312
Phone: (404) 688-2107

#2
DragonCon
Category: Arts & Entertainment
Area: Downtown
Address: 265 Peachtree Center Avenue
Atlanta, GA 30321

#3
Krog Street Tunnel
Category: Attraction
Address: 1 Krog St
Atlanta, GA 30307

#4
Dad's Garage Theatre Company
Category: Performing Arts,
Comedy Club
Area: Little Five Points
Address: 1105 Euclid Ave NE
Atlanta, GA 30307

#5
Bob Callan Trail
Category: Attraction
Address: 342-398 Interstate N Pkwy SE
Atlanta, GA 30339

#6
Atlanta Botanical Garden
Category: Botanical Gardens
Address: 1345 Piedmont Ave NE
Atlanta, GA 30309

#7
Ivy Hall
Category: Education, Attraction
Address: 179 Ponce De Leon Ave
Atlanta, GA 30308
Phone: (404) 253-2332

#8
Martin Luther King Jr Center
Category: Museum
Address: 449 Auburn Ave NE
Atlanta, GA 30312

#9
CNN Center
Category: Attraction
Address: 190 Marietta St NW
Atlanta, GA 30303
Phone: (404) 827-2300

#10
TOTEM - Cirque du Soleil
Category: Performing Arts
Area: Atlantic Station
Address: 20th St N W
Atlanta, GA 30363

#11
Pemberton Place
Category: Attraction
Address: 320 Centennial Olympic Park Dr
NW, Atlanta, GA 30313

#12
Starlight Drive-In Theatre
Category: Cinema
Address: 2000 Moreland Ave SE
Atlanta, GA 30316

#13
Buford Highway
Category: Attraction
Address: Buford Hwy
Atlanta, GA 30329

#14
The Goat Farm
Category: Music Venues, Coffee, Tea
Area: Westside / Home Park
Address: 1200 Foster St
Atlanta, GA 30318

#15
Terminus
Category: Attraction
Address: 790 Windsor St SW
Atlanta, GA 30315

#16
Shakespeare Tavern
Category: Performing Arts
Area: Downtown
Address: 499 Peachtree St NE
Atlanta, GA 30308

#17
Center For Puppetry Arts
Category: Performing Arts, Museum
Area: Midtown
Address: 1404 Spring St NW
Atlanta, GA 30309

#18
Fifth Street Bridge
Category: Attraction
Address: 101 5th St NW
Atlanta, GA 30313

#19
The Atlanta History Center
Category: Museum, Venues
Area: West Paces Ferry / Northside
Address: 130 W Paces Ferry Rd NW
Atlanta, GA 30305

#20
Michael C Carlos Museum of Emory University
Category: Museum, Cultural Center
Address: 571 S Kilgo Cir NE
Atlanta, GA 30322

#21
Cirque Du Soleil - Kooza
Category: Performing Arts
Address: Under the Grand Chapiteau
Atlanta, GA 30319
Phone: (404) 523-3141

#22
Heritage Sandy Springs
Category: Attraction
Address: 6110 Blue Stone Rd NE
Atlanta, GA 30328
Phone: (404) 851-9111

#23
Kennesaw Mountain
Category: Park, Attraction, Hiking
Address: 900 Kennesaw Mountain Dr
Kennesaw, GA 30152
Phone: (770) 422-3696

#24
Whole World Improv Theatre
Category: Performing Arts
Area: Midtown
Address: 1216 Spring St NW
Atlanta, GA 30309

#25
Marietta Square
Category: Attraction
Area: Marietta, GA
Address: XOX
Phone: (800) 450-1480

#26
Fox Theatre Atlanta
Category: Performing Arts, Music Venues
Area: Midtown
Address: 660 Peachtree St Ne
Atlanta, GA 30308

#27
High Museum of Art
Category: Museum
Area: Midtown
Address: 1280 Peachtree St NE
Atlanta, GA 30309
Phone: (404) 874-5299

#28
Tech Square
Category: Attraction
Address: 79 5th St NW
Atlanta, GA 30308

#29
East Point Historical Society
Category: Attraction
Address: 1685 Norman Berry Dr
Atlanta, GA 30344
Phone: (404) 767-4656

#30
Joystick Gamebar
Category: Arcades, Cocktail Bar
Address: 427 Edgewood Ave
Atlanta, GA 30312
Phone: (404) 814-4000

#31
Tabernacle
Category: Music Venues, Venues
Area: Downtown
Address: 152 Luckie St
Atlanta, GA 30303

#33
Cin'Bistro at Town Brookhaven
Category: American, Cinema, Lounge
Address: 1004 Town Blvd NE
Atlanta, GA 30319

#32
The Drunken Unicorn
Category: Music Venues
Area: Virginia Highland, Old Fourth Ward
Address: 736 Ponce De Leon Ave
Atlanta, GA 30306
Phone: (404) 881-2100

#34
Crowley Family Mausoleum
Category: Attraction, Cemetery
Address: 3580 Memorial Dr
Decatur, GA 30032

#35
City of Chamblee
Category: Attraction
Address: 5468 Peachtree Rd
Chamblee, GA 30341
Phone: (770) 452-0902

#36
Inman Park Festival
Category: Festival
Area: Inman Park
Address: 167 Elizabeth St NE
Atlanta, GA 30307

#37
The Gilbert House
Category: Attraction
Address: 2238 Perkerson Rd SW
Atlanta, GA 30315
Phone: (404) 817-6815

#38
Variety Playhouse
Category: Music Venues
Area: Little Five Points
Address: 1099 Euclid Avenue
Atlanta, GA 30307

#39
Historic Downtown Norcross
Category: Attraction
Address: 65 Lawrenceville St
Norcross, GA 30071
Phone: (770) 448-2122

#40
Atlanta Rollergirls
Category: Professional Sport Team
Area: Midtown, Old Fourth Ward
Address: 400 Ponce De Leon Ave NE
Atlanta, GA 30308

#41
World of Coca Cola
Category: Museum
Area: Downtown
Address: 121 Baker St NW
Atlanta, GA 30313
Phone: (404) 524-7354

#42
Dekalb County Recorders Court
Category: Attraction
Address: 3630 Camp Cir
Decatur, GA 30032
Phone: (404) 371-3272

#43
The Earl
Category: Dive Bar, American, Music Venues
Area: East Atlanta Village
Address: 488 Flat Shoals Ave SE
Atlanta, GA 30316
Phone: (404) 676-5151

#44
Blind Willie's
Category: Jazz & Blues
Area: Virginia Highland
Address: 828 N Highland Ave
Atlanta, GA 30306
Phone: (404) 873-2583

#45
Marietta National Cemetary
Category: Attraction
Address: 500 Washington Ave
Marietta, GA 30060

#46
Donna Van Gogh's Artist Market
Category: Art Gallery
Area: Candler Park
Address: 1651 McLendon Ave NE
Atlanta, GA 30307
Phone: (404) 370-1003

#47
The Basement Theatre
Category: Performing Arts, Comedy Club
Address: 175 W Wieuca Rd NE
Atlanta, GA 30342

#48
Flicks on 5th
Category: Cinema
Area: Midtown
Address: Technology Square 5th St
Atlanta, GA 30308
Phone: (404) 894-2805

#49
Living Walls
Category: Art Gallery
Area: Reynoldstown
Address: 170 Chester Ave SE
Atlanta, GA 30316
Phone: (404) 000-0000

#50
Prohibition
Category: Lounge, Jazz & Blues
Area: Buckhead
Address: 56 E Andrews Dr NW
Atlanta, GA 30305
Phone: (404) 869-1132

#51
Taste of the Highlands
Category: Festival
Area: Virginia Highland
Address: John Howell Park
Atlanta, GA 30306

#52
Taste of Atlanta
Category: Festival
Area: Midtown
Address: Tech Square
Atlanta, GA 30308
Phone: (404) 875-4434

#53
Philips Arena
Category: Arena
Area: Downtown
Address: 1 Philips Dr
Atlanta, GA 30303
Phone: (404) 249-6400

#54
AMC Phipps Plaza 14
Category: Cinema
Area: Buckhead
Address: 3500 Peachtree Road NE
Atlanta, GA 30326
Phone: (404) 231-1492

#55
Atlanta Dogwood Festival
Category: Festival
Address: 400 Park Drive
Atlanta, GA 30306

#56
Horizon Theatre Company
Category: Performing Arts
Address: 1083 Austin Ave NE
Atlanta, GA 30307
Phone: (404) 584-7450

#57
Plaza Theatre
Category: Cinema
Area: Poncey-Highland
Address: 1049 Ponce De Leon Ave NE
Atlanta, GA 30306
Phone: (404) 873-1939

#58
The Jimmy Carter Library & Museum
Category: Museum, Libraries
Area: Poncey-Highland
Address: 441 Freedom Pkwy
Atlanta, GA 30307
Phone: (404) 865-7100

#59
Chomp and Stomp
Category: Festival
Area: Cabbagetown
Address: Cabbagetown Park
Atlanta, GA 30316

#60
Eyedrum
Category: Art Gallery, Music Venues, Performing Arts
Area: Downtown
Address: 115 Martin Luther King Jr Dr
Atlanta, GA 30303
Phone: (404) 522-0655

#61
Atlanta Cyclorama & Civil War Museum
Category: Museum
Area: Grant Park
Address: 800 Cherokee Ave SE
Atlanta, GA 30315
Phone: (404) 658-7625

#62
The Village Theatre
Category: Performing Arts, Comedy Club
Address: 349 Decatur St
Atlanta, GA 30312

#63
Cinefest Film Theatre
Category: Cinema
Area: Downtown
Address: 66 Courtland St SE
Atlanta, GA 30303
Phone: (404) 413-1798

#64
The Children's Museum of Atlanta
Category: Museum
Area: Downtown
Address: 275 Centennial Olympic Park Dr NW, Atlanta, GA 30313
Phone: (404) 659-5437

#65
Fernbank Museum of Natural History
Category: Museum
Address: 767 Clifton Rd NE
Atlanta, GA 30307

#66
Sips n Strokes
Category: Art Gallery, Art School
Address: 3019 N Druid Hills Rd NE
Atlanta, GA 30329

#67
East Atlanta Beer Festival
Category: Festival
Area: East Atlanta Village
Address: Brownwood Park
Atlanta, GA 30316

#68
Bodies: The Exhibition
Category: Museum
Area: Atlantic Station
Address: 265 18th St
Atlanta, GA 30363
Phone: (404) 496-4274

#69
Wren's Nest House Museum
Category: Museum
Area: West End
Address: 1050 Ralph David Abernathy Blvd
SW, Atlanta, GA 30310
Phone: (404) 753-7735

#70
Swan House
Category: Museum
Area: West Paces Ferry / Northside
Address: 130 W Paces Ferry Rd NW
Atlanta, GA 30305
Phone: (404) 814-4000

#71
Star Community Bar
Category: Music Venues, Bar
Area: Little Five Points
Address: 437 Moreland Ave NE
Atlanta, GA 30307
Phone: (404) 681-9018

#72
Buckhead Club
Category: Social Club
Area: Buckhead
Address: 3344 Peachtree Rd NE
Atlanta, GA 30326
Phone: (404) 262-2262

#73
Atlanta Jazz Festival
Category: Jazz & Blues
Address: 1071 Piedmont Ave NE
Atlanta, GA 30309

#74
14th Street Playhouse
Category: Performing Arts
Area: Midtown
Address: 173 14th St NE
Atlanta, GA 30309
Phone: (404) 733-4537

#75
Atlanta Wine School
Category: Winery, Wine Bar, Restaurant
Address: 4478 Chamblee Dunwoody Rd
Atlanta, GA 30338

#76
Masquerade
Category: Music Venues
Area: Old Fourth Ward
Address: 695 North Ave NE
Atlanta, GA 30308
Phone: (404) 577-8178

#77
Cineprov!
Category: Cinema, Performing Arts, Comedy Club
Area: Morningside / Lenox Park
Address: 1049 Ponce De Leon Ave
Atlanta, GA 30306
Phone: (678) 825-5381

#78
Beep Beep Gallery
Category: Art Gallery
Area: Midtown, Old Fourth Ward
Address: 696 Charles Allen Dr
Atlanta, GA 30308
Phone: (404) 429-3320

#79
gallery1526
Category: Art Gallery
Area: Candler Park
Address: 1526 Dekalb Ave NE
Atlanta, GA 30307
Phone: (404) 484-2871

#80
QUAD @ Spring4th Complex
Category: Music Venues, Soul Food
Area: Midtown
Address: 714 Spring St NW
Atlanta, GA 30308
Phone: (404) 870-0040

#81
David J.
Category: Museum
Address: 1600 Clifton Rd Northeast
Atlanta, GA 30329

#82
Carter Center
Category: Museum
Address: 453 Freedom Pkwy NE
Atlanta, GA 30307

#83
Regal Atlantic Station Stadium 16
Category: Cinema
Area: Atlantic Station
Address: 261 19th St NW
Atlanta, GA 30363
Phone: (404) 347-9894

#84
7 Stages
Category: Performing Arts, Cinema
Area: Little Five Points
Address: 1105 Euclid Ave NE
Atlanta, GA 30307
Phone: (404) 522-0911

#85
Sixthman
Category: Event Planning & Services
Area: Grant Park
Address: 1040 Blvd SE
Atlanta, GA 30312
Phone: (404) 525-0222

#86
AMC Fork & Screen Buckhead
Category: Cinema
Area: Buckhead
Address: 3340 Peachtree Rd. NE
Atlanta, GA 30326
Phone: (404) 467-9619

#87
D'AIR
Category: Performing Arts
Area: Grant Park
Address: 575 Blvd SE
Atlanta, GA 30312
Phone: (404) 622-3247

#88
McCamish Pavilion
Category: Pavilion
Area: Georgia Tech
Address: 965 Fowler St
Atlanta, GA 30318
Phone: (888) 832-4849

#89
Gotta Dance Atlanta
Category: Performing Arts, Dance Studio
Address: 1778 Ellsworth Industrial Dr
Atlanta, GA 30318

#90
Landmark Midtown Art Cinema
Category: Cinema
Area: Midtown
Address: 931 Monroe Dr
Atlanta, GA 30308
Phone: (404) 879-0160

#91
Spring Festival On Ponce
Category: Performing Arts, Festival
Area: Druid Hills
Address: 1451 Ponce de Leon Ave
Atlanta, GA 30306
Phone: (404) 845-0793

#92
Vanquish Lounge
Category: Dance Club, Music Venues
Area: Midtown
Address: 1029 Peachtree St NE
Atlanta, GA 30309
Phone: (404) 898-1703

#93
Buckhead Spring Arts Festival
Category: Festival, Arts, Crafts, Jewelry
Address: 4001 Powers Ferry Rd NW
Atlanta, GA 30342

#94
Center For Civil and Human Rights
Category: Cultural Center, Museum
Address: 100 Ivan Allen Jr Blvd
Atlanta, GA 30313

#95
Music Midtown
Category: Festival
Area: Old Fourth Ward
Address: 395 Piedmont Ave NE
Atlanta, GA 30308
Phone: (404) 347-9453

#96
Dark Horse Tavern
Category: Music Venues, American, Pub
Area: Virginia Highland
Address: 816 N Highland Ave
Atlanta, GA 30306
Phone: (404) 873-3607

#97
Game-X
Category: Arcades
Area: Downtown
Address: 275 Baker St
Atlanta, GA 30313
Phone: (404) 525-0728

#98
Skyview Atlanta
Category: Amusement Park, Arts & Entertainment
Area: Downtown
Address: 168 Luckie St NW
Atlanta, GA 30303
Phone: (678) 949-9023

#99
Buckhead Theatre
Category: Music Venues
Area: Buckhead
Address: 3110 Roswell Rd NE
Atlanta, GA 30305
Phone: (404) 843-2825

#100
The Basement
Category: Music Venues
Area: East Atlanta Village
Address: 1245 Glenwood Ave SE
Atlanta, GA 30316
Phone: (404) 622-8686

#101
Churchill Grounds
Category: Jazz & Blues, Lounge
Area: Midtown
Address: 660 Peachtree St NE
Atlanta, GA 30308
Phone: (404) 876-3030

#102
Academy Ballroom
Category: Performing Arts
Area: Lindbergh
Address: 800 Miami Cir NE
Atlanta, GA 30324
Phone: (404) 846-3201

#103
Anime Weekend Atlanta
Category: Festival
Address: 2450 Galleria Pkwy
Atlanta, GA 30339

#104
Regal Cinemas Hollywood 24
Category: Cinema
Address: 3265 Northeast Expy NE
Atlanta, GA 30341

#105
Phipps Plaza 14 AMC Theatres
Category: Cinema
Area: Downtown
Address: Phipps Plz
Atlanta, GA 30303
Phone: (404) 816-4262

#106
Dance 411 Studio
Category: Performing Arts, Venues, Dance Studio
Address: 475 Moreland Ave SE
Atlanta, GA 30316

#107
Turner Magic & Keynotes
Category: Party & Event Planning, Performing Arts, Magicians
Area: Buckhead
Address: 2870 Peachtree Rd NW
Atlanta, GA 30305
Phone: (404) 644-6791

#108
Belly Dance Studio at Little 5 Points
Category: Performing Arts, Dance Studio, Dance School
Area: Candler Park
Address: 1394 McLendon Ave NE
Atlanta, GA 30307
Phone: (404) 638-6530

#109
Union
Category: Music Venues, Pub
Area: East Atlanta Village
Address: 485 Flat Shoals Ave
Atlanta, GA 30316
Phone: (678) 387-8354

#110
King Tut Exhibition
Category: Museum
Area: Old Fourth Ward
Address: 395 Piedmont Ave NE
Atlanta, GA 30308
Phone: (404) 523-6275

#111
Famous Pub
Category: Sports Bar, Music Venues, American
Address: 2947 N Druid Hills Rd NE
Atlanta, GA 30329

#112
Hard Rock Caf'
Category: Burgers, American, Music Venues
Area: Downtown
Address: 215 Peachtree Street NE
Atlanta, GA 30303
Phone: (404) 688-7625

#113
Ballroom Dance Club of Atlanta
Category: Dance School, Social Club
Address: 887 W Marietta St NW
Atlanta, GA 30318

#114
Atlanta Contemporary Art Center
Category: Art Gallery
Address: 535 Means St NW
Atlanta, GA 30318

#115
Martinis and IMAX
Category: Museum
Address: 767 Clifton Rd NE
Atlanta, GA 30307

#116
Universoul Circus
Category: Performing Arts
Address: 510 Whitehall St SW
Atlanta, GA 30303

#117
Seed & Feed Marching Abominable
Category: Local Flavor, Performing Arts
Area: Inman Park
Address: 1083 Austin Ave NE
Atlanta, GA 30307
Phone: (404) 688-6688

#118
42 Degrees South
Category: Art Gallery, Accessories
Area: Little Five Points
Address: 453 Moreland Ave NE
Atlanta, GA 30307
Phone: (404) 521-3420

#119
Tunes From The Tombs
Category: Festival
Address: 248 Oakland Ave SE
Atlanta, GA 30312

#120
Winter Beer Carnival
Category: Festival
Area: Atlantic Station
Address: 2410 20th St
Atlanta, GA 30363

#121
Atlanta Silverbacks
Category: Professional Sport Team
Address: 3299 Northcrest Rd.
Atlanta, GA 30340

#122
The Family Dog
Category: Bar, Performing Arts, American
Area: Morningside / Lenox Park
Address: 1402 N Highland Ave
Atlanta, GA 30306
Phone: (404) 249-0180

#123
The Granite Room
Category: Venues, Art Gallery
Area: Castleberry Hill
Address: 211 Peters St
Atlanta, GA 30313
Phone: (404) 221-0201

#124
Atlanta Streets Alive
Category: Festival
Address: 655 Highland Ave NE
Atlanta, GA 30304

#125
Regal Perimeter Point Stadium 10
Category: Cinema
Address: 1155 Mount Vernon Hwy
Atlanta, GA 30338

#126
The Music Room
Category: Music Venues
Address: 327 Edgewood Ave
Atlanta, GA 30312

#127
Cirque du Soleil Dralion
Category: Performing Arts
Area: Downtown
Address: Philips Arena
Atlanta, GA 30303
Phone: (800) 678-5440

#128
William Breman Jewish Heritage Museum
Category: Museum, Synagogues
Area: Midtown
Address: 1440 Spring St NW
Atlanta, GA 30309
Phone: (678) 222-3700

#129
Sandy Springs Funhouse
Category: Arcades
Address: 6650B Roswell Rd NE
Atlanta, GA 30328

#130
Aaron's Amphitheatre
Category: Music Venues
Address: 2002 Lakewood Way
Atlanta, GA 30315

#131
Red Light Cafe
Category: Music Venues, American
Area: Virginia Highland
Address: 553 Amsterdam Ave NE
Atlanta, GA 30306
Phone: (404) 874-7828

#132
Automatic Improv
Category: Performing Arts, Comedy Club
Area: Westside / Home Park
Address: 999 Brady Ave
Atlanta, GA 30318
Phone: (678) 590-1386

#133
Piedmont Driving Club
Category: Venues, Social Club
Address: 1215 Piedmont Ave NE
Atlanta, GA 30309

#134
Backyard Barbecue & Brews
Category: Festival
Area: Midtown
Address: 400 Park Drive
Atlanta, GA 30306

#135
Titanic: the Aritifacts Exhibition
Category: Museum
Area: Atlantic Station
Address: 265 18th St, 2nd Fl
Atlanta, GA 30363
Phone: (404) 496-4274

#136
King of Pops Field Day
Category: Festival
Area: Old Fourth Ward
Address: 695 North Ave NE
Atlanta, GA 30308

#137
Chambers of Horror
Category: Arts & Entertainment
Address: 695 North Ave.
Atlanta, GA 30354

#138
The Loft
Category: Music Venues
Area: Midtown
Address: 1374 W Peachtree St
Atlanta, GA 30309
Phone: (404) 885-1365

#139
Atlanta Food and Wine Festival
Category: Festival, Local Flavor
Area: Midtown
Address: 1065 Peachtree St
Atlanta, GA 30307
Phone: (404) 745-5000

#140
Mardi Gras Cafe Restaurant & Lounge
Category: Lounge, Music Venues
Address: 886 Martin Luther King Jr Dr SW, Atlanta, GA 30314

#141
Professional Actor's Studio
Category: Performing Arts
Area: Buckhead
Address: 2849 Piedmont Rd
Atlanta, GA 30305
Phone: (404) 943-1873

#142
The Neal Boortz Show
Category: Performing Arts
Address: 1601 W Peachtree St
Atlanta, GA 30309

#143
Atlanta Pride Parade
Category: Festival, Local Flavor
Area: Midtown
Address: 1071 Piedmont Ave NE
Atlanta, GA 30309

#144
Georgia's Governor's Mansion
Category: Museum, Art Gallery
Address: 391 W Paces Ferry Rd NW
Atlanta, GA 30305

#145
Georgia Tech Baseball
Category: Stadium
Area: Georgia Tech
Address: 255 5th St
Atlanta, GA 30313

#146
Phoenix & Dragon Bookstore
Category: Bookstore, Jewelry, Psychics & Astrologers
Address: 5531 Roswell Rd NE
Atlanta, GA 30342

#147
Under the Couch
Category: Music Venues
Area: Centennial Place
Address: 350 Ferst Dr NW
Atlanta, GA 30332

#148
East Andrews Cafe & Bar
Category: Dance Club, Pub, Music Venues
Area: Buckhead
Address: 56 E Andrews Dr NW
Atlanta, GA 30305
Phone: (404) 869-1132

#149
Martin Luther King Jr Center
Category: Museum
Address: 449 Auburn Ave NE
Atlanta, GA 30312

#150
Cabbagetown Clay & Glass Works
Category: Art Gallery
Area: Grant Park
Address: 588 Woodward Avenue
Atlanta, GA 30312
Phone: (678) 778-7082

#151
Circus Arts Institute
Category: Performing Arts, Art School
Area: Edgewood
Address: 206 Rogers St NE
Atlanta, GA 30317
Phone: (404) 549-3000

#152
Hillside Pumpkin Patch
Category: Arts, Crafts, Arts & Entertainment
Area: Morningside / Lenox Park
Address: 1301 Monroe Dr
Atlanta, GA 30306

#153
The Northside Tavern
Category: Jazz & Blues, Dive Bar
Area: Westside / Home Park
Address: 1058 Howell Mill Rd NW
Atlanta, GA 30318
Phone: (404) 874-8745

#154
PushPush Theater
Category: Performing Arts
Area: Decatur
Address: 121 New St
Atlanta, GA 30030
Phone: (404) 377-6332

#155
Candler Park Fall Fest
Category: Festival
Area: Candler Park
Address: 599 Candler Park Dr
Atlanta, GA 30307

#156
The Walking Dead Escape
Category: Arts & Entertainment
Area: Downtown
Address: 1 Philips Dr
Atlanta, GA 30303

#157
Atlanta Falcons
Category: Professional Sport Team
Area: Downtown
Address: One Georgia Dome Drive Nw
Atlanta, GA 30313
Phone: (404) 223-8444

#158
Global Winter Wonderland
Category: Festival, Amusement Park
Address: 755 Hank Aaron Dr
Atlanta, GA 30315

#159
Family Feud Taping
Category: Performing Arts
Area: Old Fourth Ward
Address: 395 Piedmont Ave NE
Atlanta, GA 30308
Phone: (818) 880-8200

#160
Great Gatsby's
Category: Art Gallery, Interior Design
Address: 5180 Peachtree Industrial Blvd
Atlanta, GA 30341

#161
Distant Worlds: Music From Final Fantasy
Category: Performing Arts
Area: Downtown
Address: 1280 Peachtree St NE
Atlanta, GA 30308
Phone: (404) 733-4900

#162
Dr. Conundrum's Cabaret of Miracles
Category: Performing Arts, Magicians
Area: Midtown
Address: 1140 Crescent Ave
Atlanta, GA 30309
Phone: (404) 604-0034

#163
Shaky Knees Music Festival
Category: Festival
Area: Atlantic Station
Address: 1380 Atlantic Dr NW
Atlanta, GA 30363
Phone: (404) 600-6428

#164
The Dinner Detective
Category: Performing Arts
Area: Midtown
Address: 35 14th St NE
Atlanta, GA 30309
Phone: (888) 959-6590

#165
ABV Creative Agency and Gallery
Category: Art Gallery
Area: Old Fourth Ward
Address: 659 Auburn Ave
Atlanta, GA 30312
Phone: (213) 915-6448

#166
Baconfest
Category: Festival, Cinema
Area: Inman Park
Address: 280 Elizabeth St C 101
Atlanta, GA 30307
Phone: (404) 523-3141

#167
Midsummer Music and Food Fest
Category: Festival
Area: Lake Claire
Address: Candler Park
Atlanta, GA 30307

#168
SweetWater 420 Fest
Category: Festival
Area: Candler Park
Address: Candler Park
Atlanta, GA

#169
Herndon Home
Category: Museum
Address: 587 University Pl NW
Atlanta, GA 30314

#170
Kiang Projects
Category: Art Gallery
Address: 1011A Marietta St
Atlanta, GA 30318

#171
Millennium Gate Museum
Category: Museum
Area: Atlantic Station
Address: 395 17th St NW
Atlanta, GA 30363
Phone: (404) 881-0900

#172
Starlight Six Drive-in Theatre Flea Market
Category: Cinema
Address: 2000 Moreland Ave SE
Atlanta, GA 30316

#173
Speakeasy Cocktail Festival
Category: Festival
Area: Downtown
Address: 285 Andrew Young International Blvd NW
Atlanta, GA 30313

#174
Atlanta Ballet Centre for Dance Education - Buckhead Centre
Category: Dance Studio, Opera & Ballet
Area: Buckhead
Address: 4279 Roswell Rd
Atlanta, GA 30342
Phone: (404) 303-1501

#175
Terminal West
Category: Music Venues
Address: 887 W Marietta St NW, Studio C,
Atlanta, GA 30318

#176
SAS Atlanta Sky Lounge
Category: Venues, Music Venues,
Recording & Rehearsal Studio
Address: 1676 Defoor Cir NW
Atlanta, GA 30318

#177
Emerging Art Scene
Category: Art Gallery, Venues
Area: Castleberry Hill
Address: 321 Nelson St SW
Atlanta, GA 30313
Phone: (404) 890-0532

#178
Nelson Street Gallery
Category: Art Gallery
Area: Castleberry Hill
Address: 364 Nelson St SW
Atlanta, GA 30313

#179
A Handy Little Company
Category: Party & Event Planning,
Performing Arts, Psychics & Astrologers
Address: 3545 Broad St
Atlanta, GA 30366

#180
Atlanta BBQ Festival
Category: Festival, Barbeque,
Street Vendor
Area: Atlantic Station
Address: 20th St
Atlanta, GA 30363

#181
Synchronicity Performance Group
Category: Performing Arts
Address: 1105 Euclid Ave
Atlanta, GA 30307

#182
Marcia Wood Gallery
Category: Art Gallery
Area: Castleberry Hill
Address: 263 Walker St SW
Atlanta, GA 30313
Phone: (404) 827-0030

#183
MomoCon
Category: Arts & Entertainment
Area: Downtown
Address: 265 Peachtree Center Ave
Atlanta, GA 30303

#184
Out of Hand Theater
Category: Performing Arts
Area: Grant Park
Address: 880 Glenwood Ave
Atlanta, GA 30316
Phone: (404) 462-8836

#185
Woodruff Arts Center
Category: Performing Arts, Art Gallery
Area: Midtown
Address: 1280 Peachtree St NE
Atlanta, GA 30309
Phone: (404) 733-4200

#186
Sweet Auburn Festival
Category: Festival
Address: 301 Auburn Ave NE
Atlanta, GA 30312

#187
The Defoor Centre
Category: Venues, Art Gallery
Address: 1710 Defoor Ave NW
Atlanta, GA 30318

#188
Apex Museum
Category: Museum
Area: Downtown
Address: 135 Auburn Ave NE
Atlanta, GA 30303
Phone: (404) 523-2739

#189
Sugar Hill
Category: Music Venues
Area: Downtown
Address: 50 Upper Alabama St SW
Atlanta, GA 30303
Phone: (404) 658-0068

#190
Primal
Category: Dance Club,
Jazz & Blues, Bar
Area: Midtown
Address: 960 Spring St
Atlanta, GA 30309
Phone: (404) 745-9494

#191
3 Hill Productions
Category: Performing Arts
Address: 1984 Howell Mill Rd
Atlanta, GA 30318

#192
Chastain Park Arts Festival
Category: Arts & Entertainment
Address: Director, Patrick Dennis
Atlanta, GA 30342

#193
MINT Gallery
Category: Art Gallery
Area: Old Fourth Ward
Address: 684B John Wesley Dobbs Ave
Atlanta, GA 30312

#194
Oglethorpe University Museum of Art
Category: Museum
Address: 4484 Peachtree Rd NE
Atlanta, GA 30319

#195
Ticket Alternative
Category: Ticket Sales
Area: Midtown
Address: 1369 Spring St NW
Atlanta, GA 30309
Phone: (877) 725-8849

#196
Atlanta Civic Center
Category: Performing Arts, Music Venues
Area: Old Fourth Ward
Address: 395 Piedmont Ave
Atlanta, GA 30308
Phone: (404) 523-6275

#197
Lips Down On Dixie
Category: Performing Arts, Cinema
Area: Poncey-Highland
Address: 1049 Ponce De Leon Ave NE
Atlanta, GA 30306

#198
Atlantic Station Open Air Market
Category: Arts & Entertainment
Area: Atlantic Station
Address: 171 17th St NW
Atlanta, GA 30363

#199
Andrews Upstairs
Category: Music Venues, Lounge
Area: Buckhead
Address: 56 E Andrews Dr NW
Atlanta, GA 30305
Phone: (404) 869-1132

#200
Trois Gallery
Category: Art Gallery
Area: Midtown
Address: 1600 Peachtree St NW
Atlanta, GA 30309
Phone: (404) 253-3100

#201
Studio Dionne School of Dance & Music
Category: Performing Arts, Dance Studio
Area: Buckhead
Address: 524 Plasters Ave NE
Atlanta, GA 30324
Phone: (404) 877-0005

#202
Hagedorn Foundation Gallery
Category: Art Gallery
Area: Lindbergh
Address: 425 Peachtree Hills Ave NE
Atlanta, GA 30305
Phone: (404) 492-7718

#203
Gems of Africa Gallery
Category: Art Gallery, Home Decor
Area: Poncey-Highland
Address: 630 N Highland Ave NE
Atlanta, GA 30306
Phone: (404) 876-8200

#204
Atlanta Music Guide
Category: Music Venues
Area: Midtown
Address: 1369 Spring St NW
Atlanta, GA 30309
Phone: (877) 725-8849

#205
Avatar Events Group
Category: Music Venues, Video/Film Production
Area: Virginia Highland
Address: 503 Amsterdam Ave
Atlanta, GA 30306
Phone: (404) 589-9450

#206
Frabel Glass Art Studio
Category: Art Gallery
Area: Buckhead
Address: 309 E Paces Ferry Road NE
Atlanta, GA 30305
Phone: (404) 467-9464

#207
Powercore
Category: Social Club
Area: Buckhead
Address: 3060 Pharr Ct NW
Atlanta, GA 30305
Phone: (404) 816-3377

#208
United Artists Midtown Cinema
Category: Cinema
Area: Midtown
Address: 931 Monroe Dr NE
Atlanta, GA 30308
Phone: (404) 872-6100

#209
The Great Frame Up
Category: Art Gallery
Address: 2810 Paces Ferry Rd SE
Atlanta, GA 30339

#210
Atlanta Diamond Buyer & Jewelry Buyer
Category: Art Gallery, Jewelry, Pawn Shop
Area: Buckhead
Address: 3455 Peachtree Rd NE
Atlanta, GA 30326
Phone: (404) 995-6782

#211
Ponce de Leon Beer Festival
Category: Festival
Area: Midtown, Old Fourth Ward
Address: 400 Ponce De Leon Ave NE
Atlanta, GA 30308

#212
Freeze Dried Monkey
Category: Performing Arts
Area: Virginia Highland
Address: 816 N Highland Ave NE
Atlanta, GA 30306
Phone: (404) 606-2040

#213
The Atlanta School of Burlesque
Category: Dance Studio, Performing Arts, Dance School
Address: 1745 Defoor Pl
Atlanta, GA 30318

#214
Modern Now
Category: Bookstore, Art Gallery
Area: Old Fourth Ward
Address: 659 Auburn Ave NE
Atlanta, GA 30312
Phone: (855) 278-2665

#215
Walk Now For Autism Speaks
Category: Festival
Area: Georgia Tech
Address: 240 20th St
Atlanta, GA 30363
Phone: (770) 451-0570

#216
Atlanta Streets Alive
Category: Festival
Area: Old Fourth Ward
Address: 660 Peachtree St
Atlanta, GA 30308

#217
Myott Studio
Category: Art Gallery
Address: 1360 Boyd Ave NW
Atlanta, GA 30318

#218
Pinch n' Ouch Theatre
Category: Performing Arts
Area: Poncey-Highland
Address: 1085 Ponce De Leon Ave NE
Atlanta, GA 30306
Phone: (800) 838-3006

#219
IMAGE Film and Video Center
Category: Performing Arts
Address: 535 Means Street
Atlanta, GA 30318

#220
The Barbara Archer Gallery
Category: Art Gallery
Area: Inman Park
Address: 280 Elizabeth St NE
Atlanta, GA 30307
Phone: (404) 523-1845

#221
Atlanta Greek Festival
Category: Festival, Local Flavor
Address: 2500 Clairmont Rd NE
Atlanta, GA 30329

#222
Metro Gallery and Framing
Category: Art Gallery, Framing
Area: Old Fourth Ward
Address: 659 Auburn Ave
Atlanta, GA 30312
Phone: (404) 433-3262

#223
True Colors Theatre Company
Category: Performing Arts, Cinema
Area: Old Fourth Ward
Address: 659 Auburn Ave NE Apt 257
Atlanta, GA 30312
Phone: (404) 588-0308

#224
The Soul Food Museum
Category: Museum
Address: 372 Auburn Ave NE
Atlanta, GA 30312

#225
The Little House of Art
Category: Art Gallery,
Child Care & Day Care
Area: Brookhaven
Address: 1418 Dresden Dr NE
Atlanta, GA 30319
Phone: (404) 814-1910

#226
Tim Barrett Designs
Category: Art Gallery
Area: Inman Park
Address: 10 Krog Street NE Apt F
Atlanta, GA 30307
Phone: (404) 522-5308

#227
Krog Street Tunnel in Atlanta
Category: Art Gallery
Area: Inman Park
Address: Krog Street NE
Atlanta, GA 30316
Phone: (678) 534-7363

#228
Atlantix Ticket Services
Category: Ticket Sales
Area: Downtown
Address: 65 Upper Alabama St
Atlanta, GA 30303
Phone: (404) 588-9890

#229
Flux Night
Category: Nightlife, Local Flavor,
Arts & Entertainment
Area: Castleberry Hill
Address: 345-381 Markham St Sw
Atlanta, GA 30313

#230
Hushpuppy Gallery
Category: Art Gallery
Area: Grant Park
Address: 379 Woodward Ave SE
Atlanta, GA 30312
Phone: (404) 468-0769

#231
Ivan Allen Jr Braves Museum & Hall of Fame @ Turner Field
Category: Amusement Park,
Museum, Tours
Address: 755 Hank Aaron Dr SW
Atlanta, GA 30315

#232
Mayercraft Carrier
Category: Music Venues
Area: Grant Park
Address: 1040 Boulevard, Suite J
Atlanta, GA 30312
Phone: (877) 749-8462

#233
Summerfest
Category: Festival
Area: Virginia Highland
Address: Virginia-Highland
Atlanta, GA 30306

#234
Sabra Gallery East Atlanta
Category: Art Gallery
Area: East Atlanta Village
Address: 465 Flat Shoals Ave
Atlanta, GA 30316
Phone: (404) 588-9222

#235
Siyeh Glass
Category: Art Gallery
Area: East Lake
Address: 2480 Memorial Dr
Atlanta, GA 30317
Phone: (404) 373-4729

#236
Atlanta Strings Conservatory
Category: Performing Arts, Musicians, Musical Instruments & Teachers
Address: 70 Little St SE
Atlanta, GA 30315

#237
Inspire Aerial Arts: Aerial Silks Classes In Atlanta
Category: Dance Studio, Performing Arts
Address: 675 Metropolitan Pkwy
Atlanta, GA 30310

#238
Kadts Ballroom Dancesport Studio
Category: Performing Arts
Address: 680 Murphy Ave SW
Atlanta, GA 30310

#239
Shrine of the Black Madonna Culture Center
Category: Museum
Area: West End
Address: 946 Ralph David Abernath
Atlanta, GA 30310
Phone: (404) 752-6125

#240
Georgia Shakespeare
Category: Performing Arts
Address: 4484 Peachtree Rd NE
Atlanta, GA 30319

#241
Containment
Category: Arts & Entertainment
Area: Atlantic Station
Address: 1380 Atlantic Dr NW
Atlanta, GA 30363
Phone: (404) 549-5953

#242
Summer Shade Festival
Category: Festival
Area: Grant Park
Address: 401 Memorial Dr
Atlanta, GA 30312
Phone: (404) 521-0938

#243
Caf' Circa
Category: Lounge, Caribbean, Jazz & Blues
Address: 464 Edgewood Ave
Atlanta, GA 30312

#244
Khicks Ballroom Contemporary Style
Category: Social Club, Dance Club
Address: 3335 Martin Luther King Jr Blvd, Atlanta, GA 30331

#245
An Evening With Yanni
Category: Performing Arts
Address: 2800 Cobb Galleria Pkwy
Atlanta, GA 30339

#246
Sopranos 2 by 2
Category: Performing Arts
Address: PO Box 42253
Atlanta, GA 30311

#247
Flux Night
Category: Arts & Entertainment
Area: Castleberry Hill
Address: Castleberry Hill
Atlanta, GA

#248
Movies ATL
Category: Cinema
Address: 3760 Princeton Lakes Pkwy
Atlanta, GA 30331

#249
Context
Category: Home Decor, Art Gallery
Area: Downtown
Address: 75 John Wesley Dobbs Ave
Atlanta, GA 30303
Phone: (404) 477-3301

#250
Brina Beads
Category: Arts & Entertainment, Jewelry
Area: Buckhead
Address: 3231 Cains Hill Place
Atlanta, GA 30305
Phone: (404) 816-8230

#251
Vinyl
Category: Music Venues
Area: Midtown
Address: 1374 W Peachtree St
Atlanta, GA 30309
Phone: (404) 885-1365

#252
Brookhaven Chili Cookoff
Category: Street Vendor, Festival
Address: 2740 Apple Valley Rd Ne
Atlanta, GA 30319

#253
The Wizard of Oz
Category: Performing Arts
Address: 2800 Cobb Galleria Pkwy
Atlanta, GA 30339

#254
Freedom Park Ladder Sculpture
Category: Art Gallery
Address: Moreland Ave & Freedom Pkwy,
Atlanta, GA 30307

#255
Laughing Matters
Category: Performing Arts,
Comedy Club
Address: 173 Cleveland Ave SE
Atlanta, GA 30354

#256
Tech Town @ Atlantic Station
Category: Festival
Area: Atlantic Station
Address: 1380 Atlantic Dr
Atlanta, GA 30363
Phone: (404) 733-1221

#257
Get This! Gallery
Category: Art Gallery
Area: Virginia Highland
Address: 1037 Monroe Dr NE
Atlanta, GA 30306
Phone: (678) 596-4451

#258
The Studio-Atlanta Dance
Category: Performing Arts
Area: Buckhead
Address: 3229 Cains Hill Pl NW
Atlanta, GA 30305
Phone: (404) 233-8686

#259
Sous Whisky Marin
Category: Event Planning & Services, Arts & Entertainment
Area: Castleberry Hill
Address: 263 Peters St SW
Atlanta, GA 30313
Phone: (404) 590-5975

#260
Atlanta Street Food Festival
Category: Festival
Address: Piedmont Park
Atlanta, GA 30309

#261
Kibbee Gallery
Category: Art Gallery
Area: Poncey-Highland
Address: 688 Linwood Ave NE
Atlanta, GA 30306
Phone: (404) 839-0331

#262
The B-Complex
Category: Art Gallery
Address: 1272 Murphy Ave
Atlanta, GA 31136

#263
Sunday Cinema Club
Category: Cinema
Area: Midtown
Address: 931 Monroe Drive
Atlanta, GA 30308

#264
Atlanta BAR-B-Q Festival
Category: Festival
Address: 755 Hank Aaron Dr SE
Atlanta, GA 30315

#265
TNT
Category: Television Stations,
Arts & Entertainment
Area: Westside / Home Park
Address: 1010 Techwood Dr NW
Atlanta, GA 31136

#266
So and So and His Imaginary Friends
Category: Performing Arts
Area: Westside / Home Park
Address: 380 14th St NW
Atlanta, GA 30318
Phone: (404) 343-0347

#267
Monte Carlo Productions
Category: Casino,
Party & Event Planning
Area: Westside / Home Park
Address: 767 Trabert Ave NW
Atlanta, GA 30318
Phone: (404) 351-9012

#268
Empire Tickets
Category: Arts & Entertainment, Shopping
Area: Buckhead
Address: 3 W Paces Ferry Rd
Atlanta, GA 30305
Phone: (404) 467-0227

#269
Kat's Cafe
Category: American, Music Venues
Area: Midtown
Address: 970 Piedmont Ave
Atlanta, GA 30306
Phone: (404) 347-2263

#270
Atlanta Pride Parade
Category: Festival
Area: Midtown
Address: 951-999 Peachtree St NE
Atlanta, GA 30309

#271
East West Jewelers
Category: Watches, Art Gallery, Jewelry
Area: Buckhead
Address: 3005 Peachtree Rd Ne
Atlanta, GA 30305
Phone: (404) 869-9935

#272
STUDIO PHILISA
Category: Hair Salon, Art Gallery
Area: Old Fourth Ward
Address: 659 Auburn Ave
Atlanta, GA 30312
Phone: (678) 234-3016

#273
Smoove Salsero
Category: Performing Arts
Address: 800 Miami Cir
Atlanta, GA 30324

#274
Fay Gold Gallery
Category: Art Gallery
Area: Lindbergh
Address: 764 Miami Cir NE
Atlanta, GA 30324
Phone: (404) 233-3843

#275
Verizon Wireless Amphitheatre
Category: Cinema
Area: Midtown
Address: 1280 Peachtree St NE
Atlanta, GA 30309
Phone: (404) 733-5929

#276
OutsiderInsideArt
Category: Art Gallery
Area: Morningside / Lenox Park
Address: 1393 N Highland Ave
Atlanta, GA 30306
Phone: (404) 876-1393

#277
Dewberry Gallery
Category: Art Gallery
Area: Midtown
Address: 1545 Peachtree St
Atlanta, GA 30309

#278
Draft on Taft
Category: Festival
Area: Midtown
Address: Charles Allen Dr
Atlanta, GA 30309

#279
Margaret Mitchell House & Movie Museum
Category: Museum
Area: Midtown
Address: 990 Peachtree St NE
Atlanta, GA 30309
Phone: (404) 249-7015

#280
Festival On Ponce
Category: Festival
Area: Virginia Highland
Address: Atlanta, GA 30306
Phone: (404) 845-0793

#281
Razor Gator
Category: Ticket Sales
Area: Buckhead
Address: 1745 Peachtree Rd
Atlanta, GA 30309
Phone: (800) 542-4466

#282
Atlanta Winter Beer Festival
Category: Festival
Area: Old Fourth Ward
Address: 695 North Ave NE
Atlanta, GA 30308

#283
Artlantis Arts and Music Festival
Category: Festival
Area: Poncey-Highland
Address: 1085 Ponce de Leon Ave
Atlanta, GA 30306

#284
Sky View Atlanta
Category: Arts & Entertainment
Area: Downtown
Address: 168 Luckie St NW
Atlanta, GA 30303

#285
Healium Center
Category: Art Gallery
Area: Candler Park
Address: 344 Candler Park Dr
Atlanta, GA 30307
Phone: (404) 216-8877

#286
The Atlanta Film Festival
Category: Cinema
Area: Downtown
Address: 25 Park Pl NE
Atlanta, GA 30303
Phone: (678) 929-8103

#287
Chastain Arts Center
Category: Cultural Center
Area: Downtown
Address: 135 W Wieuca Rd
Atlanta, GA 30303
Phone: (404) 252-2927

#288
ZogSports
Category: Amateur Sports Team, Sports Club, Social Club
Area: Downtown
Address: 2875 Northside Dr NW
Atlanta, GA 30305
Phone: (678) 974-1772

#289
NAIO Gallery
Category: Art Gallery
Area: East Atlanta Village
Address: 477 Flat Shoals Ave SE
Atlanta, GA 30316
Phone: (404) 521-2283

#290
Hammonds House Museum
Category: Museum
Area: West End
Address: 503 Peeples Street, SW
Atlanta, GA 30310
Phone: (404) 612-0481

#291
The Legend Of Zelda Symphony Of The Goddesses
Category: Performing Arts
Address: 2800 Cobb Galleria Pkwy
Atlanta, GA 30339

#292
Georgia Dome
Category: Stadium
Area: Downtown
Address: One Georgia Dome Drive Nw
Atlanta, GA 30313
Phone: (404) 223-4636

#293
Cinevision Corporation
Category: Cinema
Address: 3300 Northeast Expy NE
Atlanta, GA 30341

#294
Starlite Drive-in Theater
Category: Cinema
Address: Moreland Ave
Atlanta, GA 30315

#295
Heritage Green
Category: Arts & Entertainment
Address: 6110 Bluestone Road
Atlanta, GA 30328

#296
pb&j gallery
Category: Art Gallery
Area: Kirkwood
Address: 35 Howard St SE
Atlanta, GA 30317
Phone: (404) 606-1856

#297
Young Blood Boutique
Category: Art Gallery, Jewelry, Gift Shop
Area: Poncey-Highland
Address: 632 N Highland Ave NE
Atlanta, GA 30306
Phone: (404) 254-4127

#298
United Artists Tara Cinema
Category: Cinema
Address: 2345 Cheshire Bridge Rd NE
Atlanta, GA 30324

#299
Lagerquist Gallery
Category: Art Gallery
Area: Buckhead
Address: 3235 Paces Ferry Pl NW
Atlanta, GA 30305
Phone: (404) 261-8273

#300
Hapeville Depot Museum
Category: Museum
Address: 620 S Central Ave
Atlanta, GA 30354

#301
Atlanta Camping & RV Show
Atlanta Expo Center South
Category: Festival
Address: 3850 Jonesboro Rd SE
Atlanta, GA 30354

#302
UA Tara Cinemas
Category: Cinema
Address: 2345 Cheshire Bridge Rd Ne
Atlanta, GA 30324

#303
American Top Teams Atlanta
Category: Professional Sport Team
Address: 2110 Faulkner Rd NE
Atlanta, GA 30324

#304
Museum of Design Atlanta
Category: Museum
Area: Midtown
Address: 1315 Peachtree St
Atlanta, GA 30309
Phone: (404) 979-6455

#305
Piedmont Park Green Concert
Category: Festival
Area: Midtown
Address: 1071 Piedmont A
Atlanta, GA 30309

#306
MidSummer Music Festival
Category: Festival
Area: Candler Park
Address: 1400 McLendon Ave NE
Atlanta, GA 30307

#307
Dance Stop Studio
Category: Performing Arts
Address: 1299 Johnson Ferry Rd
Atlanta, GA 30303

#308
Atlanta Civic Center
The Boisfauillet Jones
Category: Performing Arts
Area: Old Fourth Ward
Address: 395 Piedmont Ave NE
Atlanta, GA 30308
Phone: (404) 523-6275

#309
Atlanta Spirit
Category: Stadium
Area: Downtown
Address: 101 Marietta St NW
Atlanta, GA 30303
Phone: (404) 878-3000

#310
Amnesia Club & Lounge
Category: Bar, Social Club
Address: 3220 Butner Rd
Atlanta, GA 30331

#311
Southwest Arts Center
Category: Performing Arts
Address: 915 New Hope Road
Atlanta, GA 30331

#312
Venue Gallery
Category: Art Gallery
Address: 1254 Murphy Ave
Atlanta, GA 30310

#313
Hottie Hawg's Smokin BBQ
Category: Barbeque, Music Venues
Address: 2061 Main St NW
Atlanta, GA 30318

#314
Emory, Arts at
Category: Music Venues, Performing Arts
Address: 1700 N Decatur Rd
Atlanta, GA 30322

#315
Acoustix Jazz Restaurant and Lounge
Category: Jazz & Blues
Address: 840 Marietta St
Atlanta, GA 30318

#316
Amanda's Psychic Readings & Love Spells
Category: Psychics & Astrologers
Area: Little Five Points
Address: 1118 Euclid Ave
Atlanta, GA 30307
Phone: (404) 863-4129

#317
LivingSocial's Craft Beerfest
Category: Festival
Area: Atlantic Station
Address: 241 20th St
Atlanta, GA 30363
Phone: (877) 521-4191

#318
Vaknin Gallery
Category: Art Gallery
Area: Midtown
Address: 905 Juniper St NE
Atlanta, GA 30309
Phone: (404) 513-0169

#319
The Mission Motif
Category: Furniture Store, Art Gallery
Area: Lindbergh
Address: 747-A Miami Circle NE
Atlanta, GA 30324
Phone: (404) 370-1505

#320
First Thursday Art Walk
Category: Art Gallery
Area: Downtown
Address: 50 Hurt Plz
Atlanta, GA 30303
Phone: (404) 658-1877

#321
Unique Events Atlanta
Category: Performing Arts, Party & Event Planning
Address: 2622 Paces View
Atlanta, GA 30339

#322
Janke Studio
Category: Art Gallery, Arts, Crafts
Area: Old Fourth Ward
Address: 659 Auburn Ave NE
Atlanta, GA 30312
Phone: (404) 584-0305

#323
Fastframe
Category: Framing, Interior Design, Art Gallery
Area: Lindbergh
Address: 2625 Piedmont Rd NE
Atlanta, GA 30324
Phone: (404) 261-1213

#324
Kai Lin Art
Category: Art Gallery, Arts, Crafts, Jewelry
Area: Buckhead
Address: 999 Brady Ave
Atlanta, GA 30318
Phone: (404) 408-4248

#325
Picaflor Studio
Category: Arts & Entertainment
Area: Edgewood
Address: 195 Arizona Ave
Atlanta, GA 30307
Phone: (404) 247-6432

#326
AMC Parkway Pointe 15
Category: Cinema
Address: 3101 Cobb Pkwy.
Atlanta, GA 30339

#327
PeraDance Studio
Category: Venues, Performing Arts, Dance Studio
Address: 1015-B Collier Rd
Atlanta, GA 30318

#328
Wonderroot
Category: Music Venues, Art Gallery, Cultural Center
Area: Reynoldstown
Address: 982 Memorial Dr
Atlanta, GA 30316
Phone: (404) 254-5955

#329
Theatrical Outfit
Category: Performing Arts
Area: Downtown
Address: 84 Luckie St NW
Atlanta, GA 30303
Phone: (404) 577-5257

#330
Art By The Glazz
Category: Arts & Entertainment
Address: 3652 Roswell Rd NW
Atlanta, GA 30305

#331
Center Stage Theatre
Category: Performing Arts, Music Venues
Area: Midtown
Address: 1374 W Peachtree St. Nw
Atlanta, GA 30309
Phone: (404) 885-1365

#332
Netherworld Haunted House
Category: Arts & Entertainment
Address: 6624 Dawson Blvd Norcross, GA 30093

#333
Studio 281
Category: Jazz & Blues, Lounge
Area: Castleberry Hill
Address: 281 Peters St SW
Atlanta, GA 30313
Phone: (404) 524-7247

#334
Vita Hill Social Club
Category: Social Club, Videos, Video Game Rental
Area: Old Fourth Ward
Address: 800 Peachtree St
Atlanta, GA 30308

#335
Food Truck Nation
Category: Festival
Area: Old Fourth Ward
Address: 930 Spring St
Atlanta, GA 30308

#336
Thomas Deans Fine Art
Category: Art Gallery
Area: Lindbergh
Address: 690 Miami Cir NE
Atlanta, GA 30324
Phone: (404) 814-1811

#337
Gallery 515
Category: Art Gallery
Area: Buckhead
Address: 515 E Paces Ferry Rd
Atlanta, GA 30305
Phone: (404) 233-2911

#338
Studio No.7
Category: Lounge, Tapas, Art Gallery
Address: 393 Marietta St NW
Atlanta, GA 30313

#339
Atlanta Rockstar Rehearsals
Category: Music Venues, Recording & Rehearsal Studio
Area: Buckhead
Address: 255 B Ottley Dr
Atlanta, GA 30324
Phone: (770) 296-5530

#340
Sweet Auburn Music Fest
Category: Festival
Address: 312 Auburn Ave
Atlanta, GA 30312

#341
Tees & Quotes
Category: Screen Printing, T-Shirt Printing, Art Gallery
Area: Castleberry Hill
Address: 244 Peters St
Atlanta, GA 30313
Phone: (404) 963-1553

#342
Michael C Carlos Museum At Emory University
Category: Museum
Area: Midtown
Address: 1447 Peachtree St NE
Atlanta, GA 30309
Phone: (404) 881-1109

#343
The Museum of Contemporary Art of Georgia
Category: Museum, Art Gallery
Address: 75 Bennett St NW
Atlanta, GA 30309

#344
Matter Boutique
Category: Antiques, Furniture Store, Art Gallery
Address: 1082 Huff Rd
Atlanta, GA 30318

#345
The Music Class
Category: Performing Arts, Musical Instruments & Teachers
Address: 2991A N Druid Hills Rd
Atlanta, GA 30329

#346
Healium Center
Category: Art Gallery
Area: Candler Park
Address: 344 Candler Park Dr
Atlanta, GA 30307
Phone: (404) 216-8877

#347
Club Solstice
Category: Dance Club, Music Venues
Area: Buckhead
Address: 4279 Roswell Rd
Atlanta, GA 30342
Phone: (404) 202-6000

#348
Margaret Mitchell House
Category: Museum
Area: Midtown
Address: 990 Peachtree St NE
Atlanta, GA 30309
Phone: (404) 249-7015

#349
Actor's Express
Category: Performing Arts
Address: 887 W Marietta St,Ste J-107
Atlanta, GA 30318

#350
Eddie's Attic
Category: Music Venues, American
Area: Decatur
Address: 515-B N McDonough St Decatur, GA 30030
Phone: (404) 377-4976

#351
David Gallery
Category: Art Gallery
Area: Buckhead
Address: 365 Peachtree Hills Ave NE Ste 103, Atlanta, GA 30305
Phone: (404) 841-5500

#352
Drama Inc
Category: Performing Arts
Address: 650 Hamilton Ave SE
Atlanta, GA 30312

#353
ASCAP
Category: Professional Services, Arts & Entertainment
Address: 950 Joseph E. Lowery Blvd. NW, Atlanta, GA 30318

#354
Little Five Points Halloween Parade and Festival
Category: Festival
Area: Lake Claire
Address: Euclid/Moreland
Atlanta, GA 30307

#355
Screen on the Green
Category: Cinema
Area: Downtown
Address: 1071 Piedmont Ave NE
Atlanta, GA 31136
Phone: (404) 875-7275

#356
Calo Gitano Flamenco Dance Company
Category: Performing Arts
Area: Kirkwood
Address: 1963 Hosea L Williams R
Atlanta, GA 30317
Phone: (404) 966-1347

#357
Atlanta Symphony Orchestra
Category: Performing Arts
Area: Midtown
Address: 1280 Peachtree St NE
Atlanta, GA 30309
Phone: (404) 733-4900

#358
VoiceoverCity
Category: Performing Arts, Educational Services, Adult Education
Address: 1810 Water Pl
Atlanta, GA 30339

#359
BYBOW - Adult Big Wheel Race - Summerhill Fall Festival
Category: Festival
Address: 161 Little St
Atlanta, GA 30315

#360
Atlanta Aliens
Category: Professional Sport Team
Area: Buckhead
Address: 2911 Piedmont Rd
Atlanta, GA 30305
Phone: (888) 901-8421

#361
Modern Models Inc
Category: Employment Agency, Performing Arts
Area: Buckhead
Address: 347 E Paces Ferry Rd Ne
Atlanta, GA 30305
Phone: (404) 783-3464

#362
Match in Six
Category: Social Club
Area: Buckhead
Address: 596 E Paces Ferry Rd
Atlanta, GA 30324
Phone: (404) 507-6338

#363
Lips
Category: Nightlife, Performing Arts
Address: 3011 Buford Highway
Atlanta, GA 30329

#364
Jai Shanti Yoga
Category: Yoga, Performing Arts
Area: Candler Park
Address: 1630-D Dekalb Ave NE
Atlanta, GA 30307
Phone: (404) 370-0579

#365
PJ's Coffee
Category: Coffee, Tea, Winery, Bakery
Area: Downtown
Address: 232 19th St
Atlanta, GA 31132
Phone: (404) 745-4215

#366
Perimeter Pointe 10 Theater
Category: Cinema
Address: 1155 Mt. Vernon Hwy
Atlanta, GA 30338

#367
Sips n Strokes
Category: Art School, Art Gallery
Address: 230 Hammond Dr Sandy Springs, GA 30328

#368
BigHouse Gallery
Category: Art Gallery, Venues
Area: Castleberry Hill
Address: 211 Peters St
Atlanta, GA 30313
Phone: (404) 221-0201

#369
Sky Gym
Category: Dance Studio, Performing Arts
Address: 6780 Roswell Rd NE
Sandy Springs, GA 30328

#370
Atlanta Braves
Category: Professional Sport Team, Amusement Park, Museum, Tours
Address: 755 Hank Aaron Drive
Atlanta, GA 30315

#371
Tribal Bellydance Center of Atlanta
Category: Venues, Performing Arts, Dance School
Address: 2861 Henderson Mill Rd
Atlanta, GA 30341

#372
Atlanta Ballroom Dance Centre
Category: Dance Studio, Performing Arts
Address: 6125 Roswell Rd Ne
Atlanta, GA 30328

#373
Jerry Farber's Side Door
Category: Music Venues, Comedy Club
Address: 3652 Roswell Rd NW
Atlanta, GA 30305

#374
Park Bench
Category: American, Music Venues, Pub
Area: Buckhead
Address: 34 Irby Ave NW
Atlanta, GA 30305
Phone: (404) 262-3624

#375
Blue Mark Studio
Category: Venues, Art Gallery
Address: 892 Jefferson St
Atlanta, GA 30318

#376
Turner Field
Category: Stadiums & Arenas
Address: 755 Hank Aaron Drive
Atlanta, GA 30315

#377
Spruill Center Gallery
Category: Museum, Art Gallery
Address: 4681 Ashford Dunwoody Road
Atlanta, GA 30338

#378
NCG Marietta Cinemas
Category: Cinema
Address: 1050 Powder Springs St Marietta, GA 30064

#379
Movie Tavern at Northlake Festival
Category: Cinema, American
Address: 4043 LaVista Rd
Tucker, GA 30084

#380
Alan Avery Art Company
Category: Art Gallery, Venues
Area: Buckhead
Address: 315 E Paces Ferry Rd
Atlanta, GA 30305
Phone: (404) 237-0370

#381
Pal's Lounge & Restaurant
Category: Dive Bar, Music Venues
Area: Downtown
Address: 254 Auburn Ave NE
Atlanta, GA 30303
Phone: (404) 748-1004

#382
Tula Richard Showrooms & Studio
Category: Art Gallery
Address: 75 Bennett St NW
Atlanta, GA 30309

#383
Respect
Category: Performing Arts
Address: 173 14th St
Atlanta, GA 30309

#384
Stuart McClean Gallery
Category: Art Gallery
Area: Old Fourth Ward
Address: 684 John Wesley Dobbs Ave NE, Atlanta, GA 30312
Phone: (404) 420-1312

#385
20-21 Collections
Category: Art Gallery
Area: Buckhead
Address: 309 E Paces Ferry Rd NE
Atlanta, GA 30305
Phone: (404) 816-9977

#386
Opera Nightclub
Category: Bar, Dance Club, Music Venues
Area: Midtown
Address: 1150 B Peachtree St NE
Atlanta, GA 30309
Phone: (404) 874-3006

#387
Cobb Energy Performing Arts Centre
Category: Performing Arts, Music Venues
Address: 2800 Cobb Galleria Parkway
Atlanta, GA 30339

#388
Atlanta Arts Festival
Category: Festival
Area: Midtown
Address: 1071 Piedmont Ave NE
Atlanta, GA 30309
Phone: (770) 941-9660

#389
MudFire
Category: Arts & Entertainment
Address: 175 Laredo Dr
Decatur, GA 30030

#390
Dave & Buster's
Category: American, Arcades
Address: 2215 D&B Dr
Marietta, GA 30067

#391
Friday Jazz
Category: Jazz & Blues
Area: Midtown
Address: 1280 Peachtree St NE
Atlanta, GA 30309
Phone: (404) 733-4444

#392
East Point Possums
Category: Performing Arts
Address: 2727 E Point St
East Point, GA 30344

#393
Oklahoma!
Category: Performing Arts
Address: 2800 Cobb Galleria Parkway
Atlanta, GA 30339

#394
Vinings Gallery
Category: Art Gallery
Address: 4686 S Atlanta Rd SE
Smyrna, GA 30080

#395
Screenworks 12
Category: Cinema
Area: Decatur
Address: 2801 Candler Rd
Decatur, GA 30036
Phone: (404) 241-3131

#396
Young Audiences, Woodruff Arts Center
Category: Local Services, Performing Arts, Elementary School
Area: Midtown
Address: 1280 Peachtree Street NE
Atlanta, GA 30309
Phone: (404) 733-5293

#397
Darwin's Burgers and Blues
Category: Bar, Music Venues, Burgers
Address: 1598 Roswell Rd
Marietta, GA 30062

#398
Chastain Park Amphitheatre
Category: Park, Music Venues
Address: 4469 Stella Drive
Atlanta, GA 30342

#399
Atlanta Zombie Apocalypse
Category: Arts & Entertainment
Address: 4215 Thurman Rd
Conley, GA 30288

#400
Anne Frank Exhibit & Museum
Category: Museum
Address: 5920 Roswell Rd, Ste 209 Sandy Springs, GA 303328

#401
MoonShadow Tavern
Category: Pub, Music Venues
Address: 3976 Lawrenceville Hwy Tucker, GA 30084

#402
1/2 Street Market
Category: Arts & Entertainment
Area: Atlantic Station
Address: 1380 Atlantic Dr
Atlanta, GA 30318
Phone: (404) 733-1221

#403
DeKalb History Center: Old Courthouse on the Square
Category: Museum, Venues
Area: Decatur
Address: 101 E Court Sq
Decatur, GA 30030
Phone: (404) 373-1088

#404
Infinite Arts
Category: Performing Arts
Address: 1040 Fisher Rd
Atlanta, GA 30316

#405
AMC North DeKalb Mall 16
Category: Cinema
Address: 2050 Lawrenceville Hwy. Decatur, GA 30033

#406
Wild Oats & Billy Goats
Category: Art Gallery, Jewelry, Gift Shop
Area: Decatur
Address: 112 E Ponce de Leon
Decatur, GA 30030
Phone: (404) 378-4088

#407
Fabrefaction Theatre Company
Category: Performing Arts, Venues
Area: Westside / Home Park
Address: 999 Brady Avenue
Atlanta, GA 30318
Phone: (404) 876-9468

#408
Mad Mad Whirled
Category: Arcades
Address: 2854 Delk Rd
Marietta, GA 30067

#409
Taste of Marietta
Category: Festival
Address: 4 Depot St NE
Marietta, GA 30060

#410
Dance 101
Category: Dance Studio, Performing Arts
Address: 2480 Briarcliff Rd Atlanta, GA 30329

#411
Just Kiln' Time
Category: Art Gallery
Address: 27 Atlanta St SE Marietta, GA 30060

#412
120 Tavern & Music Hall
Category: Sports Bar, Music Venues
Address: 1440 Roswell Rd Marietta, GA 30062

#413
Rialto Center for the Arts
Category: Performing Arts, Music Venues, Art Gallery
Area: Downtown
Address: 80 Forsyth St Atlanta, GA 30303
Phone: (404) 413-9849

#414
Cafe 290
Category: Jazz & Blues, American
Address: 290 Hilderbrand Dr NE Atlanta, GA 30328

#415
The Waffle House Museum
Category: Museum
Address: 2719 E College Ave Decatur, GA 30030

#416
Spruill Center For the Arts
Category: Art School, Art Gallery
Address: 5339 Chamblee Dunwoody Rd Atlanta, GA 30338

#417
Sandler Hudson Gallery
Category: Art Gallery
Address: 1009 Marietta St NW Atlanta, GA 30318

#418
Onstage Atlanta
Category: Performing Arts
Address: 2969 E Ponce de Leon Ave Decatur, GA 30030

#419
Delta Flight Museum
Category: Museum
Address: 1060 Delta Blvd Hapeville, GA 30354

#420
Red Sky Tapas
Category: Tapas Bar, Music Venues, Bar
Address: 1255 Johnson Ferry Rd Marietta, GA 30068

#421
The Moog Gallery & Custom Framing
Category: Art Gallery, Framing
Area: Candler Park
Address: 1653 McClendon Ave Atlanta, GA 30307
Phone: (404) 668-9678

#422
Marietta Museum of History
Category: Museum
Address: 1 Depot St Marietta, GA 30060

#423
Decatur Craft Beer Festival
Category: Festival, Local Flavor
Area: Decatur
Address: Decatur Square Decatur, GA 30030

#424
Eggtoberfest
Category: Arts & Entertainment
Address: 3417 Lawrenceville Hwy Tucker, GA 30084

#425
ATL Music Room
Category: Social Club, Music Venues
Address: 4300 Chamblee Tucker Rd Tucker, GA 30340

#426
A R T Station
Category: Art Supplies, Art Gallery
Address: 5384 Manor Dr Stone Mountain, GA 30083

#427
Syrens of the South Productions
Category: Performing Arts, Venues
Address: 2842 Franklin St Avondale Estates, GA 30002

#428
Beyond Toys
Category: Toy Store, Flowers, Gifts, Art Gallery
Address: 2841 Greenbriar Pkwy SW
Atlanta, GA 30331

#429
Decatur Wine Festival
Category: Festival
Area: Decatur
Address: PO Box 401
Decatur, GA 30031
Phone: (404) 371-9583

#430
Oakhurst Community Garden
Category: Botanical Gardens
Area: Decatur
Address: 435 Oakview Rd
Decatur, GA 30030
Phone: (404) 371-1920

#431
Decatur Glassblowing
Category: Art Classes, Art Gallery
Area: Decatur
Address: 250 Freeman St
Decatur, GA 30030
Phone: (404) 849-0301

#432
Lefont Theatres
Category: Cinema
Address: 5920 Roswell Rd NE
Atlanta, GA 30328

#433
Circus Camp
Category: Performing Arts
Address: 862 Columbia Dr
Decatur, GA 30030

#434
GTC Merchants Walk Cinema
Category: Cinema
Address: 1301 Johnson Ferry Rd Marietta, GA 30068

#435
GAS-ART GIFTS
Category: Bookstore, Art Gallery
Address: 2050 Lawrenceville Hwy Decatur, GA 30033

#436
Atlanta Lyric Theatre
Category: Performing Arts
Address: 548 S Marietta Pkwy
Marietta, GA 30060

#437
Smyrna Frame & Art Gallery
Category: Art Gallery, Framing
Address: 1154 Concord Rd SE
Smyrna, GA 30080

#438
HotShotRC Raceway and Hobbystore
Category: Arts & Entertainment
Address: 1050-C Industrial Park Dr
Marietta, GA 30062

#439
HalfBakedArt
Category: Art Gallery
Address: 1843 Village Mill Rd Dunwoody, GA 30338

#440
Earl Smith Strand Theatre
Category: Performing Arts
Address: 117 N Park Sq
Marietta, GA 30060

#441
The Atlanta Opera
Category: Performing Arts
Address: 1575 Northside Dr, N.W.
Atlanta, GA 30318

#442
MaSani Gourmet Southern Cuisine
Category: Jazz & Blues, Southern, Soul Food
Address: 915 Cobb Pkwy N
Marietta, GA 30060

#443
Good Acting Studio
Category: Performing Arts, Art School
Address: 507 Roswell St
Marietta, GA 30060

#444
Vibes
Category: Lounge, Music Venues
Address: 4469 Glenwood Rd
Decatur, GA 30032

#445
Corkscrews and Canvas
Category: Art Gallery, Art Classes
Address: 800 Whitlock Ave NW
Marietta, GA 30064

#446
Bella's Pizzeria
Category: Pizza, Music Venues
Address: 3599 Atlanta Rd SE
Smyrna, GA 30080

#447
Gone With the Wind Museum
Category: Museum
Address: 18 Whitlock Ave
Marietta, GA 30060

#448
Act3 Productions
Category: Performing Arts
Address: 6285 Roswell Rd
Sandy Springs, GA 30328

#449
Origin Nile Studio
Category: Arts & Entertainment
Address: 3026 miller rd
Lithonia, GA 30038

#450
Atlanta Duplicate Bridge Club
Category: Social Club
Address: 6761 Peachtree Industrial Blvd
Norcross, GA 30360

#451
Fright Club Haunted House
Category: Arts & Entertainment
Address: 142 S Park Square
Marietta, GA 30060

#452
Smith's Olde Bar
Category: Music Venues,
Pool Hall, Burgers
Area: Morningside / Lenox Park
Address: 1578 Piedmont Ave NE
Atlanta, GA 30324
Phone: (404) 875-1522

#453
Jazz Bar
Category: Jazz & Blues
Address: 2801 Candler Rd
Decatur, GA 30034

#454
dk Gallery
Category: Art Gallery, Venues
Address: 25 W Park Sq NE
Marietta, GA 30060

#455
Georgia Metropolitan Dance Theatre
Category: Performing Arts
Address: 49 W Park Sq
Marietta, GA 30060

#456
Root House the
Category: Museum
Address: 145 Denmead St NE
Marietta, GA 30060

#457
Legend Cafe
Category: Cafe, Music Venues
Address: 6259 Peachtree Industrial Blvd
Doraville, GA 30360

#458
The Big Dance Concert Series
Category: Performing Arts
Area: Downtown
Address: 265 Park Ave W
Northwest Atlanta, GA 30313

#459
Seven Arts Center
Category: Art Gallery
Address: 2879 E Point St
East Point, GA 30344

#460
CORE
Category: Performing Arts,
Dance Studio, Venues
Area: Decatur
Address: 133 Sycamore St
Decatur, GA 30030
Phone: (404) 373-4154

#461
Pryor Fine Art
Category: Art Gallery
Area: Lindbergh
Address: 764 Miami Cir
Atlanta, GA 30324
Phone: (404) 352-8775

#462
Atlanta Ballet
Category: Opera & Ballet
Address: 1695 Marietta Blvd NW
Atlanta, GA 30318

#463
Ichiyo Art
Category: Art School, Arts & Entertainment, Florist
Address: 1224 Converse Dr NE
Atlanta, GA 30324

#464
Sandy Springs Artsapalooza
Category: Festival
Address: 174 Johnson Ferry Rd
Sandy Springs, GA 30328

#465
South Dekalb Stadium 12 & Jazz Bar
Category: Cinema
Address: 2801 Candler Rd
Decatur, GA 30034

#466
Plaster Zone
Category: Arts & Entertainment, Tutoring Center, Active Life
Address: 5675 Jimmy Carter Blvd Norcross, GA 30071

#467
Whitespace Gallery
Category: Art Gallery
Area: Inman Park
Address: 814 Edgewood Ave
Atlanta, GA 30307
Phone: (404) 688-1892

#468
Out of Box Theatre
Category: Performing Arts
Address: 585 Cobb Pkwy S Marietta, GA 30060

#469
Apache Caf'
Category: Art Gallery, Music Venues
Area: Midtown
Address: 64 3rd St NW
Atlanta, GA 30308
Phone: (404) 876-5436

#470
1763
Category: Social Club
Address: 1763 Montreal Cir
Tucker, GA 30084

#471
Smyrna Wine Stroll
Category: Festival, Local Flavor
Address: 2840 Atlanta Rd
Smyrna, GA 30080

#472
Muse For Life
Category: Performing Arts, Specialty School, Tea Rooms
Address: 205 Hilderbrand Dr NE
Sandy Springs, GA 30328

#473
Zuffy's Place
Category: Bar, Music Venues
Address: 1860 Corporate Blvd NE
Atlanta, GA 30329

#474
Lefont Theatre Sandy Springs
Category: Cinema
Address: Sandy Springs Cir NE
Sandy Springs, GA 30358

#475
Twin Cinemas at Buford Hwy
Category: Adult Entertainment, Cinema
Address: 5805 Buford Hwy
Doraville, GA 30340

#476
Maylia Art Gallery
Category: Art Gallery
Area: Brookhaven
Address: 1442 Dresden Dr NE
Atlanta, GA 30319
Phone: (678) 995-3899

#477
Guitar Decatur
Category: Arts & Entertainment
Area: Decatur
Address: 117 N McDonough St
Decatur, GA 30030
Phone: (404) 915-4599

#478
Art on 5
Category: Art Gallery
Area: Downtown
Address: 2001 Martin Luther King Jr. Drive, Atlanta, GA 31132
Phone: (404) 564-4799

#479
Alley Stage
Category: Performing Arts
Address: 11 Anderson St
Marietta, GA 30060

#480
The Atlanta Indie Market
Category: Festival
Address: 134 Maple St
Decatur, GA 30030

#481
Alliance Theatre
Category: Performing Arts, Art School
Area: Midtown
Address: 1280 Peachtree St NE
Atlanta, GA 30309
Phone: (404) 733-4650

#482
East Marietta National Little League
Category: Professional Sport Team
Address: 2085 Lower Roswell Rd
Marietta, GA 30068

#483
Dance Tonight Atlanta
Category: Dance Studio, Performing Arts
Address: 2000 Powers Ferry Rd SE
Marietta, GA 30067

#484
StubHub
Category: Ticket Sales
Area: Downtown
Address: 101 Marietta St NW
Atlanta, GA 30303
Phone: (866) 788-2482

#485
Objet d'Art Gallery & Studio
Category: Art School, Art Gallery
Address: 5270 Peachtree Pkwy
Peachtree Corners, GA 30092

#486
Marietta/Cobb Museum Of Art
Category: Museum
Address: 30 Atlanta St SE
Marietta, GA 30060

#487
Emily Amy Gallery
Category: Art Gallery
Address: 1000 Marietta St
Atlanta, GA 30318

#488
Avisca Fine Art
Category: Art Gallery
Address: 507 Roswell St
Marietta, GA 30060

#489
Bellydance By Samora
Category: Performing Arts
Area: Decatur
Address: 519 N McDonough St
Decatur, GA 30030

#490
Marietta Indoor Sports
Category: Street Soccer Indoor
Address: 316-B Cobb Pkwy S
Marietta, GA 30060

#491
Taylor Academy of Fine Arts
Category: Performing Arts
Address: 4898 LaVista Rd
Tucker, GA 30084

#492
Enomatic
Category: Winery
Address: 5555 Oakbrook Pkwy
Norcross, GA 30093

#493
Bobby Dodd Stadium at Grant Field
Category: Stadium
Area: Georgia Tech
Address: 155 N Ave NW
Atlanta, GA 30313

#494
Lisa's Dance Spot
Category: Performing Arts
Address: 6205 Veterans Memorial Hwy
Austell, GA 30168

#495
Avery Gallery
Category: Art Gallery
Address: 390 Roswell St SE
Marietta, GA 30060

#496
Mason Murer Fine Art
Category: Art Gallery, Venues
Area: Buckhead
Address: 199 Armour Dr NE
Atlanta, GA 30324
Phone: (404) 879-1500

#497
Jackson Fine Art Gallery
Category: Art Gallery
Area: Buckhead
Address: 3115 E Shadowlawn Ave NE
Atlanta, GA 30305
Phone: (404) 233-3739

#498
Cobb Landmarks & Historical Society
Category: Museum
Address: 145 Denmead St NE
Marietta, GA 30060

#499
Catacombs Coffee House
Category: Music Venues, Churches
Address: 5100 South Old Peachtree Road
Berkeley Lake, GA 30092

#500
Quilts and Sheets
Category: Local Flavor, Art Gallery
Address: 395 Mt Vernon Hwy NE
Atlanta, GA 30328

TOP 500 NIGHTLIFE

The Most Recommended by Locals & Trevelers
(From #1 to #500)

#1
Clermont Lounge
Category: Adult Entertainment, Dive Bar
Average price: Inexpensive
Area: Virginia Highland, Old Fourth Ward, Poncey-Highland
Address: 789 Ponce De Leon Ave NE
Atlanta, GA 30306
Phone: (404) 874-4783

#2
Blind Willie's
Category: Jazz & Blues
Average price: Modest
Area: Virginia Highland
Address: 828 N Highland Ave
Atlanta, GA 30306
Phone: (404) 873-2583

#3
Dad's Garage Theatre Company
Category: Performing Arts, Comedy Club
Average price: Modest
Area: Little Five Points
Address: 1105 Euclid Ave NE
Atlanta, GA 30307
Phone: (404) 523-3141

#4
The Northside Tavern
Category: Jazz & Blues, Dive Bar
Average price: Inexpensive
Area: Westside / Home Park
Address: 1058 Howell Mill Rd NW
Atlanta, GA 30318
Phone: (404) 874-8745

#5
Tabernacle
Category: Music Venues
Average price: Modest
Area: Downtown
Address: 152 Luckie St
Atlanta, GA 30303
Phone: (404) 659-9022

#6
Joystick Gamebar
Category: Arcades, Cocktail Bar
Average price: Inexpensive
Address: 427 Edgewood Ave
Atlanta, GA 30312
Phone: (404) 525-3002

#7
MJQ Concourse
Category: Dance Club, Lounge
Average price: Inexpensive
Area: Virginia Highland, Old Fourth Ward
Address: 736 Ponce De Leon Ave NE
Atlanta, GA 30307
Phone: (404) 870-0575

#8
The Porter Beer Bar
Category: American, Pub
Average price: Modest
Area: Little Five Points
Address: 1156 Euclid Ave NE
Atlanta, GA 30307
Phone: (404) 223-0393

#9
Halo
Category: Lounge, Dance Club, Venues
Average price: Modest
Area: Midtown
Address: 817 W Peachtree St
Atlanta, GA 30308
Phone: (404) 962-7333

#10
The Earl
Category: Dive Bar, American, Music Venues
Average price: Inexpensive
Area: East Atlanta Village
Address: 488 Flat Shoals Ave SE
Atlanta, GA 30316
Phone: (404) 522-3950

#11
Variety Playhouse
Category: Music Venues
Average price: Modest
Area: Little Five Points
Address: 1099 Euclid Avenue
Atlanta, GA 30307
Phone: (404) 524-7354

#12
Two Urban Licks
Category: Bar, American
Average price: Expensive
Area: Old Fourth Ward, Poncey-Highland
Address: 820 Ralph McGill Blvd NE
Atlanta, GA 30306
Phone: (404) 522-4622

#13
Wrecking Bar Brewpub
Category: Gastropub, Pub, Brewery
Average price: Modest
Area: Little Five Points
Address: 292 Moreland Ave NE
Atlanta, GA 30307
Phone: (404) 221-2600

#14
Terminal West
Category: Music Venues
Average price: Modest
Address: 887 W Marietta St NW,
Studio C, Atlanta, GA 30318
Phone: (404) 876-5566

#15
The Bookhouse Pub
Category: Pub
Average price: Modest
Area: Virginia Highland, Old Fourth Ward
Address: 736 Ponce de Leon Ave NE
Atlanta, GA 30306
Phone: (404) 254-1176

#16
Ormsby's
Category: Pub
Average price: Modest
Area: Westside / Home Park
Address: 1170 Howell Mill Rd NW
Atlanta, GA 30318
Phone: (404) 968-2033

#17
Fado Irish Pub & Restaurant
Category: Pub, Irish
Average price: Modest
Area: Buckhead
Address: 273 Buckhead Ave
Atlanta, GA 30305
Phone: (404) 841-0066

#18
Prohibition
Category: Lounge, Jazz & Blues
Average price: Expensive
Area: Buckhead
Address: 56 E Andrews Dr NW
Atlanta, GA 30305
Phone: (404) 869-1132

#19
The Local
Category: Bar
Average price: Inexpensive
Area: Virginia Highland, Old Fourth Ward
Address: 758 Ponce De Leon Ave NE
Atlanta, GA 30306
Phone: (404) 873-5002

#20
Star Community Bar
Category: Music Venues, Bar
Average price: Inexpensive
Area: Little Five Points
Address: 437 Moreland Ave NE
Atlanta, GA 30307
Phone: (404) 681-9018

#21
El Bar
Category: Lounge
Average price: Inexpensive
Area: Virginia Highland
Address: 939 Ponce de Leon Ave NE
Atlanta, GA 30306
Phone: (208) 545-1176

#22
Krog Bar
Category: Tapas Bar, Wine Bar
Average price: Modest
Area: Old Fourth Ward, Inman Park
Address: 112 Krog St
Atlanta, GA 30307
Phone: (404) 524-1618

#23
The Basement Theatre
Category: Performing Arts,
Comedy Club
Average price: Inexpensive
Address: 175 W Wieuca Rd NE
Atlanta, GA 30342
Phone: (404) 277-3071

#24
Onyx
Category: Adult Entertainment,
Dance Club
Average price: Expensive
Area: Morningside / Lenox Park
Address: 1888 Cheshire Bridge Rd
Atlanta, GA 30324
Phone: (404) 876-9992

#25
Cheetah Lounge
Category: Adult Entertainment
Average price: Expensive
Area: Midtown
Address: 887 Spring St NW
Atlanta, GA 30308
Phone: (404) 892-3037

#26
Center Stage Theatre
Category: Performing Arts
Average price: Modest
Area: Midtown
Address: 1374 W Peachtree St.
NW Atlanta, GA 30309
Phone: (404) 885-1365

#27
Cosmo Lava Lounge
Category: Dance Club, Lounge, Venues
Average price: Modest
Area: Midtown
Address: 45 13th St NE
Atlanta, GA 30309
Phone: (404) 873-6189

#28
Righteous Room
Category: American, Bar
Average price: Modest
Area: Virginia Highland
Address: 1051 Ponce De Leon Ave NE
Atlanta, GA 30306
Phone: (404) 874-0939

#29
Anatolia Cafe & Hookah Lounge
Category: Turkish, Hookah Bar
Average price: Modest
Area: Downtown
Address: 52 Peachtree St NW
Atlanta, GA 30303
Phone: (404) 589-8008

#30
SkyLounge
Category: Lounge
Average price: Modest
Address: 110 Marietta St
Atlanta, GA 30303
Phone: (404) 521-2250

#31
Divan Restaurant & Hookah Lounge
Category: Hookah Bar, Persian/Iranian
Average price: Modest
Address: 3125 Piedmont Rd NE
Atlanta, GA 30305
Phone: (404) 467-4297

#33
Graveyard Tavern
Category: Bar, American
Average price: Modest
Area: East Atlanta Village
Address: 1245 Glenwood Ave SE
Atlanta, GA 30316
Phone: (404) 622-8686

#32
Sister Louisa's Church of the Living Room & Ping Pong Emporium
Category: Bar
Average price: Inexpensive
Address: 466 Edgewood Ave
Atlanta, GA 30312
Phone: (404) 522-8275

#34
Laughing Skull Lounge
Category: Comedy Club
Average price: Modest
Area: Midtown
Address: 878 Peachtree St
Atlanta, GA 30309
Phone: (877) 523-3288

#35
Cin'Bistro at Town Brookhaven
Category: American, Cinema, Lounge
Average price: Modest
Address: 1004 Town Blvd NE
Atlanta, GA 30319
Phone: (404) 333-0740

#36
Magic City
Category: Adult Entertainment
Average price: Expensive
Area: Downtown
Address: 241 Forsyth St SW
Atlanta, GA 30303
Phone: (404) 584-5847

#37
The Euclid Avenue Yacht Club
Category: Restaurant, Dive Bar
Average price: Inexpensive
Area: Little Five Points
Address: 1136 Euclid Ave NE
Atlanta, GA 30307
Phone: (404) 688-2582

#38
Marlow's Tavern
Category: Pub, American
Average price: Modest
Address: 2355 Cumberland Pkwy
Atlanta, GA 30339
Phone: (770) 432-2526

#39
The Shed at Glenwood
Category: American, Bar
Average price: Modest
Address: 475 Bill Kennedy Way
Atlanta, GA 30316
Phone: (404) 835-4363

#40
Oasis Goodtime Emporium
Category: Adult Entertainment, Dance Club, Bar
Average price: Modest
Address: 6363 Peachtree Industrial Blvd
Atlanta, GA 31132
Phone: (770) 454-8065

#41
Bantam Pub
Category: American, Pub
Average price: Modest
Area: Old Fourth Ward
Address: 737 Ralph McGill Blvd NE
Atlanta, GA 30312
Phone: (404) 223-1500

#42
Meehan's Public House
Category: Pub, Irish
Average price: Modest
Address: 2810 Paces Ferry Rd SE
Atlanta, GA 30339
Phone: (770) 433-1920

#43
Three Sheets
Category: Lounge
Average price: Modest
Address: 6017 Sandy Springs Cir
Atlanta, GA 30328
Phone: (404) 303-8423

#44
Highland Tap
Category: Steakhouse, Bar
Average price: Modest
Area: Virginia Highland
Address: 1026 N Highland Ave NE
Atlanta, GA 30306
Phone: (404) 875-3673

#45
Ink & Elm
Category: American, Lounge, Gastropub
Average price: Expensive
Area: Emory Village
Address: 1577 N Decatur Rd NE
Atlanta, GA 30307
Phone: (678) 244-7050

#46
Limerick Junction
Category: Pub
Average price: Modest
Area: Virginia Highland
Address: 822 N Highland Ave NE
Atlanta, GA 30306
Phone: (404) 874-7147

#47
Whiskey Blue
Category: Lounge, Wine Bar, Cocktail Bar
Average price: Expensive
Address: 3377 Peachtree Rd NE
Atlanta, GA 30326
Phone: (678) 500-3190

#48
The Basement
Category: Music Venues
Average price: Modest
Area: East Atlanta Village
Address: 1245 Glenwood Ave SE
Atlanta, GA 30316
Phone: (404) 622-8686

#49
East Side Lounge
Category: Lounge
Average price: Inexpensive
Area: East Atlanta Village
Address: 485A Flat Shoals Ave
Atlanta, GA 30316
Phone: (404) 521-9666

#50
Compound
Category: Dance Club
Average price: Modest
Area: Westside / Home Park
Address: 1008 Brady Ave
Atlanta, GA 30318
Phone: (404) 898-1702

#51
Little 5 Corner Tavern
Category: Bar, American
Average price: Modest
Area: Little Five Points
Address: 1174 Euclid Ave NE
Atlanta, GA 30307
Phone: (404) 521-0667

#52
Vine & Tap
Category: Wine Bar, Tapas
Average price: Modest
Address: 2770 Lenox Rd NE
Atlanta, GA 30324
Phone: (404) 600-5820

#53
Sanctuary
Category: Dance Club
Average price: Modest
Area: Buckhead
Address: 3209 Paces Ferry Pl NW
Atlanta, GA 30305
Phone: (404) 262-1377

#54
Apache Cafe
Category: Art Gallery, Music Venues
Average price: Modest
Area: Midtown
Address: 64 3rd St NW
Atlanta, GA 30308
Phone: (404) 876-5436

#55
MOTHER
Category: Bar, American, Dance Club
Average price: Modest
Address: 447 Edgewood Ave SE
Atlanta, GA 30312
Phone: (404) 524-4605

#56
Masquerade
Category: Music Venues
Average price: Modest
Area: Old Fourth Ward
Address: 695 North Ave NE
Atlanta, GA 30308
Phone: (404) 577-8178

#57
Johnny's Hideaway
Category: Dance Club, Lounge
Average price: Modest
Area: Buckhead
Address: 3771 Roswell Rd NE
Atlanta, GA 30342
Phone: (404) 233-8026

#58
Vanquish Lounge
Category: Dance Club, Venues, Music Venues
Average price: Expensive
Area: Midtown
Address: 1029 Peachtree St NE
Atlanta, GA 30309
Phone: (404) 898-1703

#59
Park 75 Lounge and Terrace
Category: Lounge, Tapas Bar
Average price: Exclusive
Area: Midtown
Address: 75 14th St NE
Atlanta, GA 30309
Phone: (404) 253-3840

#60
Establishment
Category: Cocktail Bar
Average price: Expensive
Address: 3167 Peachtree Rd NE
Atlanta, GA 30305
Phone: (404) 816-9897

#61
Taproom Coffee
Category: Coffee, Tea, Bar
Average price: Inexpensive
Area: Kirkwood
Address: 1963 Hosea L Williams Dr
Atlanta, GA 30317
Phone: (404) 464-5435

#62
The Punchline
Category: Comedy Club
Average price: Modest
Address: 280 Hilderbrand Dr
Atlanta, GA 30328
Phone: (404) 252-5233

#63
The Sound Table
Category: Dance Club, Tapas, Diner
Average price: Modest
Area: Old Fourth Ward
Address: 483 Edgewood Ave
Atlanta, GA 30312
Phone: (404) 835-2534

#64
529
Category: Bar, Dance Club
Average price: Inexpensive
Area: East Atlanta Village
Address: 529 Flat Shoals Ave
Atlanta, GA 30316
Phone: (404) 228-6769

#65
George's Restaurant & Bar
Category: Bar
Average price: Inexpensive
Area: Virginia Highland
Address: 1041 N Highland Ave NE
Atlanta, GA 30306
Phone: (404) 892-3648

#66
The Independent
Category: Bar, Pool Hall
Average price: Inexpensive
Area: Midtown
Address: 931 Monroe Dr NE
Atlanta, GA 30308
Phone: (404) 249-9869

#67
Pink Pony
Category: Adult Entertainment
Average price: Modest
Address: 1837 Corporate Blvd NE
Atlanta, GA 30329
Phone: (404) 634-6396

#68
The Albert
Category: Bar, American
Average price: Modest
Area: Inman Park
Address: 918 Austin Ave
Atlanta, GA 30307
Phone: (404) 872-4990

#69
Bourbon Bar
Category: Lounge
Average price: Modest
Area: Buckhead
Address: 3315 Peachtree Rd NE
Atlanta, GA 30326
Phone: (404) 946-9060

#70
Union
Category: Music Venues, Pub
Average price: Modest
Area: East Atlanta Village
Address: 485 Flat Shoals Ave
Atlanta, GA 30316
Phone: (678) 387-8354

#71
Park Bench
Category: American, Music Venues, Pub
Average price: Inexpensive
Area: Buckhead
Address: 34 Irby Ave NW
Atlanta, GA 30305
Phone: (404) 262-3624

#72
Havana Club
Category: Dance Club, Lounge
Average price: Modest
Area: Buckhead
Address: 3112 Piedmont Rd
Atlanta, GA 30305
Phone: (404) 869-8484

#73
Tongue & Groove
Category: Dance Club
Average price: Modest
Area: Lindbergh
Address: 565 Main St NE
Atlanta, GA 30324
Phone: (404) 261-2325

#74
Reign Nightclub
Category: Lounge, Dance Club, Venues
Average price: Modest
Address: 1021 Peachtree St NE
Atlanta, GA 30309
Phone: (404) 898-1704

#75
Publik Draft House
Category: Pub, American
Average price: Modest
Area: Midtown
Address: 654 Peachtree St
Atlanta, GA 30308
Phone: (404) 885-7505

#76
Drinkshop
Category: Lounge
Average price: Expensive
Area: Downtown
Address: 45 Ivan Allen Jr Blvd NW
Atlanta, GA 30308
Phone: (404) 582-5800

#77
R' R' Irish Pub
Category: Irish, Pub
Average price: Modest
Area: Midtown
Address: 1080 Peachtree St NE
Atlanta, GA 30309
Phone: (404) 477-1700

#78
Elmyr
Category: Mexican, Dive Bar
Average price: Inexpensive
Area: Little Five Points
Address: 1091 Euclid Ave NE
Atlanta, GA 30307
Phone: (404) 588-0250

#79
Rooftop 866
Category: Lounge
Average price: Modest
Area: Midtown
Address: 866 W Peachtree St NW
Atlanta, GA 30308
Phone: (678) 412-2402

#80
The Loft
Category: Music Venues
Average price: Modest
Address: 1374 W Peachtree St
Atlanta, GA 30309
Phone: (404) 885-1365

#81
The Glenwood
Category: Pub, American
Average price: Modest
Area: East Atlanta Village
Address: 1263 Glenwood Ave SE
Atlanta, GA 30316
Phone: (404) 748-1984

#82
Black Bear Tavern
Category: Pub
Average price: Inexpensive
Area: Buckhead
Address: 1931 Peachtree Rd NE
Atlanta, GA 30309
Phone: (404) 355-9089

#83
Trapeze
Category: Adult Entertainment
Average price: Exclusive
Address: 4470 Commerce Dr SW
Atlanta, GA 30336
Phone: (404) 699-0100

#84
Strip
Category: Sushi Bar, Steakhouse, Lounge
Average price: Modest
Area: Atlantic Station
Address: 245 18th St
Atlanta, GA 30363
Phone: (404) 385-2005

#85
Velvet Room
Category: Dance Club, Venues
Average price: Expensive
Address: 3358 Chamblee Tucker Rd
Atlanta, GA 30341
Phone: (404) 874-4460

#86
Elder Tree Public House
Category: Irish, Sports Bar, Gastropub
Average price: Modest
Area: East Atlanta Village
Address: 469 Flat Shoals Ave
Atlanta, GA 30316
Phone: (404) 658-6108

#87
Cloud IX Restaurant and Lounge
Category: Caribbean, Lounge
Average price: Modest
Area: Castleberry Hill
Address: 177 Peters St
Atlanta, GA 30313
Phone: (404) 681-4626

#88
Smith's Olde Bar
Category: Music Venues, Pool Hall
Average price: Modest
Area: Morningside / Lenox Park
Address: 1578 Piedmont Ave NE
Atlanta, GA 30324
Phone: (404) 875-1522

#89
East Point Corner Tavern
Category: Bar, American
Average price: Modest
Address: 2783 Main St
Atlanta, GA 30344
Phone: (404) 768-0007

#90
Lobby at Twelve
Category: Bar
Average price: Modest
Area: Atlantic Station
Address: 361 17th St
Atlanta, GA 30363
Phone: (404) 961-7370

#91
QUAD @ Spring4th Complex
Category: Music Venues, Venues
Average price: Modest
Area: Midtown
Address: 714 Spring St NW
Atlanta, GA 30308
Phone: (404) 870-0040

#92
Swinging Richards
Category: Adult Entertainment, Gay Bar
Average price: Modest
Area: Westside / Home Park
Address: 1400 Northside Dr NW
Atlanta, GA 30318
Phone: (404) 352-0532

#93
The Daiquiri Factory
Category: Bar, Karaoke
Average price: Inexpensive
Address: 889 W Peachtree St NW
Atlanta, GA 30309
Phone: (404) 881-8188

#94
Wonderroot
Category: Music Venues, Art Gallery, Cultural Center
Average price: Inexpensive
Area: Reynoldstown
Address: 982 Memorial Dr
Atlanta, GA 30316
Phone: (404) 254-5955

#95
The Village Theatre
Category: Performing Arts, Comedy Club
Average price: Inexpensive
Address: 349 Decatur St
Atlanta, GA 30312
Phone: (404) 688-8858

#96
Therapy Lounge
Category: Cafe, Hookah Bar
Average price: Modest
Address: 3145 Briarcliff Rd Ne
Atlanta, GA 30329
Phone: (404) 320-2040

#97
Jungle Atlanta
Category: Dance Club, Gay Bar
Average price: Modest
Address: 2115 Faulkner Rd NE
Atlanta, GA 30324
Phone: (404) 844-8800

#98
Frank Ski's Restaurant & Lounge
Category: Southern, Lounge, American
Average price: Modest
Area: Buckhead
Address: 2110 Peachtree Rd
Atlanta, GA 30309
Phone: (404) 603-8344

#99
Lips Atlanta
Category: Bar, American
Average price: Modest
Address: 3011 Buford Hwy NE
Atlanta, GA 30329
Phone: (404) 315-7711

#100
Olde Blind Dog
Category: Irish, Pub
Average price: Modest
Address: 705 Town Blvd
Atlanta, GA 30319
Phone: (404) 816-5739

#101
Brewhouse Cafe
Category: Pub, Sports Bar
Average price: Modest
Area: Little Five Points
Address: 401 Moreland Ave NE
Atlanta, GA 30307
Phone: (404) 525-7799

#102
The BQE Restaurant & Lounge
Category: Southern, Soul Food, Lounge
Average price: Modest
Area: Downtown
Address: 262 Edgewood Ave NE
Atlanta, GA 30303
Phone: (404) 996-6159

#103
Terra Terroir
Category: Wine Bar, American, Cocktail Bar
Average price: Modest
Area: Brookhaven
Address: 3974 Peachtree Rd
Atlanta, GA 30319
Phone: (404) 841-1032

#104
Sidebar
Category: Bar
Average price: Inexpensive
Area: Downtown
Address: 79 Poplar St NW
Atlanta, GA 30303
Phone: (404) 588-1850

#105
Pub 71
Category: Pub, Irish
Average price: Modest
Area: Brookhaven
Address: 4058 Peachtree Rd NE
Atlanta, GA 30319
Phone: (404) 467-8271

#106
The Point of View Lounge
Category: Lounge
Average price: Expensive
Area: Downtown
Address: 255 Courtland St NE
Atlanta, GA 30308
Phone: (404) 659-2000

#107
Ecco
Category: European, Cocktail Bar
Average price: Expensive
Area: Midtown
Address: 40 7th Street NE
Atlanta, GA 30308
Phone: (404) 347-9555

#108
Moondogs
Category: Bar, American
Average price: Modest
Address: 3179 Peachtree Rd NE
Atlanta, GA 30305
Phone: (404) 231-4223

#109
Treehouse Restaurant and Pub
Category: Restaurant, Pub
Average price: Modest
Address: 7 Kings Cir NE
Atlanta, GA 30305
Phone: (404) 266-2732

#110
Pour Bistro
Category: Wine Bar, American
Average price: Expensive
Area: Brookhaven
Address: 1418 Dresden Ave
Atlanta, GA 30319
Phone: (404) 254-5277

#111
Mint Ultra Lounge
Category: Lounge, Beer, Wine, Spirits
Average price: Inexpensive
Address: 3092 Briarcliff Rd NE
Atlanta, GA 30329
Phone: (404) 287-3131

#112
The Bat & Ball Pub
Category: Pub
Average price: Modest
Address: 2150 B Johnson Ferry Rd
Atlanta, GA 30319
Phone: (770) 986-0410

#113
Fox Theatre Atlanta
Category: Performing Arts, Music Venues
Average price: Expensive
Area: Midtown
Address: 660 Peachtree St Ne
Atlanta, GA 30308
Phone: (404) 881-2100

#114
Sutra Lounge
Category: Lounge, Dance Club
Average price: Modest
Address: 1136 Crescent Ave NE
Atlanta, GA 30309
Phone: (404) 607-1160

#115
The Improv Comedy Club & Dinner Theatre
Category: Comedy Club
Average price: Modest
Area: Buckhead
Address: 56 E Andrews Dr NW
Atlanta, GA 30305
Phone: (678) 244-3612

#116
Pulse Bar
Category: Lounge
Average price: Modest
Area: Downtown
Address: 265 Peachtree Ctr Ave
Atlanta, GA 30303
Phone: (404) 586-6081

#117
Java Lords
Category: Coffee, Tea, Bar
Average price: Inexpensive
Area: Little Five Points
Address: 1105 Euclid Ave NE
Atlanta, GA 30307
Phone: (404) 477-0921

#118
Red Pepper Taquer'a
Category: Mexican, Sports Bar, Latin American
Average price: Modest
Address: 2149 Briarcliff Rd
Atlanta, GA 30329
Phone: (404) 325-8151

#119
La Rumba
Category: Dance Club
Average price: Modest
Address: 4300 Buford Hwy
Atlanta, GA 30345
Phone: (678) 789-2888

#120
Inserection
Category: Adult Entertainment
Average price: Modest
Area: Morningside / Lenox Park
Address: 1739 Cheshire Bridge Rd NE
Atlanta, GA 30324
Phone: (404) 875-9200

#121
Marlow's Tavern
Category: Pub, American
Average price: Modest
Area: Midtown
Address: 950 W Peachtree St NE
Atlanta, GA 30309
Phone: (404) 815-0323

#122
Bar One
Category: Lounge, Tapas Bar
Average price: Modest
Area: Grant Park
Address: 687 Memorial Dr
Atlanta, GA 30316
Phone: (404) 522-0999

#123
Bigelow's
Category: Bar, American
Average price: Inexpensive
Address: 2564 Gresham Rd SE
Atlanta, GA 30316
Phone: (404) 241-5777

#124
Automatic Improv
Category: Performing Arts, Comedy Club
Average price: Inexpensive
Area: Westside / Home Park
Address: 999 Brady Ave
Atlanta, GA 30318
Phone: (678) 590-1386

#125
Vinyl
Category: Music Venues
Average price: Inexpensive
Area: Midtown
Address: 1374 W Peachtree St
Atlanta, GA 30309
Phone: (404) 885-1365

#126
Main Stage Gentlemen's Club
Category: Adult Entertainment, Bar
Average price: Modest
Address: 5275-A Roswell Rd
Atlanta, GA 30342
Phone: (404) 847-1440

#127
Churchill Grounds
Category: Jazz & Blues, Lounge
Average price: Modest
Area: Midtown
Address: 660 Peachtree St NE
Atlanta, GA 30308
Phone: (404) 876-3030

#128
Opera Nightclub
Category: Bar, Dance Club, Music Venues
Average price: Expensive
Area: Midtown
Address: 1150 B Peachtree St NE
Atlanta, GA 30309
Phone: (404) 874-3006

#129
Harold's Chicken & Ice Bar
Category: Chicken Wings, Bar
Average price: Modest
Address: 349 Edgewood Ave SE
Atlanta, GA 30312
Phone: (404) 577-0001

#130
Sun Dial Bar
Category: Bar
Average price: Expensive
Address: 210 Peachtree St
Atlanta, GA 30303
Phone: (404) 659-1400

#131
Living Room
Category: Lounge
Average price: Expensive
Area: Midtown
Address: 188 14th St
Atlanta, GA 30361
Phone: (404) 724-2559

#132
Tijuana Garage
Category: Pub, Tex-Mex, Burgers
Average price: Modest
Area: Little Five Points
Address: 351 Moreland Ave NE
Atlanta, GA 30307
Phone: (404) 475-8888

#133
Club Ellery's
Category: Bar, Dance Club, American
Average price: Inexpensive
Address: 2008 Campbellton Rd
Atlanta, GA 30311
Phone: (404) 755-2040

#134
Padriac's
Category: Pub, American
Average price: Modest
Address: 2460 Cumberland Pkwy
Atlanta, GA 30339
Phone: (770) 433-2398

#135
Twin Peaks
Category: Sports Bar, American
Average price: Modest
Area: Buckhead
Address: 3365 Piedmont Rd NE
Atlanta, GA 30305
Phone: (404) 961-8946

#136
The Ivy Buckhead
Category: Bar, American
Average price: Modest
Area: Buckhead
Address: 3717 Roswell Rd NE
Atlanta, GA 30342
Phone: (404) 941-3081

#137
Purple Corkscrew
Category: American, Wine Bar
Average price: Modest
Area: Emory Village
Address: 1445 Oxford Rd NE
Atlanta, GA 30307
Phone: (404) 373-3263

#138
Edgewood Speakeasy
Category: Bar
Average price: Modest
Address: 327 Edgewood Ave SE
Atlanta, GA 30312
Phone: (404) 343-4404

#139
Gold Room
Category: Lounge, Dance Club
Average price: Modest
Area: Lindbergh
Address: 2416 Piedmont Rd NE
Atlanta, GA 30324
Phone: (404) 693-9693

#140
Red Door Tavern
Category: Dive Bar
Average price: Inexpensive
Area: Buckhead
Address: 3180 Roswell Rd NW
Atlanta, GA 30305
Phone: (404) 846-6525

#141
The Highlander
Category: Dive Bar, American
Average price: Modest
Area: Midtown
Address: 931 Monroe Dr NE
Atlanta, GA 30308
Phone: (404) 872-0060

#142
Mardi Gras Atlanta
Category: Adult Entertainment
Average price: Modest
Address: 6300 Powers Ferry Rd NW
Atlanta, GA 30339
Phone: (770) 955-1638

#143
Benchwarmer's
Category: American, Sports Bar
Average price: Modest
Address: 2775 Clairmont Rd
Atlanta, GA 30329
Phone: (404) 321-0303

#144
Cafe 290
Category: Jazz & Blues, American
Average price: Modest
Address: 290 Hilderbrand Dr NE
Atlanta, GA 30328
Phone: (404) 256-3942

#145
MAX's Wine Dive
Category: American, Wine Bar
Average price: Modest
Area: Midtown
Address: 77 12th St. NE,
Atlanta, GA 30309
Phone: (404) 249-0445

#146
Six Feet Under Pub & Fish House
Category: Seafood, Pub
Average price: Modest
Area: Westside / Home Park
Address: 685 11th St
Atlanta, GA 30318
Phone: (404) 810-0040

#147
Neighbor's Pub
Category: Bar, American
Average price: Modest
Area: Virginia Highland
Address: 752 N Highland Ave NE
Atlanta, GA 30306
Phone: (404) 872-5440

#148
Wine Shoe
Category: Wine Bar
Average price: Modest
Area: Castleberry Hill
Address: 339 Nelson St SW
Atlanta, GA 30313
Phone: (404) 577-2000

#149
Hand in Hand
Category: Pub, Burgers
Average price: Modest
Area: Virginia Highland
Address: 752 N Highland Ave NE
Atlanta, GA 30306
Phone: (404) 872-1001

#150
The Warren
Category: Lounge, Venues, Breakfast & Brunch
Average price: Modest
Area: Virginia Highland
Address: 818 N Highland Ave NE
Atlanta, GA 30306
Phone: (404) 475-1991

#151
The Museum Bar
Category: Lounge
Average price: Modest
Address: 181 Ralph David Abernathy Blvd
Atlanta, GA 30312
Phone: (404) 343-2086

#152
Noche
Category: Tapas Bar
Average price: Modest
Area: Virginia Highland
Address: 1000 Virginia Ave NE
Atlanta, GA 30306
Phone: (404) 815-9155

#153
Wet Willie's
Category: Sports Bar, Karaoke
Average price: Modest
Area: Lindbergh
Address: 2450 Piedmont Rd NE
Atlanta, GA 30324
Phone: (404) 816-0151

#154
My Sister's Room
Category: Restaurant, Gay Bar
Average price: Modest
Area: Grant Park
Address: 1271 Glenwood Ave
Atlanta, GA 30316
Phone: (678) 705-4585

#155
Milltown Arms Tavern
Category: Pub
Average price: Inexpensive
Area: Cabbagetown
Address: 180 Carroll St SE
Atlanta, GA 30312
Phone: (404) 827-0434

#156
Xo Bar
Category: Bar
Average price: Modest
Area: Buckhead
Address: 3315 Peachtree Rd NE
Atlanta, GA 30326
Phone: (404) 946-9060

#157
Mixx Atlanta
Category: Gay Bar
Average price: Modest
Address: 1492 Piedmont Ave
Atlanta, GA 30309
Phone: (404) 228-4372

#158
Club Wax
Category: Adult Entertainment
Average price: Inexpensive
Address: 4375 Commerce Dr SW
Atlanta, GA 30336
Phone: (404) 696-1440

#159
The Hole In the Wall
Category: Dance Club
Average price: Inexpensive
Area: Buckhead
Address: 3177 Peachtree Rd NE
Atlanta, GA 30305
Phone: (404) 233-9801

#160
Cameli's Pizza
Category: Pizza, Bar, Italian
Average price: Modest
Area: Little Five Points
Address: 337 Moreland Ave NE
Atlanta, GA 30307
Phone: (404) 522-1624

#161
Park Bar
Category: Bar, Burgers
Average price: Modest
Area: Downtown
Address: 150 Walton St
Atlanta, GA 30303
Phone: (404) 524-0444

#162
The Music Room
Category: Music Venues
Average price: Inexpensive
Address: 327 Edgewood Ave
Atlanta, GA 30312
Phone: (404) 343-0111

#163
Model T
Category: Gay Bar
Average price: Inexpensive
Area: Old Fourth Ward, Poncey-Highland
Address: 699 Ponce De Leon Ave NE
Atlanta, GA 30308
Phone: (404) 872-2209

#164
255 Tapas Lounge
Category: Tapas Bar, Lounge
Average price: Modest
Area: Castleberry Hill
Address: 255 Peters St
Atlanta, GA 30313
Phone: (404) 522-2612

#165
S Teamshouse Lounge
Category: Seafood, Dive Bar
Average price: Modest
Area: Midtown
Address: 1051 W Peachtree St NW
Atlanta, GA 30309
Phone: (404) 233-7980

#166
La Urbana Tequila & Mezcal Bar
Category: Mexican, Cocktail Bar
Average price: Modest
Address: 1133 Huff Rd NW
Atlanta, GA 30318
Phone: (404) 464-5250

#167
The Hideaway
Category: Gay Bar
Average price: Modest
Address: 1544 Piedmont Ave
Atlanta, GA 30324
Phone: (404) 874-8247

#168
Pearl Restaurant & Lounge
Category: Seafood, Lounge
Average price: Modest
Area: Castleberry Hill
Address: 253 Peters St
Atlanta, GA 30313
Phone: (404) 523-2121

#169
Doll House
Category: Adult Entertainment, Bar
Average price: Modest
Address: 2050 Cheshire Bridge Rd NE
Atlanta, GA 30324
Phone: (404) 634-0666

#170
Hammer's Good Time Emporium
Category: Dive Bar
Average price: Inexpensive
Address: 898 Virginia Ave
Atlanta, GA 30354
Phone: (404) 768-5200

#171
Acoustix Jazz Restaurant and Lounge
Category: Jazz & Blues
Average price: Expensive
Address: 840 Marietta St
Atlanta, GA 30318
Phone: (404) 879-0111

#172
Mardi Gras Cafe Restaurant & Lounge
Category: Lounge, Music Venues
Average price: Modest
Address: 886 Martin Luther King Jr Dr SW
Atlanta, GA 30314
Phone: (404) 228-2737

#173
595 North Event Venue & Lounge
Category: Venues, Lounge
Average price: Inexpensive
Address: 595 North Ave NW
Atlanta, GA 30318
Phone: (404) 835-2329

#174
Uptown Comedy Club
Category: Comedy Club
Average price: Modest
Address: 800 Marietta St
Atlanta, GA 30318
Phone: (404) 881-0200

#175
Hard Rock Cafe
Category: Burgers, Music Venues
Average price: Modest
Area: Downtown
Address: 215 Peachtree Street NE
Atlanta, GA 30303
Phone: (404) 688-7625

#176
Cream Ultra Lounge
Category: Dance Club
Average price: Modest
Address: 3249 Buford Hwy
Atlanta, GA 30319
Phone: (678) 949-9005

#177
ilounge
Category: Hookah Bar, Champagne Bar, Lounge
Average price: Modest
Area: East Atlanta Village
Address: 1287 Glenwood Ave SE
Atlanta, GA 30316
Phone: (404) 627-9339

#178
TakoBAR
Category: Lounge
Average price: Modest
Area: Midtown
Address: 818 Juniper St
Atlanta, GA 30308
Phone: (404) 532-1944

#179
Shout
Category: Bar, American, Sushi Bar
Average price: Modest
Area: Midtown
Address: 1197 Peachtree St NE
Atlanta, GA 30361
Phone: (404) 846-2000

#180
The Tavern at Phipps
Category: Bar, American
Average price: Modest
Area: Buckhead
Address: 3500 Peachtree Rd NE
Atlanta, GA 30326
Phone: (404) 814-9640

#181
Mr C's
Category: Restaurant, Dive Bar
Average price: Inexpensive
Address: 1983 Howell Mill Rd NE
Atlanta, GA 30318
Phone: (404) 605-0888

#182
Bowlmor Atlanta
Category: Bowling, Bar
Average price: Modest
Address: 2175 Savoy Dr
Atlanta, GA 30341
Phone: (770) 451-8605

#183
House of Hookah
Category: Hookah Bar
Average price: Modest
Area: Westside / Home Park
Address: 398 14th St NW
Atlanta, GA 30318
Phone: (404) 748-1379

#184
Koo Koo Room
Category: Dance Club, Lounge
Average price: Modest
Area: Midtown
Address: 1140 Crescent Ave
Atlanta, GA 30309
Phone: (404) 985-5775

#185
Boogalou
Category: American, Lounge
Average price: Modest
Area: Midtown, Old Fourth Ward
Address: 239 Ponce de Leon Ave Ne
Atlanta, GA 30308
Phone: (678) 827-1946

#186
Whiskey Park
Category: Lounge, Wine Bar, Cocktail Bar
Average price: Expensive
Area: Midtown
Address: 188 14th St NE
Atlanta, GA 30361
Phone: (404) 724-2560

#187
Mr Cue's Billiards II
Category: Pool Hall
Average price: Inexpensive
Address: 3541 Chamblee Tucker Rd
Atlanta, GA 30341
Phone: (770) 454-7665

#188
Tilted Kilt Pub & Eatery
Category: Sports Bar, American, Pub
Average price: Modest
Address: 2960 Cobb Pkwy
Atlanta, GA 30339
Phone: (678) 741-5292

#189
Red Light Cafe
Category: Music Venues, American
Average price: Inexpensive
Area: Virginia Highland
Address: 553 Amsterdam Ave NE
Atlanta, GA 30306
Phone: (404) 874-7828

#190
Buckhead Saloon
Category: Sports Bar, American
Average price: Inexpensive
Area: Buckhead
Address: 3227 Roswell Rd NE
Atlanta, GA 30305
Phone: (404) 963-7739

#191
High Velocity
Category: Sports Bar
Average price: Modest
Area: Downtown
Address: 265 Peachtree Center Ave
Atlanta, GA 30303
Phone: (404) 586-6174

#192
Maduros Cigars
Category: Tobacco Shop, Lounge
Average price: Inexpensive
Address: 2997 Cumberland Blvd
Atlanta, GA 30339
Phone: (770) 434-4804

#193
Rose Bar
Category: Lounge, Dance Club
Average price: Modest
Area: Buckhead
Address: 3115 Piedmont Rd
Atlanta, GA 30305
Phone: (404) 869-1090

#194
Goldrush Show Bar
Category: Bar
Average price: Expensive
Address: 2608 Metropolitan Pkwy SW
Atlanta, GA 30315
Phone: (404) 766-2532

#195
Tin Lizzy's Cantina
Category: Mexican, Bar, Tex-Mex
Average price: Modest
Address: 1540 Ave Pl
Atlanta, GA 30329
Phone: (404) 537-5355

#196
The Painted Pin
Category: Bowling, Bar
Average price: Modest
Area: Lindbergh
Address: 737 Miami Circle Northeast
Atlanta, GA 30324
Phone: (404) 814-8736

#197
Churchill's British Pub
Category: Pub
Average price: Inexpensive
Area: Buckhead
Address: 3223 Cains Hill Pl NW
Atlanta, GA 30305
Phone: (404) 233-5633

#198
Enat Ethiopian Cafe
Category: Ethiopian, Lounge, Hookah Bar
Average price: Modest
Area: Morningside / Lenox Park
Address: 1999 Cheshire Bridge Rd NE
Atlanta, GA 30324
Phone: (404) 685-9291

#199
La Costilla Grill
Category: Mexican, Beer, Wine, Spirits, Sports Bar
Average price: Modest
Address: 3979 Buford Hwy
Atlanta, GA 30345
Phone: (678) 702-0856

#200
Aspen Bartini
Category: Dance Club, American, Piano Bar
Average price: Modest
Area: Buckhead
Address: 322 E Paces Ferry Rd
Atlanta, GA 30305
Phone: (404) 549-8700

#201
Mix Lounge
Category: Dance Club, Lounge, Hookah Bar
Average price: Modest
Address: 3375 Buford Hwy
Atlanta, GA 30329
Phone: (404) 399-9246

#202
Trader Vic's
Category: Hawaiian, Lounge, Asian Fusion
Average price: Expensive
Area: Downtown
Address: 255 Courtland St NE
Atlanta, GA 30303
Phone: (404) 221-6339

#203
Follies
Category: Adult Entertainment
Average price: Inexpensive
Address: 4075 Buford Hwy NE
Atlanta, GA 30345
Phone: (404) 248-9979

#204
Bar Eleven
Category: Lounge
Average price: Expensive
Area: Midtown
Address: 1065 Peachtree St
Atlanta, GA 30309
Phone: (404) 745-5000

#205
Taboo 2 Bistro & Bar
Category: Dance Club, Bar, Seafood
Average price: Modest
Address: 6075 Roswell Rd NE
Atlanta, GA 30328
Phone: (404) 255-4911

#206
Famous Pub
Category: Sports Bar, Music Venues
Average price: Inexpensive
Address: 2947 N Druid Hills Rd NE
Atlanta, GA 30329
Phone: (404) 633-3555

#207
Bucket Shop Cafe
Category: American, Bar
Average price: Modest
Area: Buckhead
Address: 3475 Lenox Rd NE
Atlanta, GA 30326
Phone: (404) 261-9244

#208
Maggie's Neighborhood Bar & Grill
Category: Bar
Average price: Inexpensive
Address: 2937 N Druid Hills Rd NE
Atlanta, GA 30329
Phone: (404) 636-5300

#209
Stagecoach
Category: Bar
Average price: Inexpensive
Area: Buckhead
Address: 34 Irby Ave
Atlanta, GA 30305
Phone: (404) 550-4169

#210
Blue Flame Lounge
Category: Adult Entertainment
Average price: Modest
Address: 1097 Harwell Rd NW
Atlanta, GA 30318
Phone: (404) 794-1446

#211
Aurum Lounge
Category: Lounge, Venues
Average price: Modest
Area: Midtown
Address: 108 8th St
Atlanta, GA 30309
Phone: (404) 941-8960

#212
Meehan's Public House
Category: Irish, Pub
Average price: Modest
Area: Downtown
Address: 200 Peachtree St
Atlanta, GA 30303
Phone: (404) 214-9821

#213
Harlem Nights Ultra Lounge
Category: Lounge, Dance Club
Average price: Modest
Area: Downtown
Address: 201 Courtland St
Atlanta, GA 30303
Phone: (678) 927-9267

#214
Oscar's Atlanta
Category: Gay Bar
Average price: Modest
Address: 1510 Piedmont Ave NE
Atlanta, GA 30324
Phone: (404) 815-8841

#215
Eleven
Category: American, Bar
Average price: Expensive
Area: Midtown
Address: 1065 Peachtree St NE
Atlanta, GA 30309
Phone: (404) 745-5745

#216
Hangovers Buckhead
Category: Dive Bar, Pizza
Average price: Inexpensive
Area: Buckhead
Address: 3188 Roswell Rd
Atlanta, GA 30305
Phone: (404) 846-8989

#217
Flip Flops
Category: Bar, Pizza
Average price: Modest
Area: Midtown
Address: 1140 Crescent Ave NE
Atlanta, GA 30309
Phone: (678) 705-3891

#218
Stooges Sports Bar & Grill
Category: Sports Bar, American
Average price: Inexpensive
Address: 857 Collier Rd
Atlanta, GA 30318
Phone: (404) 355-5445

#219
Buckhead Theatre
Category: Music Venues
Average price: Modest
Area: Buckhead
Address: 3110 Roswell Rd NE
Atlanta, GA 30305
Phone: (404) 843-2825

#220
Felix's On the Square
Category: Restaurant, Gay Bar
Average price: Inexpensive
Address: 1510 Piedmont Ave NE
Atlanta, GA 30324
Phone: (404) 249-7899

#221
The Drunken Penguin
Category: Sports Bar
Average price: Inexpensive
Address: 272 14th St NE
Atlanta, GA 30309
Phone: (404) 717-9876

#222
Flashers
Category: Adult Entertainment
Average price: Modest
Address: 6420 Roswell Rd NE
Atlanta, GA 30328
Phone: (404) 843-1167

#223
Moe's and Joe's
Category: Dive Bar, American
Average price: Inexpensive
Area: Virginia Highland
Address: 1033 N Highland Ave NE
Atlanta, GA 30306
Phone: (404) 873-6090

#224
The Mansion Elan
Category: Dance Club, Venues
Average price: Modest
Address: 3595 Clairmont Rd
Atlanta, GA 30319
Phone: (404) 997-6900

#225
Morgan Falls Billiards
Category: Pool Hall
Average price: Inexpensive
Address: 7875 Roswell Rd
Atlanta, GA 30350
Phone: (770) 394-9383

#226
La Tagliatella
Category: Italian, Pizza, Wine Bar
Average price: Modest
Address: 1540 Avenue Pl
Atlanta, GA 30329
Phone: (678) 608-4210

#227
The Reserve
Category: Bar
Average price: Modest
Address: 464 Edgewood Ave SE
Atlanta, GA 30312
Phone: (404) 477-0008

#228
East Andrews Cafe & Bar
Category: Dance Club, Pub, Music Venues
Average price: Expensive
Area: Buckhead
Address: 56 E Andrews Dr NW
Atlanta, GA 30305
Phone: (404) 869-1132

#229
Mingles Martini Bar & Grill
Category: American, Lounge
Average price: Modest
Area: Downtown
Address: 182 Courtland St NE
Atlanta, GA 30303
Phone: (404) 525-5151

#230
Bada Bings! Sports Food & Fun
Category: Sports Bar, Pub, Burgers
Average price: Modest
Address: 349 Decatur St SE
Atlanta, GA 30312
Phone: (404) 600-6484

#231
Shooter Alley
Category: Adult Entertainment
Average price: Modest
Address: 5803 Buford Hwy NE
Atlanta, GA 30340
Phone: (770) 457-0776

#232
Hooters
Category: American, Sports Bar, Chicken Wings
Average price: Modest
Address: 2977 Cobb Pkwy
Atlanta, GA 30339
Phone: (770) 984-0287

#233
Hot Jam Swings
Category: Dance Club
Average price: Inexpensive
Area: Buckhead
Address: 307 Pine Tree Dr NE
Atlanta, GA 30305
Phone: (678) 665-6462

#234
Escorpi'n
Category: Latin American, Bar
Average price: Modest
Area: Midtown
Address: 800 Peachtree St NE
Atlanta, GA 30308
Phone: (678) 666-5198

#235
Dantanna's Downtown
Category: Sports Bar, Steakhouse
Average price: Modest
Area: Downtown
Address: One CNN Center
Atlanta, GA 30303
Phone: (404) 522-8873

#236
Club Babes
Category: Adult Entertainment
Average price: Modest
Address: 304 Fulton Industrial Cir
Atlanta, GA 30336
Phone: (404) 691-7636

#237
Zo's Kitchen
Category: Bar, Mediterranean
Average price: Inexpensive
Address: 2490 Briarcliff Rd
Atlanta, GA 30329
Phone: (404) 728-0052

#238
The Pub Perimeter
Category: British, Bar, Sandwiches
Average price: Modest
Address: 4400 Ashford Dunwoody Rd
Atlanta, GA 30346
Phone: (770) 557-0883

#239
Dark Horse Tavern
Category: Music Venues, American, Pub
Average price: Modest
Area: Virginia Highland
Address: 816 N Highland Ave
Atlanta, GA 30306
Phone: (404) 873-3607

#240
TEN Atlanta
Category: Bar, American
Average price: Modest
Area: Midtown
Address: 990 Piedmont Ave
Atlanta, GA 30309
Phone: (404) 347-3360

#241
Kamal's 21
Category: Adult Entertainment, Sports Bar
Average price: Exclusive
Area: Morningside / Lenox Park
Address: 1905 Piedmont Rd
Atlanta, GA 30324
Phone: (404) 892-0063

#242
Kat's Cafe
Category: American, Music Venues
Average price: Modest
Area: Midtown
Address: 970 Piedmont Ave
Atlanta, GA 30306
Phone: (404) 347-2263

#243
Laseters Tavern at Vinings
Category: Restaurant, Sports Bar
Average price: Inexpensive
Address: 4355 Cobb Pkwy
Atlanta, GA 30339
Phone: (770) 850-8570

#244
Bone Lick BBQ
Category: Barbeque, Bar
Average price: Modest
Address: 1133 Huff Rd NW
Atlanta, GA 30318
Phone: (404) 343-6574

#245
Tap
Category: Pub, Sandwiches, Gastropub
Average price: Modest
Area: Midtown
Address: 1180 Peachtree St NE
Atlanta, GA 30309
Phone: (404) 347-2220

#246
Lost Dog Tavern
Category: Bar
Average price: Inexpensive
Area: Buckhead
Address: 3182 Roswell Rd NW
Atlanta, GA 30305
Phone: (404) 254-3341

#247
Aquarius Lounge
Category: Lounge
Average price: Modest
Address: 3050 Martin Luther King Jr Dr SW,
Atlanta, GA 30311
Phone: (404) 505-7280

#248
Room Service Lounge
Category: Dance Club, Lounge, American
Average price: Modest
Address: 1937 Piedmont Cir NE
Atlanta, GA 30324
Phone: (404) 249-7775

#249
Prive Nightclub
Category: Dance Club
Average price: Expensive
Area: Midtown
Address: 960 Spring St
Atlanta, GA 30309
Phone: (404) 220-9599

#250
Friday Jazz
Category: Jazz & Blues
Average price: Modest
Area: Midtown
Address: 1280 Peachtree St NE
Atlanta, GA 30309
Phone: (404) 733-4444

#251
Stilettos
Category: Adult Entertainment, Lounge
Average price: Modest
Address: 806 Marietta St
Atlanta, GA 30318
Phone: (404) 724-0401

#252
The Cockpit
Category: Gay Bar
Average price: Modest
Address: 465 Blvd SE
Atlanta, GA 30312
Phone: (404) 343-2450

#253
The Ultimate Bar and Grill
Category: American, Sports Bar
Average price: Modest
Address: 3515 Camp Creek Pkwy
Atlanta, GA 30344
Phone: (404) 349-2642

#254
Gibney's Pub
Category: Pub
Average price: Modest
Area: Downtown
Address: 231 Peachtree Ctr NE
Atlanta, GA 30303
Phone: (404) 688-0928

#255
Bliss Atlanta
Category: Adult Entertainment
Average price: Modest
Address: 2284 Cheshire Bridge Rd
Atlanta, GA 30324
Phone: (404) 320-1924

#256
Arif Cafe
Category: Cafe, Hookah Bar
Average price: Inexpensive
Address: 2793 Clairmont Rd
Atlanta, GA 30329
Phone: (404) 748-6015

#257
d'vine Wine Bar & Shop
Category: Wine Bar, American
Average price: Modest
Address: 5486 Chamblee Dunwoody Rd
Atlanta, GA 30338
Phone: (770) 350-9463

#258
Elliott Street Deli & Pub
Category: Deli, Sandwiches, Pub
Average price: Modest
Area: Castleberry Hill
Address: 51 Elliott St SW
Atlanta, GA 30313
Phone: (404) 523-2174

#259
Coronet
Category: Nightlife
Average price: Modest
Address: 5275 Roswell Rd NE
Atlanta, GA 30342
Phone: (404) 250-1534

#260
Stats
Category: American, Sports Bar
Average price: Modest
Area: Downtown
Address: 300 Marietta St NW
Atlanta, GA 30313
Phone: (404) 885-1472

#261
The Dive Bar
Category: Dive Bar
Average price: Modest
Area: Buckhead
Address: 3184 Roswell Rd NW
Atlanta, GA 30305
Phone: (678) 510-7765

#262
Organix Lounge
Category: Lounge
Average price: Modest
Area: Midtown, Old Fourth Ward
Address: 239 Ponce De Leon Ave NE
Atlanta, GA 30308
Phone: (678) 827-1946

#263
The Family Dog
Category: Bar, Performing Arts, American
Average price: Modest
Area: Morningside / Lenox Park
Address: 1402 N Highland Ave
Atlanta, GA 30306
Phone: (404) 249-0180

#264
Morris Restaurant & Lounge
Category: Dive Bar, American
Average price: Inexpensive
Area: Kirkwood
Address: 2254 Oakview Rd SE
Atlanta, GA 30317
Phone: (404) 378-9262

#265
The Imperial
Category: Pub
Average price: Modest
Area: Decatur
Address: 726 W College Ave
Atlanta, GA 30030
Phone: (404) 464-5698

#266
Moe's Original Bar B Que
Category: Barbeque, Sports Bar
Average price: Modest
Area: Westside / Home Park
Address: 349 14th St
Atlanta, GA 30318
Phone: (404) 249-0707

#267
The Midway Pub
Category: Pub
Average price: Modest
Area: East Atlanta Village
Address: 552 Flat Shoals Ave
Atlanta, GA 30316
Phone: (404) 584-0335

#268
Bar Amalfi
Category: Bar
Average price: Modest
Area: Westside / Home Park
Address: 1077 Hemphill Ave NW
Atlanta, GA 30318
Phone: (404) 844-2707

#269
97 Estoria
Category: Pub
Average price: Inexpensive
Address: 727 Wylie St SE
Atlanta, GA 30316
Phone: (404) 522-0966

#270
Amnesia Club & Lounge
Category: Bar, Social Club
Average price: Modest
Address: 3220 Butner Rd
Atlanta, GA 30331
Phone: (404) 343-4475

#271
The Anchor Bar & Tattoo Studio
Category: Hookah Bar, Lounge
Average price: Modest
Address: 1878 Piedmont Ave NE
Atlanta, GA 30324
Phone: (404) 892-6868

#272
E'Villa
Category: Ethiopian, Cocktail Bar, Hookah Bar
Average price: Modest
Area: Downtown
Address: 495 Peachtree St NE
Atlanta, GA 30308
Phone: (404) 254-5011

#273
Aaron's Amphitheatre
Category: Music Venues
Average price: Expensive
Address: 2002 Lakewood Way
Atlanta, GA 30315
Phone: (800) 745-3000

#274
Del Frisco's Grille
Category: American, Wine Bar
Average price: Expensive
Area: Buckhead
Address: 3376 Peachtree Rd NE
Atlanta, GA 30326
Phone: (404) 537-2828

#275
Stillhouse Craft Burgers & Moonshine
Category: Cocktail Bar, Burgers
Average price: Modest
Area: Buckhead
Address: 56 E Andrews Dr NW
Atlanta, GA 30305
Phone: (678) 244-3601

#276
Rose and Crown Tavern
Category: Pub, American, British
Average price: Modest
Address: 1931 Powers Ferry Rd SE
Atlanta, GA 30339
Phone: (770) 933-5595

#277
Blu Cantina
Category: Hookah Bar, Mexican
Average price: Modest
Area: Castleberry Hill
Address: 257 Peters St
Atlanta, GA 30313
Phone: (404) 963-2454

#278
Tattletale Lounge
Category: Adult Entertainment
Average price: Modest
Area: Morningside / Lenox Park
Address: 2075 Piedmont Rd N E
Atlanta, GA 30324
Phone: (404) 873-2294

#279
Zocalo Mexican Kitchen and Cantina
Category: Mexican, Lounge
Average price: Modest
Area: Midtown
Address: 187 10th Street NE
Atlanta, GA 30309
Phone: (404) 249-7575

#280
Cafe Intermezzo
Category: Cafe, Bar, Crepes
Average price: Modest
Area: Midtown
Address: 1065 Peachtree St NE
Atlanta, GA 30309
Phone: (404) 355-0411

#281
Hudson Grille
Category: American, Sports Bar
Average price: Modest
Area: Midtown
Address: 942 Peachtree St NE
Atlanta, GA 30309
Phone: (404) 892-0892

#282
Josephine
Category: Lounge, American
Average price: Modest
Address: 6325 Peachtree Industrial Blvd
Atlanta, GA 30360
Phone: (678) 973-4441

#283
Deadwood Saloon
Category: Bar
Average price: Modest
Address: 66 12th St NE
Atlanta, GA 30309
Phone: (404) 671-4290

#284
SOHO Restaurant
Category: American, Wine Bar
Average price: Expensive
Area: Vinings
Address: 4300 Paces Ferry Road
Atlanta, GA 30339
Phone: (770) 801-0069

#285
Laughing Matters
Category: Performing Arts, Comedy Club
Average price: Modest
Address: 173 Cleveland Ave SE
Atlanta, GA 30354
Phone: (404) 225-5000

#286
Five Paces Inn
Category: Dive Bar
Average price: Inexpensive
Area: Buckhead
Address: 41 Irby Ave NW
Atlanta, GA 30305
Phone: (404) 365-0777

#287
Southern Nights Adult Video
Category: Adult Entertainment, Videos, Video Game Rental
Average price: Expensive
Address: 2205 Cheshire Bridge
Atlanta, GA 30324
Phone: (404) 728-0701

#288
Velvet Room
Category: Sports Bar
Average price: Expensive
Address: 3358 Chamblee Tucker Rd
Atlanta, GA 30341
Phone: (770) 220-8686

#289
Meehan's Public House
Category: Pub, Irish
Average price: Modest
Area: Atlantic Station
Address: 232 19th St NW
Atlanta, GA 30363
Phone: (404) 249-7812

#290
Woofs on Piedmont
Category: Gay Bar, Sports Bar
Average price: Inexpensive
Area: Lindbergh
Address: 2425 Piedmont Rd NE
Atlanta, GA 30324
Phone: (404) 869-9422

#291
Taco Mac
Category: Burgers, Bar, American
Average price: Modest
Address: 1211 Ashford Crossing
Atlanta, GA 30346
Phone: (678) 336-1381

#292
La Parrilla Mexican Restaurant
Category: Mexican, Sports Bar
Average price: Modest
Address: 2945 N Druid Hills Rd
Atlanta, GA 30329
Phone: (678) 403-3831

#293
Jr Crickets
Category: Sports Bar, Barbeque
Average price: Modest
Area: Midtown
Address: 1197 Peachtree St NE
Atlanta, GA 30361
Phone: (404) 685-9464

#294
Friends On Ponce
Category: Gay Bar, Lounge
Average price: Inexpensive
Area: Virginia Highland, Old Fourth Ward
Address: 736 Ponce De Leon Ave NE
Atlanta, GA 30306
Phone: (404) 817-3820

#295
Pure
Category: Dance Club
Average price: Expensive
Address: 2793 Clairmont Rd
Atlanta, GA 30329
Phone: (404) 633-5020

#296
The Atlanta Eagle
Category: Gay Bar, Dance Club
Average price: Inexpensive
Area: Midtown, Old Fourth Ward
Address: 306 Ponce De Leon Ave NE
Atlanta, GA 30308
Phone: (404) 873-2453

#297
Dugan's
Category: American, Sports Bar
Average price: Modest
Area: Virginia Highland, Old Fourth Ward, Poncey-Highland
Address: 777 Ponce de Leon Ave NE
Atlanta, GA 30306
Phone: (404) 885-1217

#298
Hangbok - Happy Karaoke
Category: Restaurant, Karaoke
Average price: Inexpensive
Address: 5425 Buford Hwy NE
Atlanta, GA 30340
Phone: (770) 458-8661

#299
Meehan's Public House
Category: Restaurant, Pub, Irish Pub
Average price: Modest
Address: 227 Sandy Springs Pl NE
Atlanta, GA 30328
Phone: (404) 843-8058

#300
Flatiron Restaurant & Bar
Category: Restaurant, Bar
Average price: Modest
Area: East Atlanta Village
Address: 520 Flat Shoals Ave SE
Atlanta, GA 30316
Phone: (404) 688-8864

#301
Venue Restaurant & Tapas Bar
Category: Bar, American
Average price: Modest
Area: Downtown
Address: 30 Ivan Allen Jr Blvd
Atlanta, GA 30308
Phone: (470) 299-1321

#302
The Rusty Nail Pub
Category: Burgers, American, Dive Bar
Average price: Modest
Address: 2900 Buford Hwy NE
Atlanta, GA 30329
Phone: (404) 634-6306

#303
Leverage Lounge
Category: Bar
Average price: Inexpensive
Area: West End
Address: 792 Cascade Ave SW
Atlanta, GA 30310
Phone: (404) 838-6516

#304
The Royal Peacock
Category: Dance Club
Average price: Modest
Area: Downtown
Address: 186 Auburn Ave NE
Atlanta, GA 30303
Phone: (404) 523-0579

#305
Sledge Lounge
Category: Sports Bar, Pool Hall
Average price: Inexpensive
Address: 4186 Buford Hwy NE
Atlanta, GA 30345
Phone: (678) 705-3896

#306
Tin Lizzy's Cantina
Category: Tex-Mex, Mexican, Sports Bar
Average price: Modest
Address: 121 Perimeter Ctr W
Atlanta, GA 30346
Phone: (470) 514-1050

#307
Karaoke Melody 2
Category: Karaoke, Lounge
Average price: Modest
Address: 7130 Buford Hwy
Atlanta, GA 30340
Phone: (770) 825-0088

#308
Tin Lizzy's Cantina
Category: Mexican, Bar, Tex-Mex
Average price: Modest
Area: Buckhead
Address: 3639 Piedmont Rd NE
Atlanta, GA 30305
Phone: (404) 846-6000

#309
The Shark Bar & Grille
Category: Bar, American
Average price: Inexpensive
Address: 2841 Greenbriar Pkwy
Atlanta, GA 30331
Phone: (404) 346-3406

#310
Taco Mac
Category: Sports Bar, Tex-Mex, Mexican
Average price: Modest
Area: Virginia Highland
Address: 1006 N Highland Ave NE
Atlanta, GA 30306
Phone: (404) 873-6529

#311
Atlanta Civic Center
Category: Performing Arts, Music Venues
Average price: Modest
Area: Old Fourth Ward
Address: 395 Piedmont Ave
Atlanta, GA 30308
Phone: (404) 523-6275

#312
Mardi Gras Sports Cafe
Category: Sports Bar
Average price: Modest
Address: 2040 Headland Dr
Atlanta, GA 30344
Phone: (404) 883-2931

#313
Central City Tavern
Category: Sports Bar, American
Average price: Modest
Address: 1801 Howell Mill Rd
Atlanta, GA 30318
Phone: (404) 351-1957

#314
Apres Diem
Category: Restaurant, Bar
Average price: Modest
Area: Midtown
Address: 931 Monroe Dr NE
Atlanta, GA 30308
Phone: (404) 872-3333

#315
Blush Ultra Lounge
Category: Lounge
Average price: Modest
Address: 2847 Buford Hwy
Atlanta, GA 30329
Phone: (404) 549-8195

#316
Rush Lounge
Category: Dance Club
Average price: Modest
Address: 2715 Buford Hwy NE
Atlanta, GA 30324
Phone: (678) 568-9657

#317
Sweet Auburn BBQ
Category: Cocktail Bar, Barbeque, Sandwiches
Average price: Modest
Area: Poncey-Highland
Address: 656 N Highland Ave NE
Atlanta, GA 30306
Phone: (678) 515-3550

#318
Zuffy's Place
Category: Bar, Music Venues
Average price: Inexpensive
Address: 1860 Corporate Blvd NE
Atlanta, GA 30329
Phone: (404) 343-1171

#319
Club Europe
Category: Dance Club
Average price: Modest
Address: 4001 Presidential Pkwy
Atlanta, GA 30340
Phone: (770) 452-1240

#320
Brick Store Pub
Category: Pub, American
Average price: Modest
Area: Decatur
Address: 125 E Ct Sq
Decatur, GA 30030
Phone: (404) 687-0990

#321
Intercrew Billiards and Bar
Category: Lounge
Average price: Modest
Area: Downtown
Address: 1301 Old Peachtree Rd NW
Atlanta, GA 31136
Phone: (678) 205-2937

#322
Hottie Hawg's Smokin BBQ
Category: Barbeque, Music Venues
Average price: Modest
Address: 2061 Main St NW
Atlanta, GA 30318
Phone: (404) 794-5224

#323
Condesa Coffee
Category: Sandwiches, Wine Bar
Average price: Inexpensive
Area: Old Fourth Ward
Address: 480 John Wesley Dobbs Ave
Atlanta, GA 30312
Phone: (404) 524-5054

#324
Bulldog's
Category: Gay Bar
Average price: Inexpensive
Area: Midtown
Address: 893 Peachtree St NE
Atlanta, GA 30309
Phone: (404) 872-3025

#325
Clay's Sports Cafe
Category: Dive Bar, Chicken Wings
Average price: Inexpensive
Address: 6518 Roswell Rd NE
Atlanta, GA 30328
Phone: (404) 843-1233

#326
Mojito
Category: Bar
Average price: Exclusive
Area: Midtown
Address: Wyndham Midtown
Atlanta, GA 30309
Phone: (404) 892-4440

#327
Finish Line Sports Bar
Category: Sports Bar
Average price: Modest
Address: 1031 Virginia Ave
Atlanta, GA 30354
Phone: (404) 767-9000

#328
Lunacy Black Market
Category: American, Wine Bar
Average price: Modest
Area: Downtown
Address: 231 Mitchell St SW
Atlanta, GA 30303
Phone: (404) 688-0806

#329
Taverna Fiorentina
Category: Italian, Wine Bar
Average price: Modest
Address: 3324 Cobb Pkwy SE
Atlanta, GA 30339
Phone: (770) 272-9825

#330
Studio No.7
Category: Lounge, Tapas, Art Gallery
Average price: Modest
Address: 393 Marietta St NW
Atlanta, GA 30313
Phone: (404) 549-9839

#331
Club Crucial
Category: Dance Club
Average price: Inexpensive
Address: 2517 Donald Lee Hollowell
Atlanta, GA 30318
Phone: (404) 794-2114

#332
Caf' Circa
Category: Lounge, Caribbean, Jazz & Blues
Average price: Modest
Address: 464 Edgewood Ave
Atlanta, GA 30312
Phone: (404) 477-0008

#333
RH Brands
Category: Adult Entertainment
Average price: Inexpensive
Address: 1095 Zonolite Rd NE
Atlanta, GA 30306
Phone: (404) 892-8868

#334
CafeNineteen
Category: Breakfast & Brunch, Bar
Average price: Inexpensive
Area: Atlantic Station
Address: 232 19th St
Atlanta, GA 30363
Phone: (404) 963-6189

#335
Buckhead Bottle Bar & Bistro
Category: American, Hookah Bar
Average price: Modest
Area: Buckhead
Address: 268 E Paces Ferry Rd NE
Atlanta, GA 30305
Phone: (404) 474-9892

#336
Taco Mac
Category: Sports Bar, Mexican
Average price: Modest
Area: Midtown
Address: 933 Peachtree St NE
Atlanta, GA 30309
Phone: (678) 904-7211

#337
Eddie's Attic
Category: Music Venues, American
Average price: Modest
Area: Decatur
Address: 515-B N McDonough St
Decatur, GA 30030
Phone: (404) 377-4976

#338
Publik Draft House
Category: Pub
Average price: Modest
Area: Midtown
Address: 654 Peachtree St
Atlanta, GA 30308
Phone: (404) 885-7505

#339
The Fred
Category: Bar, American
Average price: Modest
Address: 5600 Roswell Rd
Sandy Springs, GA 30342
Phone: (404) 671-3733

#340
Karaoke Melody
Category: Karaoke, Lounge
Average price: Modest
Address: 5979 Buford Hwy
Atlanta, GA 30340
Phone: (770) 986-8881

#341
656 Sports Bar & Grille
Category: Sports Bar
Average price: Modest
Address: 656 Pryor St
Atlanta, GA 30312
Phone: (678) 732-3656

#342
Java Vino
Category: Coffee, Tea, Wine Bar
Average price: Inexpensive
Area: Poncey-Highland
Address: 579 N Highland Ave
Atlanta, GA 30307
Phone: (404) 577-8673

#343
Andrews Upstairs
Category: Music Venues, Lounge
Average price: Modest
Area: Buckhead
Address: 56 E Andrews Dr NW
Atlanta, GA 30305
Phone: (404) 869-1132

#344
Pirate's Pub
Category: Pub
Average price: Modest
Address: 3979 Buford Hwy
Atlanta, GA 30345
Phone: (404) 636-4003

#345
Eleanor's
Category: Lounge
Average price: Modest
Address: 1675 Cumberland Pkwy
Smyrna, GA 30080
Phone: (770) 434-1114

#346
Stout Irish Sports Pub
Category: Pub, Irish
Average price: Modest
Area: Buckhead
Address: 56 E Andrews Dr
Atlanta, GA 30305
Phone: (404) 869-1151

#347
Lions
Category: Lounge, Ethiopian
Average price: Inexpensive
Address: 3779 Buford NE Hwy
Atlanta, GA 30345
Phone: (404) 633-4499

#348
Johnny M's Pizza Bistro
Category: Pizza, Sports Bar, Lounge
Average price: Inexpensive
Address: 904 Martin Luther King Junior Dr SW, Atlanta, GA 30318
Phone: (404) 577-9505

#349
Opus 1
Category: Gay Bar, Dive Bar
Average price: Inexpensive
Address: 1086 Alco St NE
Atlanta, GA 30324
Phone: (404) 634-6478

#350
BJ Roosters
Category: Gay Bar
Average price: Inexpensive
Address: 2345 Cheshire Bridge Rd NE
Atlanta, GA 30324
Phone: (404) 634-5895

#351
Buffalo Wild Wings
Category: Chicken Wings, American, Sports Bar
Average price: Modest
Address: 6000 N Terminal Parkway, Terminal D
Atlanta, GA 30320
Phone: (404) 763-0770

#352
Jocks N Jills Sports Bar
Category: Sports Bar
Average price: Modest
Address: 1 Galleria Pkwy SE
Atlanta, GA 30339
Phone: (770) 952-8401

#353
Thinking Man Tavern
Category: Pub
Average price: Modest
Area: Decatur
Address: 537 W Howard Ave Decatur, GA 30030, **Phone:** (404) 370-1717

#354
Mary's
Category: Gay Bar
Average price: Modest
Area: Grant Park
Address: 1287 Glenwood Ave
Atlanta, GA 30316
Phone: (404) 624-4411

#355
Locos Grill & Pub
Category: Pub, American, Sports Bar
Average price: Inexpensive
Area: Buckhead
Address: 3167 Peachtree Rd NE
Atlanta, GA 30305
Phone: (404) 816-9993

#356
Steinbeck's
Category: Bar
Average price: Modest
Area: Decatur
Address: 659 E Lake Dr
Decatur, GA 30030
Phone: (404) 373-1116

#357
Southern-Comfort Restaurant & Lounge
Category: Dive Bar, American
Average price: Inexpensive
Address: 1383 Cedar Grove Rd.
Conley, GA 30288
Phone: (404) 361-5675

#358
Dunwoody Tavern
Category: Pub, American
Average price: Modest
Address: 5488 Chamblee Dunwoody Rd
Atlanta, GA 30338
Phone: (770) 394-4164

#359
Fontaine's Oyster House
Category: Seafood, Bar
Average price: Modest
Area: Virginia Highland
Address: 1026 N Highland Ave NE
Atlanta, GA 30306
Phone: (404) 872-0869

#360
Elbow Room Bar
Category: Dive Bar, Sports Bar, Pizza
Average price: Modest
Area: Buckhead
Address: 248 Pharr Rd NE
Atlanta, GA 30305
Phone: (404) 231-3308

#361
Mac McGee
Category: Irish, Pub
Average price: Modest
Area: Decatur
Address: 111 Sycamore St
Decatur, GA 30030
Phone: (404) 377-8050

#362
Strokers Club
Category: Adult Entertainment
Average price: Modest
Address: 1353 Brockett Rd
Clarkston, GA 30021
Phone: (770) 270-0350

#363
Suite Food Lounge
Category: American, Lounge
Average price: Modest
Address: 375 Luckie St
Atlanta, GA 30313
Phone: (404) 577-2500

#364
Eyedrum
Category: Art Gallery, Music Venues, Performing Arts
Average price: Inexpensive
Area: Downtown
Address: 115 Martin Luther King Jr Dr
Atlanta, GA 30303
Phone: (404) 522-0655

#365
Yebo
Category: South African, Lounge
Average price: Modest
Area: Buckhead
Address: 3500 Peachtree Rd NE
Atlanta, GA 30326
Phone: (404) 467-4988

#366
Legends Restaurant & Lounge
Category: American, Lounge
Average price: Modest
Area: Downtown
Address: 495 Peachtree St
Atlanta, GA 30308
Phone: (404) 832-5463

#367
Twain's Billiards & Tap
Category: Pool Hall, Brewery
Average price: Modest
Area: Decatur
Address: 211 E Trinity Pl Decatur, GA 30030, **Phone:** (404) 373-0063

#368
Red Sky Tapas
Category: Tapas Bar, Music Venues
Average price: Modest
Address: 1255 Johnson Ferry Rd
Marietta, GA 30068
Phone: (770) 973-0100

#369
Copeland's Cheesecake Bistro
Category: Desserts, Bar, American
Average price: Modest
Area: Atlantic Station
Address: 265 18th St NW
Atlanta, GA 30363
Phone: (404) 815-8800

#370
Top Flr
Category: American, Wine Bar, Cocktail Bar
Average price: Modest
Area: Midtown
Address: 674 Myrtle St NE
Atlanta, GA 30308
Phone: (404) 685-3110

#371
Stem Wine Bar
Category: American, Wine Bar
Average price: Expensive
Address: 1311 Johnson Ferry Rd
Marietta, GA 30068
Phone: (678) 214-6888

#372
Colbeh Persian Kitchen & Bar
Category: Middle Eastern, Bar
Average price: Modest
Area: Decatur
Address: 123 E Court Sq
Decatur, GA 30030
Phone: (404) 373-1226

#373
45 South Cafe
Category: Wine Bar, Music Venues
Average price: Inexpensive
Address: 45 S Peachtree St
Norcross, GA 30071
Phone: (770) 409-4009

#374
Dantanna's
Category: Sports Bar, Steakhouse
Average price: Modest
Area: Buckhead
Address: 3400 Around Lenox Rd
NE Atlanta, GA 30326
Phone: (404) 760-8873

#375
Righteous Room
Category: American, Dive Bar
Average price: Inexpensive
Address: 2142 Johnson Ferry Rd
NE Brookhaven, GA 30319
Phone: (770) 559-5678

#376
Trackside Tavern
Category: Dive Bar, American, Pub
Average price: Inexpensive
Area: Decatur
Address: 313 E College Ave
Decatur, GA 30030
Phone: (404) 378-0504

#377
Eleventh Street Pub
Category: American, Pub
Average price: Modest
Area: Midtown
Address: 1041 W Peachtree St
NW Atlanta, GA 30309
Phone: (404) 724-9060

#378
Steve's Live Music
Category: Music Venues
Average price: Modest
Address: 234 Hilderbrand Dr
NE Sandy Springs, GA 30328
Phone: (404) 418-6777

#379
Cafe Istanbul
Category: Turkish, Hookah Bar
Average price: Modest
Address: 1850 Lawrenceville Hwy Decatur, GA 30033
Phone: (404) 320-0054

#380
Bistro New York
Category: Coffee, Tea, Karaoke
Average price: Modest
Address: 4126 Pleasantdale Road
Atlanta, GA 30340
Phone: (770) 263-0220

#381
The Pinewood
Category: Bar, Southern
Average price: Modest
Area: Decatur
Address: 254 W Ponce De Leon Ave
Decatur, GA 30030
Phone: (404) 373-5507

#382
The Imperial
Category: Pub
Average price: Modest
Area: Decatur
Address: 726 W College Ave
Decatur, GA 30030
Phone: (404) 464-5698

#383
Speakeasy Lounge
Category: Lounge
Average price: Modest
Area: Downtown
Address: 156 Forsyth S W St
Atlanta, GA 30303
Phone: (404) 522-9509

#384
Sahara Hookah Lounge
Category: Hookah Bar
Average price: Modest
Area: Buckhead
Address: 321 Pharr Rd NE
Atlanta, GA 30305
Phone: (404) 565-0390

#385
Suede Tapas Lounge
Category: Hookah Bar
Average price: Modest
Area: Downtown
Address: 257 Trinity Ave SW
Atlanta, GA 30303
Phone: (404) 589-1414

#386
Pin Ups
Category: Adult Entertainment
Average price: Modest
Address: 2788 E Ponce De Leon Ave
Decatur, GA 30030
Phone: (404) 373-9477

#387
Midtown Tavern
Category: Pub, Gastropub
Average price: Modest
Area: Downtown
Address: 554 Piedmont Ave NE
Atlanta, GA 30308
Phone: (404) 541-1372

#388
Three Dollar Cafe
Category: Chicken Wings, Bar
Average price: Modest
Area: Buckhead
Address: 4475 Roswell Rd NE
Atlanta, GA 30342
Phone: (404) 303-0047

#389
Johnnie MacCrackens Celtic Pub
Category: Pub
Average price: Modest
Address: 15 Atlanta St SE
Marietta, GA 30060
Phone: (678) 290-6641

#390
Mazzy's Sports Bar & Grill
Category: Sports Bar, Pool Hall
Average price: Inexpensive
Address: 2217 Roswell Rd
NE Marietta, GA 30062
Phone: (678) 213-1688

#391
Dixie Tavern
Category: Dive Bar
Average price: Modest
Address: 2319 Windy Hill Rd
SE Marietta, GA 30067
Phone: (770) 690-0090

#392
Niks Place
Category: Dive Bar, Greek
Average price: Inexpensive
Address: 645 Whitlock Ave
Marietta, GA 30006
Phone: (678) 355-1088

#393
Takorea
Category: Bar, Korean, Mexican
Average price: Modest
Area: Midtown
Address: 818 Juniper St
Atlanta, GA 30308
Phone: (404) 532-1944

#394
J's Lounge
Category: Hookah Bar, Lounge
Average price: Modest
Address: 1995 Windy Hill Rd
Smyrna, GA 30080
Phone: (678) 383-6164

#395
Darwin's Burgers and Blues
Category: Bar, Music Venues, Burgers
Average price: Inexpensive
Address: 1598 Roswell Rd
Marietta, GA 30062
Phone: (770) 509-2664

#396
Cineprov!
Category: Cinema, Performing Arts, Comedy Club
Average price: Modest
Area: Morningside / Lenox Park
Address: 1049 Ponce De Leon Ave
Atlanta, GA 30306
Phone: (678) 825-5381

#397
Joe's On Juniper
Category: Gay Bar, American
Average price: Modest
Area: Midtown
Address: 1049 Juniper St
Atlanta, GA 30309
Phone: (404) 875-6634

#398
Slice
Category: Pizza, Lounge
Average price: Inexpensive
Area: Downtown
Address: 85 Poplar St NW
Atlanta, GA 30303
Phone: (404) 917-1820

#399
H Harper Station
Category: American, Bar
Average price: Modest
Area: Reynoldstown
Address: 904 Memorial Dr SE
Atlanta, GA 30316
Phone: (678) 732-0415

#400
Vino Venue
Category: American, Wine Bar
Average price: Modest
Address: 4478 Chamblee Dunwoody Rd
Atlanta, GA 30338
Phone: (770) 668-0435

#401
Jerry Farber's Side Door
Category: Music Venues, Comedy Club
Average price: Modest
Address: 3652 Roswell Rd NW
Atlanta, GA 30305
Phone: (770) 738-3000

#402
120 Tavern & Music Hall
Category: Sports Bar, Music Venues
Average price: Modest
Address: 1440 Roswell Rd
Marietta, GA 30062
Phone: (770) 509-3320

#403
Atlanta Wine School
Category: Winery, Wine Bar, Restaurant
Average price: Exclusive
Address: 4478 Chamblee Dunwoody Rd
Atlanta, GA 30338
Phone: (770) 668-0435

#404
The Manchester Arms
Category: British, Pub
Average price: Modest
Address: 1705 Virginia Ave
College Park, GA 30337
Phone: (404) 763-9980

#405
Primal
Category: Dance Club, Jazz & Blues
Average price: Expensive
Area: Midtown
Address: 960 Spring St
Atlanta, GA 30309
Phone: (404) 745-9494

#406
Tin Roof Cantina
Category: Mexican, Bar
Average price: Inexpensive
Address: 2591 Briarcliff Rd NE
Atlanta, GA 30329
Phone: (404) 329-4700

#407
Octane
Category: Coffee, Tea,
Breakfast & Brunch, Bar
Average price: Inexpensive
Area: Grant Park
Address: 437 Memorial Dr
Atlanta, GA 30312
Phone: (404) 815-9886

#408
MoonShadow Tavern
Category: Pub, Music Venues
Average price: Inexpensive
Address: 3976 Lawrenceville Hwy
Tucker, GA 30084
Phone: (770) 674-2133

#409
Twenty-Two Storys
Category: Sports Bar, American, Lounge
Average price: Expensive
Area: Downtown
Address: 265 Peachtree St NE
Atlanta, GA 30308
Phone: (404) 460-6519

#410
The Marlay House
Category: Pub, Irish
Average price: Modest
Area: Decatur
Address: 426 W Ponce De Leon Ave
Decatur, GA 30030
Phone: (404) 270-9950

#411
The Grove Restaurant & Tavern
Category: American, Sports Bar, American
Average price: Inexpensive
Address: 2761 LaVista Rd
Decatur, GA 30033
Phone: (404) 321-4448

#412
Tin Lizzy's Cantina
Category: Mexican, Sports Bar
Average price: Modest
Area: Grant Park
Address: 415 Memorial Dr
Atlanta, GA 30312
Phone: (404) 554-8220

#413
Faces Lounge
Category: Bar, American, Karaoke
Average price: Inexpensive
Address: 138 Powers Ferry Rd SE Marietta, GA 30067
Phone: (770) 579-3801

#414
Highland Cigar
Category: Tobacco Shop, Wine Bar
Average price: Modest
Area: Old Fourth Ward, Inman Park
Address: 245 N Highland Ave
Atlanta, GA 30307
Phone: (404) 477-2415

#415
Cakes & Ale
Category: Breakfast & Brunch, Bar
Average price: Expensive
Area: Decatur
Address: 155 Sycamore St
Decatur, GA 30030
Phone: (404) 377-7994

#416
Sage Woodfire Tavern
Category: American, Bar
Average price: Modest
Address: 4505 Ashford Dunwoody
Atlanta, GA 30346
Phone: (770) 804-8880

#417
Tilted Kilt Pub & Eatery
Category: American, Sports Bar, Pub
Average price: Modest
Address: 1155 Mt. Vernon Hwy. Perimeter, GA 30338
Phone: (678) 672-4533

#418
Confetti's Bar & Grill
Category: Bar, American
Average price: Modest
Address: 6470 Spalding Dr
Norcross, GA 30092
Phone: (678) 728-0025

#419
Club 426 Restaurant & Lounge
Category: American, Lounge
Average price: Inexpensive
Address: 5469 Memorial Dr Stone Mountain, GA 30083
Phone: (404) 297-9910

#420
Chastain Park Amphitheatre
Category: Park, Music Venues
Average price: Modest
Address: 4469 Stella Drive
Atlanta, GA 30342
Phone: (800) 745-3000

#421
Dugan's Tavern
Category: Bar
Average price: Modest
Address: 5922 Memorial Dr Stone Mountain, GA 30083
Phone: (404) 297-8545

#422
Hi Life
Category: American, Bar
Average price: Modest
Address: 3380 Holcomb Bridge Rd
Norcross, GA 30092
Phone: (770) 409-0101

#423
Food Therapy
Category: Mediterranean, Lounge
Average price: Modest
Address: 3125 Briarcliff Rd
Atlanta, GA 30329
Phone: (404) 963-2905

#424
The Spot Sports Bar & Grill
Category: Sports Bar, Karaoke
Average price: Inexpensive
Address: 4578 Britt Rd
Tucker, GA 30084
Phone: (770) 934-5100

#425
O'Brian's Tavern
Category: Pub, British, Irish
Average price: Modest
Address: 2486 Mount Vernon Rd
Dunwoody, GA 30338
Phone: (770) 396-0096

#426
Mulligans
Category: Nightlife, Restaurant
Average price: Inexpensive
Address: 698 Roswell St
SE Marietta, GA 30060
Phone: (770) 499-1137

#427
Suburban Tap
Category: Restaurant, Dive Bar
Average price: Modest
Address: 1318 Johnson Ferry Rd
Marietta, GA 30068
Phone: (770) 977-4467

#428
Three Dollar Cafe
Category: American, Sports Bar
Average price: Modest
Address: 6050 Peachtree Pkwy
Norcross, GA 30092
Phone: (770) 441-8520

#429
Hudson Grille
Category: Sports Bar, American
Average price: Modest
Address: 6317 Roswell Rd
Sandy Springs, GA 30328
Phone: (404) 554-8282

#430
Tripp's Bar
Category: Gay Bar
Average price: Inexpensive
Address: 1931 Piedmont Cir NE
Atlanta, GA 30324
Phone: (404) 724-0067

#431
Ai Tunes Karaoke
Category: Karaoke, Lounge, Beer, Wine, Spirits
Average price: Modest
Address: 4771 Britt Rd
Norcross, GA 30093
Phone: (678) 218-3883

#432
Nino's Italian Restaurant
Category: Italian, Bar
Average price: Modest
Area: Morningside / Lenox Park
Address: 1931 Cheshire Bridge Rd NE
Atlanta, GA 30324
Phone: (404) 874-6505

#433
Harbour House Pub
Category: American, Pub
Average price: Modest
Area: Decatur
Address: 129 Church St
Decatur, GA 30030
Phone: (404) 371-0088

#434
Blake's On The Park
Category: Gay Bar
Average price: Modest
Area: Midtown
Address: 227 10th St NE
Atlanta, GA 30309
Phone: (404) 892-5786

#435
Front Page News
Category: American, Pub, Sports Bar
Average price: Modest
Area: Little Five Points
Address: 351 Moreland Ave NE
Atlanta, GA 30307
Phone: (404) 475-7777

#436
Tin Lizzy's Cantina
Category: Bar, Tex-Mex
Average price: Modest
Area: Midtown
Address: 1136 Crescent Ave NE
Atlanta, GA 30309
Phone: (404) 537-5060

#437
Front Row Seafood Sportsbar
Category: Sports Bar, Seafood
Average price: Modest
Address: 6365 Peachtree Industrial Blvd
Atlanta, GA 30360
Phone: (470) 299-4136

#438
Red's Timbers
Category: Chicken Wings, Dive Bar
Average price: Modest
Address: 730 Concord Rd
SE Smyrna, GA 30082
Phone: (770) 434-2432

#439
Dania's Restaurant & Lounge
Category: Middle Eastern, Lounge
Average price: Inexpensive
Area: Downtown
Address: 26 Peachtree St
NW Atlanta, GA 30303
Phone: (404) 588-0069

#440
LeBuzz
Category: Gay Bar
Average price: Inexpensive
Address: 585 Franklin Rd
SE Marietta, GA 30067
Phone: (770) 424-1337

#441
Victory Sandwich Bar
Category: Bar, American
Average price: Inexpensive
Area: Decatur
Address: 340 Church St
Decatur, GA 30030
Phone: (404) 377-9300

#442
Chili's
Category: Bar, American
Average price: Modest
Address: 4784 Ashford Dunwoody Rd
Atlanta, GA 30338
Phone: (770) 394-6175

#443
Noni's Bar & Deli
Category: Italian, Sandwiches, Lounge
Average price: Modest
Address: 357 Edgewood Ave
Atlanta, GA 30312
Phone: (404) 343-1808

#444
Gold Dust Bar and Grill
Category: Sports Bar
Average price: Inexpensive
Address: 4880 Lawrenceville Hwy
Tucker, GA 30084
Phone: (770) 493-4740

#445
ATL Music Room
Category: Social Club, Music Venues
Average price: Inexpensive
Address: 4300 Chamblee Tucker Rd
Tucker, GA 30340
Phone: (770) 362-0602

#446
HOBNOB
Category: American, Pub
Average price: Modest
Area: Morningside / Lenox Park
Address: 1551 Piedmont Ave NE
Atlanta, GA 30324
Phone: (404) 968-2288

#447
The Tavern at Medlock
Category: Pub, Sports Bar
Average price: Modest
Address: 3230 Medlock Bridge Rd
Norcross, GA 30092
Phone: (770) 242-2757

#448
Epic Lounge And Bistro
Category: Lounge
Average price: Modest
Address: 5496 Cascade Rd
Atlanta, GA 30331
Phone: (404) 963-5577

#449
Chef Rob's Caribbean Cafe & Upscale Lounge
Category: Caribbean, Hookah Bar
Average price: Modest
Address: 5920 Roswell Rd
Sandy Springs, GA 30328
Phone: (404) 250-3737

#450
Jimiz Lounge
Category: Lounge
Average price: Inexpensive
Address: 2090 Cobb Pkwy SW
Smyrna, GA 30080
Phone: (770) 541-9391

#451
U Bar
Category: Sports Bar
Average price: Modest
Address: 3515 Camp Creek Pkwy East
Point, GA 30344
Phone: (404) 349-2642

#452
2 Monkeys Tavern
Category: Pub, Dive Bar
Average price: Inexpensive
Address: 688 Whitlock Ave
Marietta, GA 30064
Phone: (770) 795-0944

#453
Brockett Pub House & Grill
Category: American, Pub
Average price: Modest
Address: 4522 East Ponce de Leon Ave
Clarkston, GA 30021
Phone: (770) 938-1080

#454
The Comeback
Category: Sports Bar
Average price: Modest
Address: 2845 Mountain Industrial Blvd
Tucker, GA 30084
Phone: (770) 934-1773

#455
Red Pepper Taqueria
Category: Sports Bar, Mexican, Cocktail Bar
Average price: Modest
Area: Buckhead
Address: 3135 Piedmont Rd
Atlanta, GA 30305
Phone: (404) 869-2773

#456
Zanza
Category: Nightlife
Average price: Inexpensive
Address: 4203 Snapfinger Woods Dr
Decatur, GA 30035
Phone: (404) 286-4500

#457
Tucker Saloon
Category: Bar, Restaurant
Average price: Inexpensive
Address: 3766 Lawrenceville Hwy
Tucker, GA 30084
Phone: (770) 864-1985

#458
Vintage Tavern
Category: American, Bar
Average price: Modest
Address: 2860 Atlanta Rd
SE Smyrna, GA 30080
Phone: (770) 803-9793

#459
South Beach Bistro & Lounge
Category: Nightlife
Average price: Inexpensive
Address: 2077 Northlake Pkwy
Tucker, GA 30084
Phone: (770) 934-4988

#460
Cellar 56
Category: Wine Bar, Tapas Bar
Average price: Modest
Area: Buckhead
Address: 56 E Andrews
Atlanta, GA 30305
Phone: (404) 869-1132

#461
Taco Mac
Category: Sports Bar, American
Average price: Modest
Area: Decatur
Address: 240 W Ponce De Leon Ave
Decatur, GA 30030
Phone: (404) 378-4140

#462
Pizza Bar
Category: Sports Bar, Pizza
Average price: Modest
Address: 1450 Veterans Memorial Hwy
SE Mableton, GA 30126
Phone: (404) 505-8200

#463
Vibes
Category: Lounge, Music Venues
Average price: Inexpensive
Address: 4469 Glenwood Rd
Decatur, GA 30032
Phone: (404) 288-8423

#464
Sportsline Bar & Grill
Category: Sports Bar
Average price: Modest
Address: 2359 Windy Hill Rd
Marietta, GA 30067
Phone: (770) 226-0111

#465
Vixn Hookah & Martini Lounge
Category: Lounge, Hookah Bar, Dance Club
Average price: Modest
Address: 2930 Ember Dr
Decatur, GA 30034
Phone: (404) 212-3800

#466
Fusion Nightclub
Category: Dance Club, Lounge
Average price: Modest
Address: 4771 Britt Rd
Norcross, GA 30093
Phone: (770) 873-0861

#467
The Square Pub
Category: Pub
Average price: Modest
Area: Decatur
Address: 115 Sycamore St
Decatur, GA 30030
Phone: (404) 844-4010

#468
Irish Bred Pub
Category: Pub, Irish, Karaoke
Average price: Modest
Address: 1155 Virginia Ave
Hapeville, GA 30354
Phone: (404) 765-0280

#469
The Other Bar
Category: Dive Bar, Karaoke
Average price: Inexpensive
Address: 3766 Lawrenceville Hwy
Tucker, GA 30084
Phone: (770) 493-8837

#470
Tanqueray Lounge
Category: Lounge
Average price: Inexpensive
Address: 4019 Glenwood Rd
Decatur, GA 30032
Phone: (404) 286-2003

#471
Royal Oak Pub
Category: Pub, Fish & Chips, British
Average price: Modest
Address: 1155 Mt. Vernon Hwy
Sandy Springs, GA 30338
Phone: (770) 390-0859

#472
Jay's Place
Category: Sports Bar
Average price: Modest
Address: 4812 Redan Rd
Stone Mountain, GA 30088
Phone: (404) 501-0430

#473
Addis X Hookah Lounge
Category: Hookah Bar, Lounge
Average price: Inexpensive
Address: 1920 Manville Dr.
Chamblee, GA 30341
Phone: (404) 944-0352

#474
Oceans Grill & Bar
Category: American, Bar
Average price: Inexpensive
Address: 5955 Jimmy Carter Blvd Norcross,
GA 30071
Phone: (770) 441-9509

#475
Fleming's Prime Steakhouse & Wine Bar
Category: Steakhouse, Wine Bar
Average price: Expensive
Address: 4501 Olde Perimeter Way
Atlanta, GA 30346
Phone: (770) 698-8112

#476
Seasons 52
Category: American, Vegetarian,
Wine Bar
Average price: Modest
Area: Buckhead
Address: 3050 Peachtree Rd NW
Atlanta, GA 30305
Phone: (404) 846-1552

#477
Rialto Center for the Arts
Category: Performing Arts,
Music Venues, Art Gallery
Average price: Expensive
Area: Downtown
Address: 80 Forsyth St
Atlanta, GA 30303
Phone: (404) 413-9849

#478
Bradley's American Cafe
Category: Sports Bar, Cafe
Average price: Inexpensive
Address: 4961 Lower Roswell Rd
Marietta, GA 30068
Phone: (770) 321-0108

#479
Hush Sports Bar and Lounge
Category: Dance Club, Lounge
Average price: Inexpensive
Address: 2077 Beaver Ruin Rd
Norcross, GA 30071
Phone: (404) 307-8032

#480
The Valley
Category: Dance Club, Bar
Average price: Modest
Address: 3400 Holcomb Bridge Rd
Norcross, GA 30092
Phone: (770) 368-1325

#481
Mezza Luna Pasta and Seafood
Category: Italian, Wine Bar
Average price: Modest
Address: 1669 Spring Rd
SE Smyrna, GA 30080
Phone: (770) 319-0333

#482
Moondog Growlers
Category: Beer, Wine, Spirits, Bar
Average price: Modest
Address: 5065 Nandina Ln
Dunwoody, GA 30338
Phone: (770) 390-0660

#483
Starship Enterprises
Category: Adult Entertainment
Average price: Modest
Address: 2365 S Cobb Dr
SE Smyrna, GA 30080
Phone: (770) 432-3274

#484
Atlanta Jazz Festival
Category: Jazz & Blues
Average price: Inexpensive
Address: 1071 Piedmont Ave NE
Atlanta, GA 30309
Phone: (404) 875-7275

#485
Hooters
Category: Chicken Wings,
Sports Bar, American
Average price: Modest
Area: Downtown
Address: 209 Peachtree St
NE Atlanta, GA 30303
Phone: (404) 522-9464

#486
The Iron Horse
Category: Pub
Average price: Inexpensive
Address: 29 Jones St Norcross, 30071
Phone: (678) 291-9220

#487
J Buffalo Wings & Bar
Category: Chicken Wings, Bar, Seafood
Average price: Inexpensive
Address: 2580 Windy Hill Rd
SE Marietta, GA 30067
Phone: (678) 483-8811

#488
The Village Corner
Category: Bakery, German, Bar
Average price: Modest
Address: 6655 James B Rivers Dr
Stone Mountain, GA 30083
Phone: (770) 498-0329

#489
Temptation Hookah Lounge
Category: Hookah Bar
Average price: Inexpensive
Address: 3677 Claremont Rd
Chamblee, GA 30341
Phone: (678) 697-7861

#490
The Comback Bar and Grill
Category: Pub, Steakhouse
Average price: Inexpensive
Address: 2845 Mountain Industrial Blvd
Tucker, GA 30084
Phone: (770) 934-1773

#491
Cobb's Smoke and Hookah
Category: Tobacco Shop, Hookah Bar
Average price: Modest
Address: 2555 Delk Rd Marietta, 30067
Phone: (770) 644-0004

#492
Spiral Bar & Grill
Category: Bar, American
Average price: Inexpensive
Address: 3183 Main St
East Point, GA 30344
Phone: (404) 748-4338

#493
Icon Ultra Lounge
Category: Dance Club
Average price: Modest
Address: 2847 Buford Hwy NE Brookhaven, GA 30329
Phone: (404) 600-2546

#494
Cafe Intermezzo
Category: Coffee, Tea, Bar, Desserts
Average price: Modest
Address: 4505 Ashford-Dunwoody Rd
Dunwoody, GA 30346
Phone: (770) 396-1344

#495
Rocco's Pub
Category: Pub, American
Average price: Modest
Address: 1477 Roswell Rd
Marietta, GA 30062
Phone: (770) 971-8806

#496
Jack's Pizza & Wings
Category: Pizza, Pub, Chicken Wings
Average price: Inexpensive
Area: Old Fourth Ward
Address: 676 Highland Ave Atlanta, GA
Phone: (404) 525-4444

#497
Flip Burger Boutique
Category: Burgers, American, Wine Bar
Average price: Modest
Address: 3655 Roswell Rd NE
Atlanta, GA 30305
Phone: (404) 549-3298

#498
Atkins Park Tavern
Category: American, Bar
Average price: Modest
Address: 2840 Atlanta Rd
SE Smyrna, GA 30080
Phone: (770) 435-1887

#499
The Bird Rotisserie and Sports
Category: Chicken Wings, Sports Bar
Average price: Modest
Address: 4719 Ashford Dunwoody Rd
Phone: (770) 804-8288

#500
The Heretic
Category: Dance Club, Gay Bar
Average price: Inexpensive
Address: 2069 Cheshire Bridge Rd NE
Atlanta, GA 30324
Phone: (404) 325-3061

8881482R00089

Printed in Great Britain
by Amazon.co.uk, Ltd.,
Marston Gate.